Lisa V. Blitz, PhD, LCSW
Mary Pender Greene, LCSW-R,

Racism and Racial Identity: Reflections on Urban Practice in Mental Health and Social Services

Racism and Racial Identity: Reflections on Urban Practice in Mental Health and Social Services has been co-published simultaneously as *Journal of Emotional Abuse*, Volume 6, Numbers 2/3 2006.

Pre-publication REVIEWS, COMMENTARIES, EVALUATIONS . . .

"**A** thoughtful and useful treatment of racial issues; it is a needed work for and from people who are frontline service providers. This book will be a valuable resource to many professionals."

Robert T. Carter, PhD
*Professor of Psychology
and Education
Department of Counseling and
Clinical Psychology
Teachers College
Columbia University*

HMTP

The Haworth Maltreatment & Trauma Press®
An Imprint of The Haworth Press, Inc.

New York • London • Victoria (AU)
www.HaworthPress.com

Racism and Racial Identity:
Reflections on Urban Practice
in Mental Health
and Social Services

Racism and Racial Identity: Reflections on Urban Practice in Mental Health and Social Services has been co-published simultaneously as *Journal of Emotional Abuse*, Volume 6, Numbers 2/3 2006.

To
Michelle
Thank you
for your support
in the struggle

Mary
78/07

Monographs from the *Journal of Emotional Abuse*™

For additional information on these and other Haworth Press titles, including descriptions, tables of contents, reviews, and prices, use the QuickSearch catalog at http://www.HaworthPress.com.

Racism and Racial Identity: Reflections on Urban Practice in Mental Health and Social Services

Lisa V. Blitz, PhD, LCSW
Mary Pender Greene, LCSW-R, ACSW
Editors

Racism and Racial Identity: Reflections on Urban Practice in Mental Health and Social Services has been co-published simultaneously as *Journal of Emotional Abuse,* Volume 6, Numbers 2/3 2006.

So Michelle
this book is a
must read. It is
a long time overdue
Enjoy Sondra Aldridge

HMTP

The Haworth Maltreatment & Trauma Press®
An Imprint of The Haworth Press, Inc.

New York • London • Victoria (AU)
www.HaworthPress.com

Published by

· ·The Haworth Maltreatment & Trauma Press, 10 Alice Street, Binghamton, NY 13904-1580 USA

The Haworth Maltreatment & Trauma Press is an imprint of The Haworth Press, Inc., 10 Alice Street, Binghamton, NY 13904-1580 USA.

Racism and Racial Identity: Reflections on Urban Practice in Mental Health and Social Services has been co-published simultaneously as *Journal of Emotional Abuse*, Volume 6, Numbers 2/3 2006.

The development, preparation, and publication of this work has been undertaken with great care. However, the publisher, employees, editors, and agents of The Haworth Press and all imprints of The Haworth Press, Inc., including The Haworth Medical Press® and The Pharmaceutical Products Press®, are not responsible for any errors contained herein or for consequences that may ensue from use of materials or information contained in this work. With regard to case studies, identities and circumstances of individuals discussed herein have been changed to protect confidentiality Any resemblance to actual persons, living or dead, is entirely coincidental.

The Haworth Press is committed to the dissemination of ideas and information according to the highest standards of intellectual freedom and the free exchange of ideas. Statements made and opinions expressed in this publication do not necessarily reflect the views of the Publisher, Directors, management, or staff of The Haworth Press, Inc., or an endorsement by them.

Cover illustration "Issues in Identity" © Eileen P. McGann. Printed with permission.

Library of Congress Cataloging-in-Publication Data

Racism and racial identity : reflections on urban practice in mental health and social services / Lisa V. Blitz, Mary Pender Greene, editors.
    p. cm.
    "Co-published simultaneously as Journal of emotional abuse, Volume 6, Numbers 2/3 2006.
Includes bibliographical references and index.
ISBN-13: 978-0-7890-3108-2 (hard cover. : alk. paper)
ISBN-10: 0-7890-3108-6 (hard cover. : alk. paper)
ISBN-13: 978-0-7890-3109-9 (soft cover. : alk. paper)
ISBN-10: 0-7890-3109-4 (soft cover. : alk. paper)
    1. Social work with minorities–United States. 2. Social work with immigrants–United States 3. Minorities–Mental health–United States. 4. Minorities–Mental Health Services–United States. 5. Social service and race relations–United States. 6. Racism in social services–United States. 7. Racism–United States–Psychological aspects. 8. City dwellers–Services for–United States. I. Blitz, Lisa V. II. Greene, Mary Pender. III. Journal of emotional abuse.
HV3176.R33 2006
362.2089'00973–dc22   2006016220

Indexing, Abstracting & Website/Internet Coverage

This section provides you with a list of major indexing & abstracting services and other tools for bibliographic access. That is to say, each service began covering this periodical during the year noted in the right column. Most Websites which are listed below have indicated that they will either post, disseminate, compile, archive, cite or alert their own Website users with research-based content from this work. (This list is as current as the copyright date of this publication.)

Abstracting, Website/Indexing Coverage . . . . Year When Coverage Began

- *Applied Social Sciences Index & Abstracts (ASSIA) (Online: ASSI via DataStar) (CDRom: ASSIA Plus) <http://www.csa.com>*. 1998
- *Biological Sciences Database (Cambridge Scientific Abstracts) <http://www.csa.com>* 2006
- *British Library Inside (The British Library) <http://www.bl.uk/services/current/inside.html>*. 2006
- *Cambridge Scientific Abstracts is a leading publisher of scientific information in print journals, online databases, CD-ROM and via the Internet <http://www.csa.com>* 1998
- *Criminal Justice Abstracts (Sage)* 1998
- *EBSCOhost Electronic Journals Service (EJS) <http://ejournals.ebsco.com>*. 1999
- *Educational Research Abstracts (ERA) (online database) <http://www.tandf.co.uk/era>*. 2002
- *Elsevier Eflow-I* 2006
- *Elsevier Scopus . . . <http://www.info.scopus.com>*. 2005
- *EMBASE (The Power of EMBASE + MEDLINE Combined) <http://www.embase.com>*. 1999
- *EMBASE/Excerpta Medica Secondary Publishing Division. Included in newsletters, review journals, major reference works, magazines & abstract journals <http://www.elsevier.nl>*. 1999
- *Environmental Sciences and Pollution Management (Cambridge Scientific Abstracts Internet Database Service) <http://www.csa.com>* 2006

(continued)

(continued)

- *Social Services Abstracts (Cambridge Scientific Abstracts)*
  <http://www.csa.com> 1998
- *Social Work Abstracts (NASW) <http://www.silverplatter.com/catalog/*
  swab.htm> 1998
- *SocIndex (EBSCO)* 2006
- *Sociological Abstracts (Cambridge Scientific Abstracts)*
  <http://www.csa.com> 1998
- *Ulrich's Periodicals Directory International Periodicals*
  Information Since 1932 (Bibliographic Access)
  <http://www.Bowkerlink.com> 2006
- *Violence and Abuse Abstracts (Sage)* 2004
- *zetoc (The British Library) <http://www.bl.uk/>* 2004

*Exact start date to come.

*Special Bibliographic Notes related to special journal issues
(separates) and indexing/abstracting:*

- indexing/abstracting services in this list will also cover material in any "separate" that is co-published simultaneously with Haworth's special thematic journal issue or DocuSerial. Indexing/abstracting usually covers material at the article/chapter level.
- monographic co-editions are intended for either non-subscribers or libraries which intend to purchase a second copy for their circulating collections.
- monographic co-editions are reported to all jobbers/wholesalers/approval plans. The source journal is listed as the "series" to assist the prevention of duplicate purchasing in the same manner utilized for books-in-series.
- to facilitate user/access services all indexing/abstracting services are encouraged to utilize the co-indexing entry note indicated at the bottom of the first page of each article/chapter/contribution.
- this is intended to assist a library user of any reference tool (whether print, electronic, online, or CD-ROM) to locate the monographic version if the library has purchased this version but not a subscription to the source journal.
- individual articles/chapters in any Haworth publication are also available through the Haworth Document Delivery Service (HDDS).

We would like to dedicate this issue to the People's Institute for Survival and Beyond, in gratitude for teaching us the powerful sociopolitical and historical analysis of racism that has enriched our knowledge, improved our practice, and fueled our antiracist organizing efforts. It is our sincere hope that others will join us in our quest to undo racism within our profession.

ABOUT THE EDITORS

Lisa V. Blitz, PhD, LCSW, is Director of JBFCS Genesis, an emergency domesitc violence shelter for families, and teaches in the JBFCS/Martha K. Selig Educational Institute for social workers and the JBFCS/Adult Milieu Training Institute for residential direct care staff. She practice has a private psychotherapy practice in New York City.

Mary Pender Greene, LCSW-R, ACSW, is practice Chief of Social Work Services at the Jewish Board of Family and Children's Services. A past president of the New York City chapter of the National Association of Social Workers, she is on the executive committee of Black Agency Executives and is a member of the New York State Education Social Work Board.

Racism and Racial Identity: Reflections on Urban Practice in Mental Health and Social Services

CONTENTS

About the Contributors

Robert Abramovitz, MD, is Chief Psychiatrist at the Jewish Board of Family and Children's Services (JBFCS), and Director of the Center for Trauma Program Innovation (CTPI). He is Adjunct Associate Professor of Psychiatry at Mount Sinai School of Medicine (MSSM) and Adjunct Research Scholar at the Columbia University School of Social Work.

Joseph Ackerman, LCSW, has had a distinguished career working with children and parents as counselor, program director, and executive. He directed a crisis program for children and mothers and developed a clinical consultation program that placed mental health, domestic violence, and substance abuse experts in child protective units so decision makers would opt to support mothers rather than remove children. Mr. Ackerman is currently Assistant Director of JBFCS' Bronx Real Services, which provides a broad range of community treatment and residential services for adults challenged by mental illness.

Dr. Nancy Boyd-Franklin, PhD, is Professor of Clinical Psychology at Rutgers University in the Graduate School of Applied and Professional Psychology. She has written on the treatment of African American families, extended family issues, spirituality and religion, home-based family therapy, group therapy for Black women, HIV and AIDS, parent and family support groups, community empowerment and the Multisystems Model. She is the author of *Black Families in Therapy: A Multisystems Approach* (Guilford Press, 1989) and an editor of *Children, Families and HIV/AIDS: Psychosocial and Psychotherapeutic Issues* (Guilford Press, 1995). Her book with Dr. Brenna Bry, *Reaching Out in Family Therapy: Home-Based, School and Community Interventions* was released by Guilford Press in 2000. Her latest book, *Boys Into Men: Raising Our African American Teenage Sons*, with A. J. Franklin and Pamela Toussaint, was published by Dutton Press in 2000.

Rene T. Chapman, MA, MSW, LCSW, also holds a Certificate in Psychoanalytic Psychotherapy and Psychoanalysis. She is Coordinator of the Clinical Consultation Program of the Jewish Board of Family and Children's Services, a program in partnership with the Administration for Children's Services in New York City providing consultation and training to child protective staff and family services workers in the areas of Mental Health, Domestic Violence, and Substance Abuse. She maintains a private psychotherapy practice in Brooklyn, NY.

Pat Churchill, LMSW, was born and raised in Harlem and has two daughters, ages 20 and 27. She earned her Bachelors degree in Forensic Psychology at John Jay College of Criminal Justice. She came to social work as a second career and, after earning her Masters degree in Social Work from New York University, specialized in the field of domestic violence as a counselor and trainer.

George Daniels, LMSW, is Director of Hawthorne Cedar Knolls, a 104-bed Residential Treatment Center at JBFCS. He has worked for JBFCS for 25 years in a variety of positions, including Milieu Counselor, Therapist, and Director of a JBFCS group home. He received his Master of Social Work degree from the Wurzweiler School of Social Work at Yeshiva University in New York City, and a Certificate from the Columbia University Graduate School of Business.

Barbara L. Edwards, LCSW-R, JD, has considerable experience in Executive Management positions with New York City Health and Human Services organizations. She has served on the faculty of several metropolitan New York Schools of Social Work. This is her sixth year as an appointed advisor to the Westchester County Executive and Legislators.

Anderson J. Franklin, PhD, is Professor of Clinical and Social Personality Psychology at The City College and Graduate School of The City University of New York. He is a psychotherapist in private practice having a specialty with African American males. He is Past President of The Society for the Psychological Study of Ethnic and Minority Issues, a Division of the American Psychological Association. Dr. Franklin lectures and consults with a variety of domestic and international organizations on diversity issues. He is co-author with Dr. Nancy Boyd-Franklin of *Boys Into Men: Raising Our African American Teenage Sons* published by Dutton. His latest book is *From Brotherhood to Manhood: How Black Men Rescue Their Relationships and Dreams from the Invisibility Syndrome* by John Wiley & Sons in 2004.

Janet A. Geller, EdD, LCSW, is Director of the Family Violence Prevention Canter at the Jewish Board of Family and Children's Services in New York City. She has a private practice since 1974 where she treats individuals, couples and groups. Her specialty is domestic violence. Dr. Geller has published extensively and presented her model of treating domestic violence at numerous conferences.

Pia Hargrove, LMSW, is a New York University alumna with a Master's degree in Social Work and a recipient of the university's Nia Award, recognizing her commitment to social justice and activism. She has served as a panelist on issues of adolescent social work and teenage pregnancy in

New York City schools. As social worker at the Jewish Board's Neptune Family Services, Pia worked with adolescents and adults conducting family therapy and facilitating psychotherapeutic groups with a predominantly Mexican-born and Spanish-speaking population.

Dadrene Hine-St. Hilaire, ABD. LCSW, is currently Director of Horizons Domestic Violence Shelter/Jewish Board of Family and Children's Services. She has worked since 1979 creating, developing, and directing clinical/social service programs for families and children impacted by mental health issues, substance abuse, sexual assault, battering, and child abuse. Her work, initially in the field of mental health as a psychotherapist, motivated her commitment to providing psychosocial and mental health services to an underserved community of lower socioeconomic level. Dadrene has worked as a college professor, and served on a number of human service boards of directors. She also maintains a private practice.

Hillel Hirshbein, LMSW, MPH, a graduate of the University of Michigan Schools of Public Health and Social Work, is Executive Associate to the CEO and the Director, Social Work Examination and Licensure Support Services at the Jewish Board of Family and Children's Services.

Linda Illidge, LCSW, is Administrative Supervisor of JBFCS Genesis. Ms. Illidge currently teaches in the JBFCS Multicultural Clinical Practice program for social work interns and has a private psychotherapy practice in New York City.

Dr. Shalonda Kelly, PhD, is Associate Professor of Clinical Psychology at the Graduate School of Applied and Professional Psychology at Rutgers, The State University of New Jersey. Her primary research interests are racial, ethnic and cultural issues, particularly in couple relationships. This focus is upon the conceptualization and measurement of racial and cultural constructs in relationship to individual and couple functioning. Her interests also extend to cognitive-behavioral and systems oriented treatment of individuals, couples and families.

Benjamin G. Kohl, Jr., PhD, LCSW, is Director of Multicultural Practice and Research and Program Director of Southern Brooklyn Family Services at the Jewish Board of Family and Children's Services. He is an adjunct faculty member at New York University School of Social Work, where he recently completed his doctorate.

Warren C. Lyons, LCSW, is a graduate of the Hunter College School of Social Work, New York, New York. He is on the staff of the Jewish Board of Family and Children's Services.

Libbe Madsen, LCSW, MSW, is Director of Staff Development, Center for Trauma Program Innovation, Jewish Board of Family and Children's Services and a clinical social worker in private practice. She is also a member of the National Association of Social Workers.

Eileen P. McGann, MA, ATR-BC, received her Master's degree in 1989 from New York University. Currently, Ms. McGann is Senior Art Therapist, with the Jewish Board of Family and Children's Services and a faculty member of the graduate art therapy program at the School of Visual Arts in New York City.

Kathleen McGlade, PhD, began her work in child welfare as a community organizer and volunteer founder of a youth program. That early perspective convinced her that a great deal of talent lay dormant in the clients and employees with whom she worked. She used her supervisory and executive roles looking out for talent and helping it unfold. Dr. McGlade is a licensed clinical social worker and currently the Corporate Compliance Director at JBFCS, a role she treasures for its focus on ethical problem solving.

Jacqueline Miller, LCSW, is Director of Family Violence at the Jewish Board of Family and Children's Services in New York. She has developed and managed programs for families at risk for over 30 years, including services for teen parents, domestic violence programs, and child abuse prevention programs. She has been a frequent lecturer and trainer on issues related to working with disorganized families, the impact of disability on families, and training modules for direct care staff.

Caroline Peacock, LMSW, is Co-Director of the Center for Trauma Program Innovation and Westchester Division Sanctuary® Project at JBFCS. She received her Master of Social Work degree from the CUNY Hunter College School of Social Work in New York City.

Lesley Samuel-Young, LMSW, is Director of the Jewish Board of Family and Children's Services/Women's Transition Center. She attended the Hunter School of Social Work in New York where she earned her Master of Social Work degree in 1989. She has worked for most of her career in adult mental health settings, in community-based agencies such as Community Access Inc. on the Lower East Side in New York and Weston United Community Renewal Inc. in Harlem, where she became Director of "Club United" (a mental health program where the clientele is very involved in the program operation using the clubhouse model). She began working at the Jewish Board of Family and Children's Services in 1999 as Director of Social Services and became Program Director of Transition Center, a domestic violence shelter in 2002. She has served on the advisory board of Caribbean Women's Health Association, an agency that focuses on HIV/AIDS issues among Caribbean women.

Alan Siskind, PhD, LCSW, is Executive Vice President and CEO of the Jewish Board of Family and Children's Services, the nation's premier voluntary mental health and family service agency, which serves over 65,000 clients annually in 185 programs in the five boroughs of New York City and in Westchester. He is an adjunct Professor at Columbia University School of Social Work and the Smith College School of Social Work, and has been named a Distinguished Practitioner by the National Academies of Practice.

Foreword:
From a Multicultural Institution to an Antiracist Institution:
A Traditional Jewish Organization Meets the Challenge

Mary Pender Greene
Alan Siskind

Racial segregation, like all other forms of cruelty and tyranny, debases all human beings–those who are its victims, those who victimize, and in quite subtle ways, those who are its accessories.

–Dr. Kenneth B. Clark (as cited in Massey & Denton, 1993)

The prologue to this volume tells the story of a proud institution, the Jewish Board of Family and Children's Services (JBFCS), with a long

---

Contributions from Robert Abramovitz, MD, and Hillel Hirshbein, LMSW, MPH, Jewish Board of Family and Children's Services, New York, NY, have also been given to the Foreword.

Address correspondence to: Mary Pender Greene, LCSW-R, ACSW:JBFCS, 120 West 57th Street, 7th Floor, New York, NY 10019 (E-mail: mpendergreene@jbfcs.org).

[Haworth co-indexing entry note]: "Foreword: From a Multicultural Institution to an Antiracist Institution: A Traditional Jewish Organization Meets the Challenge." Greene, Mary Pender, and Alan Siskind. Co-published simultaneously in *Journal of Emotional Abuse* (The Haworth Maltreatment & Trauma Press, an imprint of The Haworth Press, Inc.) Vol. 6, No. 2/3, 2006, pp. xxvii-xxxiv; and: *Racism and Racial Identity: Reflections on Urban Practice in Mental Health and Social Services* (ed: Lisa V. Blitz, and Mary Pender Greene) The Haworth Maltreatment & Trauma Press, an imprint of The Haworth Press, Inc., 2006, pp. xxi-xxviii. Single or multiple copies of this article are available for a fee from The Haworth Document Delivery Service [1-800-HAWORTH, 9:00 a.m. - 5:00 p.m. (EST). E-mail address: docdelivery@haworthpress.com].

Available online at http://www.jea.haworthpress.com
xxi

tradition of helping needy New Yorkers. But it frames the story in a way never before attempted. The backdrop to this story is neither the history of social services in New York, nor the history of poverty, nor mental illness, nor clinical practice, nor child welfare. The backdrop is race. This telling of the narrative of JBFCS acknowledges as a basic premise that the United States of America–the wealthiest and most powerful country in the world–has historical roots in slavery and genocide. The institution of slavery and the genocide of the native peoples of the land have had a fundamental influence on the way American society has evolved. The first 200 years of American history led to the development of a society that, unlike most other industrialized nations, polarized its diverse population according to a race construct.

The manifestations of the intertwined issues of race and racism are portrayed in art, myth, and social legends; this history, as lived through oral tradition, results in stories, ideals, and values that are handed down over generations. Scholars and journalists record facts, but ultimately the social construction of history is what lives on in the minds, hearts, and memories of a society's people. The biases of this socially constructed history are often reflected in education and public discourse about our nation's origins, early development, and growth to prosperity. Facts are rarely excluded outright, but deeply held convictions in the rightness of our ideals, supported by notions of manifest destiny and blessings of divine order, serve to narrow the lens through which we hear and understand these facts. The way in which we interpret facts molds our attitudes and shapes our culture. Our nation's collective pride in rugged individualism encourages us to sustain a belief that America's meritocracy functions equally for all citizens. This credo states that anyone who works hard will have success and can take satisfaction in these earned achievements. What remains unexamined is how the effects of racism and chauvinism provide unearned privileges that create invisible barriers for people of color, making their achievements harder to come by, while simultaneously supporting the success of White people.

In a complex, service-oriented society, success is obtained through negotiation with various institutions in that society. When race-based privilege becomes embedded in the structure of institutions, it becomes as invisible as the social construction of history itself. Americans share a resistance to understanding the depth and complexity of how this structural racism plays out in the work of our societal institutions. As noted by Better (2002), "to accept that racism is purposely in place within American institutions to preserve White privilege would mean to acknowledge that America is not at its roots a just and meritorious society" (p. 9). Many find that seeing the facts of American history though a different lens, one that highlights injustice and the profound benefits of White privilege, is a painful and disorienting process. As Better further explains, "it is easier to blame the victims of inequality or lunatic fringe groups than to admit the reality of basic injustice" (p. 9). Avoidance of that pain, however, is at the core of the continuation of institutional racism.

Institutional racism refers to the practices, policies, and –most important–the social culture of institutions. In a society set up to support white-skin privilege, the inherent social culture of that society's institutions will naturally reflect that bias, unless there is deliberate action to counteract that bias. In institutions where these forces of racial bias remain invisible and outside of conscious attention, the social culture of unconscious racism will influence basic policies and practices and result in overt racial discrimination in spite of explicit intentions to produce another result. Unfortunately, even in institutions that have a fairly high degree of awareness of race bias, unconscious or unexamined aspects of the institution's social culture can unintentionally reinforce dynamics that continue to privilege people with white skin. It is in this manner that American institutions remain dominated by practices that produce racial inequalities (Thompson & Neville, 1999).

JBFCS is one of the largest and most prominent non-profit mental health and social service agencies in the United States. The agency's 120 year-long tradition of helping families and children began with services to poor Jewish families and immigrants. It has expanded its mission and now annually serves more than 70,000 New Yorkers of all racial, ethnic, economic, and religious backgrounds. At its core, JBFCS is a social work organization with a staff of nearly 3,200, including social workers, psychiatrists, psychologists, milieu staff, expressive therapists, teachers, doctors, and nurses. The agency is dedicated to providing a wide spectrum of mental health and social services that ease the burdens that strain and disrupt lives. It provides a continuum of services shaped by the needs of its clients, ranging from residential services to day treatment, outpatient mental health services for adults, children, and families, and a range of services addressing family violence and other social issues. Many of our clients are people of color, and large numbers speak languages other than English, such as Spanish, Russian, Mandarin, Hebrew, Creole, Yiddish, and many other languages.

To maintain its commitment to providing the highest quality of social and mental health services, JBFCS must continue to evolve. JBFCS serves an increasingly diverse community, and to do so effectively the agency must continuously expand its competence at serving all New Yorkers. The shift taking place in the agency's work on cultural competence and antiracism can be best characterized as a journey that began with an initial mission to serve the Jewish community, developed towards the adoption of diversity and multiculturalism paradigms, and which is now directed toward an anti-racist approach.

Starting in 1991, a 25-person diversity task force was established and met monthly for three years. The group was charged with examining ways to strengthen our cultural competence to better serve all New Yorkers, and to make appropriate recommendations with regard to diversity issues. From the outset, this effort was viewed as a long-term goal of the agency that would require years of work, and for a number of years, multiculturalism was a significant theme stressed by JBFCS leadership.

Significant gains were made through the adoption of a multicultural stance, including increased representation of people of color among the agency staff. It became apparent as our own work has progressed, however, that such approaches do not go far enough in addressing numerous issues of structural inequity that pervade all of American culture and its institutions. Multiculturalism focuses on helping people of color and new immigrants achieve the goals and resources defined as important by the White society. Assimilating in this way may bring marginalized groups into the dominant culture, but does not include focus on power or decision-making roles and responsibilities from a point of view that is culturally congruent to them. Since it is based upon the belief that the diversity work is all the work that needs to be done, this assimilationist approach posits that utmost importance needs only to be given to the development of strong clinical skills and a commitment to traditional color-blind models of treatment. Race-related issues need not be given room in the workplace since they are deemed to be personal and emotional and not professionally relevant.

Our goal, however, is to go beyond multiculturalism and address the less visible issues of power and privilege that operate within institutions. Therefore, JBFCS is adopting an antiracist stance that: (a) seeks to recognize institutional bias imbedded in organizational structure; (b) works to make changes in policies and procedures that support structures that are accountable with outcomes of equity; and (c) ensures that the clinical theories and social service delivery models that guide our direct work with clients are understood and practiced through the lens of antiracism.

We acknowledge that JBFCS is an American institution, and therefore that it could not avoid having the characteristics of other American institutions. As we explored further, we accepted that our clinical practice, policies, and procedures were developed from a so-called "one type fits all," color-blind approach. That is, as our institution grew, practices that had been developed for a totally White, mostly Jewish population needed to be redesigned to accommodate the changes in the clients we serve and the staff providing the services.

We discovered that we were selecting staff, supervisors, and directors primarily to mirror those who were already on staff and to perform in their image. We became aware that our hierarchal system traditionally rewarded longevity, and sometimes overly challenged different approaches. Having become an exceedingly successful agency, seeing the limitations that may have existed in our policy and practice approaches was sometimes a difficult process.

Antiracism work, which focuses on the structural nature of institutional racism, asserts that failure to address racism serves to lend it institutional support. Therefore, the ability to offer the best possible service depends on making explicit the reinforcing, race-based structures that are vestiges of American history haunting the halls of all modern institutions. Antiracist philosophy further contends that to truly provide quality culturally-competent services, every manager, supervisor, and worker must recognize that contemporary forms of racism exist and become familiar with the various forms that racism takes in the lives of staff and clients of color. Self-awareness and effort are necessary to learn and to identify what those issues are and how they may be unintentionally perpetuated in an organization's policies, practices, and procedures. The goal is to widen the circle of influence and opportunity. JBFCS senior leadership assert that antiracist work will assist White people and people of color to better understand how institutional racism works, and will offer strategies and support for systemic change.

Managing the evolution of the JBFCS approach to issues of race is a complex and dynamic process for the top leadership of the organization. Since changes of attitude and culture are slow and gradual processes that cannot be mandated, much thought and consultation continues to be needed. Honest dialogue and an understanding that antiracist work is often a long-term process is also necessary. Leadership must consistently demonstrate their commitment to the process by setting a tone that values honest discourse and openly acknowledges uncomfortable tensions that come with discussion of race, which is a historically taboo subject in the workplace. Tension must be addressed respectfully and swiftly when possible and, simultaneously, staff must be helped to accept a degree of uncertainty and discomfort that is an inextricable characteristic of change.

JBFCS top leadership have stated that they intend the agency to be a safe place for workers to be themselves and to express their true feelings about race or any other matters. While there is still some fear and distrust about repercussions and the seriousness of the effort to move forward, there is also a feeling of hope that has been expressed by many members of the staff. Antiracist work has also created some backlash, which causes some members of the dominant group to question the value of placing so much agency time and resources into discussion of race. Other majority group members feel left out, unsatisfied, and unclear about the role that they could or should play. In addition, some majority group members are uncertain about whether there are benefits that can be gained from antiracist work and formidable opposition may arise when they themselves are asked to change. It has become clear that we cannot lead this initiative without listening and creating an open space for these divergent views on issues while maintaining clear expectations and a vision regarding desired outcomes.

A common passion about the desire to help a beloved and effective organization to move beyond multiculturalism has sustained forward movement. While staff, at this phase, vary in their readiness to fully embrace an antiracist agenda, all agree that since the organization enjoys a reputation of excellence in many different areas, mediocrity as it relates to race and race matters is unacceptable. Multiculturalism alone does not meet the standard now. Antiracism requires the sharing of influence and decision-making and presupposes that the core culture and institutional structures must fundamentally change, while recognizing that changes in our personal attitudes are also essential. An antiracist focus explicitly examines power relationships and sees the parallels, intersections, and distinctions between all forms of oppression and the ways they manifest themselves within the society and within the organization.

Our struggle now is to accept that we do not know what we do not know, and that there are others who *do* know what we do not. The challenge is to acknowledge the value of outside knowledge and incorporate it into our organizational culture, clinical practice, administration, policy decision-making, and collective wisdom. This can be achieved only if these diverse voices are consistently and prominently present at all levels of the agency. We are now working to establish policies and procedures that support institutional change, keep communication flowing, and maintain a stance that is open to hearing all sides on issues of race.

Despite the long road we know is ahead, we have already learned much. We have a model for facilitating our community's capacity to shape services for itself and we are clear about the need for heightened awareness of race and racism and how it impacts seeking help. We can use this knowledge as we reach out to communities of color. Our clients must become our active partners and not objects of rescue as they work to improve their own lives, families, and communities.

Our original goal was to attract a multicultural staff to better serve our broad array of multicultural clients, but something even bigger than that happened. Over the years, in pockets of our agency, our demographically representative work force brought fresh new perspectives. They were able to pursue and maintain clinical cases that previously all-White staff had not been able to engage. Staff of color did outreach to the community's natural support systems that the White staff would not have thought relevant or appropriate because the link to clinical treatment was not obvious to them. We have learned that having a staff of color can affect the work in terms of expanding our notions of what are "treatment" issues and taking on those issues and reframing them in creative ways, some of which we had never done before. We have also learned that a racially diverse staff can really change the substance and enhance the quality of our work. In essence, we have started to learn how to identify and analyze these culturally-based skills, beliefs, and practices so that we can learn from them and teach others. It is our continuing struggle to integrate these skills into the very core of the organization's culture.

Our pursuit of becoming an antiracist organization is a journey and not a destination. We have seen the future and want to go there. For change to be lasting in our organization, we must sustain these efforts on all levels, beginning with the leadership, reflected in supervision, and mandated in treatment. We also should be mindful of the unrealistic expectations that there will be a comfortable, harmonious atmosphere, as diverse voices explore certain truths and biases around the human condition. We anticipate a degree of discord and confusion; we anticipate that there will be desire on the part of some to let the conversation fade into the background. Disagreement is freedom's privilege and we will continue to develop a higher organizational pain threshold in order to stay the course.

The articles in this volume represent the manifestation of antiracism at work within JBFCS. The writing represents experiences within our agency, as well as the authors' experiences in private practice and past experiences with agencies that did not take on the challenge of antirac-ism. Antiracism requires discourse and dialogue. It requires permission to speak openly of race and its effects. It requires White people to rein-terpret and revise their assumptions about policy and practice that are truly effective in serving a diverse client population and that truly honor a diverse staff. While these are meritorious works in and of themselves, we ask readers to envision the antiracist work that these articles em-body. They are the scholarly byproducts of antiracism in action. They are a testament as well to a developmental process that has already and will continue to strengthen all who participate in it.

REFERENCES

Better, S. (2002). *Institutional racism: A primer on theory and strategies for social change*. Chicago: Burnham.

Massey, D. S., & Denton, N. A. (1993). *American apartheid*. Harvard University Press,

Thompson, C. E., & Neville, H. A. (1999). Racism, mental health, and mental health practice. *The Counseling Psychologist, 27*, 155-223.

Preface

By unconsciously allowing White cultural beliefs and practices to dominate, mental health and social services are just as vulnerable to embedded bias and racism as other organizations, influencing the treatment and service they provide. To counter institutional racism, agencies must understand their own culture and welcome divergent cultural orientations (Matthews, 1996). Openness to new ideas, combined with an analysis of power and hierarchy that is transformed into meaningful practice, allows the organization to become the center of multicultural learning, thus resisting racism at an institutional level.

Captured here are the insights and struggles of a group of experienced social workers as our agency took on the challenge of working toward antiracist practice. We are a diverse group with differences in race, religion, sexual identity, political ideology, and professional focus. We came together because we share a common concern that racism is taking a horrific toll on the clients we serve, the community and nation we live in, and us as citizens and professional helpers. Many of us have been impacted by workshops on Undoing Racism™ by the People's Institute for Survival and Beyond, a 25-year-old national organization based in New Orleans, LA. The editors of this volume and several contributors continue to work closely with core trainers of The People's Institute, and their analysis is the foundation for our understanding of race and racism.

Through a study of history and an analysis of this country's institutional structures, we have come to understand that race is a political construct invented to give White people advantaged social status. While bigotry and race prejudice are acts of injustice that can be committed by any individual or group, *racism* refers to the structures of our social insti-

[Haworth co-indexing entry note]: "Preface." Blitz, Lisa V., and Mary Pender Greene. Co-published simultaneously in *Journal of Emotional Abuse* (The Haworth Maltreatment & Trauma Press, an imprint of The Haworth Press, Inc.) Vol. 6, No. 2/3, 2006, pp. xxxv-xxxvi; and: *Racism and Racial Identity: Reflections on Urban Practice in Mental Health and Social Services* (ed: Lisa V. Blitz, and Mary Pender Greene) The Haworth Maltreatment & Trauma Press, an imprint of The Haworth Press, Inc., 2006, pp. xxix-xxx. Single or multiple copies of this article are available for a fee from The Haworth Document Delivery Service [1-800-HAWORTH, 9:00 a.m. - 5:00 p.m. (EST). E-mail address: docdelivery@haworthpress.com].

tutions that benefit White people and disadvantage people of color. Although racism is deeply engrained in our society, its effects are often invisible to White people unless and until Whites recognize the collective, unearned privileges that they enjoy. To "undo" racism in our society requires a profound process of collective and individual self-examination and transformation. Some people even believe that it is impossible to completely purge the culturally embedded racism in the individual until the culture itself changes. To that end, we strive to hold the Undoing Racism™ ethics and values close to our hearts, and transform our work from that of professional helpers to that of committed antiracist activist-helpers.

Throughout this volume, authors have differed in their choice to capitalize the terms "White" and "Black." Capitalizing White and Black acknowledges the political and social nature of racial identity, while terms such as "people of color" are more inclusive and do not refer to a specific community or people and are therefore not capitalized. The choice not to capitalize often reflects the fluid nature of who is considered white, black, or brown as social constructs shift, in effect gerrymandering racial lines but never eliminating the basic construct of race or the destructive power of racism.

Racism is not simply a Black-White issue, of course, since racism has a profound impact on all ethnic groups and communities of color, as well as Whites who are pulled into the role of oppressor. Further, to truly appreciate the forces of oppression at work in society, it is necessary to examine the intersections of various forms of marginalization, such as racism, anti-Semitism, patriarchy, classism, colonialism, and heterosexism. Our choice to focus on racial identity and racism, however, comes from a concern that the impact of racism makes other forms of oppression worse. A strong racial identity is the best form of individual resistance; bringing the discussion to the foreground is the beginning of collective action toward change.

Lisa V. Blitz
Mary Pender Greene

REFERENCES

Matthews, L. (1996). Culturally competent models in human services organizations. *Journal of Multicultural Social Work*, 4, 131-135.

The People's Institute for Survival and Beyond can be contacted at: www.thepeoplesinstitute.org

Acknowledgments

The development of this special volume is reflective not only of the efforts of the contributing authors and editors, but of many people who have provided their support and encouragement and who have held us accountable for a higher standard of antiracist practice. Nancy Boyd-Franklin and Anderson J. Franklin, who contributed to this work, provided extensive education, training, and guidance to our agency during the period this collection was developed. Without their help this work would not have been possible. We are indebted to the People's Institute for Survival and Beyond, particularly Ronald Chisom, David Billings, Margery Freeman, Monica Walker, and Barbara Major, for sharing their analysis of racism and organizational change strategies. Sandra Bernabei of the Antiracist Alliance of New York City has offered keen insights that have been integral to our work. Faculty of Columbia University, particularly Robert Carter and Cheryl Franks, have offered ongoing educational support to our agency staff. We are also grateful for our ongoing dialogue with many colleagues who have offered invaluable insights, including Shirley Better, George Cohen, Mahdi Fard, Phyllis Frank, Gail Golden, Kenneth Hardy, Janet Helms, Samuel Johnson, Monica McGoldrick, Kathleen Pogue-White, Elaine Pinderhughes, Anthony Porter, and David Thomas. The editors would also like to acknowledge the courage of Alan Siskind and Paul Levine, the executive leaders of the Jewish Board of Family and Children's Services, Inc., for their willingness to use an antiracist lens to engage in critical analysis of the organizational dynamics and service delivery of one of the largest mental health and social services agencies in the country. The Martha K. Selig Educational Institute of JBFCS, which provides education, training, and support to agency clinicians and continuing professional development throughout the community, has been a crucial part of this endeavor. The Institute is generously endowed and funded by the Saul Z. Cohen and Amy S. Cohen Family Foundation and named in honor of Martha K. Selig for her outstanding contribution to this important aspect of JBFCS' education and training program. Finally, we want to extend our gratitude to the many staff members of our agency who have taken personal and professional risks in the process of defining, implementing, and supporting antiracist practice.

SECTION I
THE EMOTIONAL AND PSYCHOLOGICAL IMPACT OF RACISM

Violence:
The Inarticulate Language
of Hate, Dread, and Despair:
An Introduction to Racism and Racial Identity:
Reflections on Urban Practice

Warren C. Lyons

SUMMARY. Violence, whether actual physical violence or the violence of oppression, is an inarticulate language rooted in an obscure matrix of hate, dread and despair. It connotes qualitatively discrete categories of pain–psychological, emotional, spiritual–that are beyond words, mocking our concept of human understanding. Facts are detached from reality. Reality is estranged from meaning. An academic approach to the

Address correspondence to: Warren C. Lyons, 120 Stuyvesant Place, 4th Floor, Staten Island, NY 10301.

[Haworth co-indexing entry note]: "Violence: The Inarticulate Language of Hate, Dread, and Despair: An Introduction to Racism and Racial Identity: Reflections on Urban Practice." Lyons, Warren C. Co-published simultaneously in *Journal of Emotional Abuse* (The Haworth Maltreatment & Trauma Press, an imprint of The Haworth Press, Inc.) Vol. 6, No. 2/3, 2006, pp. 1-7; and: *Racism and Racial Identity: Reflections on Urban Practice in Mental Health and Social Services* (ed: Lisa V. Blitz, and Mary Pender Greene) The Haworth Maltreatment & Trauma Press, an imprint of The Haworth Press, Inc., 2006, pp. 1-7. Single or multiple copies of this article are available for a fee from The Haworth Document Delivery Service [1-800-HAWORTH, 9:00 a.m. - 5:00 p.m. (EST). E-mail address: docdelivery@haworthpress.com].

Available online at http://jea.haworthpress.com
doi:10.1300/J135v06n02_01

subject of human violence that addresses those who commit such acts as well as those who fall victim, must engage something in and of the human experience of the irrational, but explicated from the *inside* of that experience. This is, admittedly, a quixotic proposition. Yet in the absence of such a perspective, any discussion of human violence is rendered, well, academic. doi:10.1300/J135v06n02_01   *[Article copies available for a fee from The Haworth Document Delivery Service: 1-800-HAWORTH. E-mail address: <docdelivery@haworthpress.com> Website: <http://www.HaworthPress.com> © 2006 by The Haworth Press, Inc. All rights reserved.]*

KEYWORDS. Violence, hate, dread, despair, oppression

Cruelty has a Human Heart,
And Jealousy a Human Face,
Terror the Human Form Divine,
And Secrecy the Human Dress

–William Blake

With honor and respect, I have agreed to introduce the work of a collective of writers, thinkers, educators, and clinical practitioners who are engaged in examining the issue of violence through the lens of racism. I seek to do so by way of "experiential" vignettes that, to me, go beyond the limitations of a strictly academic approach by communicating the sense of primal terror that underlies the experience of violence. This holds true whether the violence is inflicted by one against another, secretly and silently inflicted within the self, or whether it is physically or psychologically imposed or engendered by the impersonal and anonymous force of the State via neglectful and destructive social policies and practices.

Violence and love, sexuality and the terror of death are inextricably interwoven into the fabric of human experience. Attempts to articulate and clarify these interconnections inevitably evoke strange and provocative questions that penetrate to the very core of what it means to be human. I say "strange and provocative questions" because they implicate regions of the unconscious . . . the unknown. Anyone who thinks sincerely about these matters knows that this is true. The difficulties involved in this intricate and arduous pursuit explain to a considerable extent why it is avoided. Yet, I believe the anxiety aroused by these questions has something significant to do with the human propensity for violence, and that a familiarity with these weighty, brooding matters is indispensable to any who seek to negotiate this difficult psychological, emotional, and spiritual terrain.

Violence, however one opts to define it, is always opposed to love and empathy. This is so whether one takes a life or withholds that which makes a life worth living. In the following vignette, I attempt to capture the essence of a particular primal human reality, rendered in terms of the stark desolation of a soul embedded in the intractable violence of grinding poverty.

In considering an approach to this introductory piece, I had originally submitted another vignette. It was a terrifying account of a man who had brutally murdered his wife and child. Part of a larger psychodrama, the story unfolded somewhere in the deep recesses of the man's shattered mind. The vignette was rejected because of the unsettling and uncompromising level of violence and the likelihood that, as part of a volume on racism, it would have been assumed that the man was of African descent and thus would have endorsed, inadvertently perhaps, the stereotypical view of the African as enraged and given to an excess of violence.

But, what is both significant and instructive here is the fact that the piece, composed many years ago, was drawn from the headlines and that the central character was, in fact, a white, Jewish, upper-middle-class lawyer. Moreover, as horrifying as his actions was the tacit, vicarious violence of the social order itself, which by omission aided and abetted in the murder. "Animal!" "Beast!" "Monster!"–the headlines screamed. But what is the hidden meaning of this drama? What does it reveal that we dare not look at? What is a Nigger? A Kike? A Mick? A Spic? A Wop? What are they? Where do they live? And most importantly, where do they go–and what do they do–when we are sleeping? We are dealing here with the notion of projection.

Is it possible that this propensity for projection is, ineluctably, structured into our psychological being, perhaps as an aspect of the death side of the life force? If this is so, then our willingness to contain and confront the rejected and split-off parts of ourselves may be our only means of checking the violence we commit in the shadows of our projections. The violence I depicted, whether directed against the other or against the self, was not gratuitous. Instead, it was written in order to strip bare a reality that is intolerable to contemplate, despite the fact that it surrounds each of us as water surrounds the sea.

What confronts us here is a profound problem of human dimensions that simultaneously embraces and exceeds the dubious boundaries of race, gender, class, religion, or culture. Although these divisions may at once appear grounded in reality–psychological, political, social, economic, cultural, linguistic–they in no way can, even if taken together, encompass the degree of nuance that typifies the whole of a single human experience. Indeed, at the same time that we are faced with the bullet-riddled body of Amadou Diallo or the headless remains of James Byrd scattered along a lonesome stretch of Texas roadway, we are also faced with a dismembered history, with ignorant, inaccurate, and confusing thoughts and feelings that render useless almost any conceptual construct that purports to make the reality of human living in its depth and breadth comprehensible. The record of genocide and atrocity as well as human acts of violence against the process of life itself is the inadmissible evidence of our collective capacity to act irrationally in the grip of hate, dread, and despair. And yet, as a species, we try, despite hate, despite fear, and, most importantly, despite despair, to comprehend the incomprehensible. There is a stained and resplendent glory in this truth.

In what follows, my second vignette, I attempt to address a primal human reality. It is a visceral, not an intellectual, sense that I attempt to exploit. This category of experience is more to the point when seen from the inside of that experience. As such, the protagonist in the piece is exactly what she is; and so, she supercedes interpretation. I like the way in which the telling closes the distance between the character we would study, and the reality she contains that mocks the relevance of such a study. For beneath the ambient strangeness of the vignette lies something deep, secret, and terrifying about the nature of the human heart and soul. This "something," however, is felt at its most inarticulate moment of knowing. Here, the multifarious manifestations of human diversity and the ways in which evil operates in the world are not denied, but are instead incorporated as elements of a transcendent human truth which, while eluding analysis, nonetheless invites an order of contemplation that approaches the conditions of prayer. There are those moments when, in the depths of a kind of psychological and spiritual "ground zero," this is the only response we can offer, because it is the only response, short of an irrational impulse to destroy, that we can have.

It is inconceivable that one could trust anyone to help them out of this wasteland/promised land if that "guide" lacks sufficient intelligence, courage, emotional integrity, and stamina of spirit to recognize such states of consciousness as part of the human condition. I hope that what

I have presented will situate the material in the pages that follow, in a
helpful, albeit uncanny, light. And I hope, too, that this will enhance the
urgency of their message and relevance of these dedicated writers who,
through their thoughts and actions, continue to courageously grapple
with the large and difficult questions of our tormented and tormenting
times.

She lived alone
She lived alone with the cries of the child
The child's crushed in belly had been choked by an endless hunger
The paint was peeling off of the walls and the ceiling
Roaches and mice scurried about the tiny ice-coated apartment
in search of scraps of food, traces of warmth
She sat in a chair
She sat in a chair in a corner under a low intensity light
She sat against the backdrop of the endless cries of the child
She sat, this starving mother, amid a chaos of unending sorrows,
amid retreating memories of love, amid the gathering night of an inex-
pressible dread and hatred of herself and of living.
She lit a cigarette
She lit a cigarette and hung it on the corner of her chapped lips without
smoking it
It just hung there, its pale blue smoke clouding her vision and smooth-
ing the jagged edges of the child's shrill screams and cries
For weeks the piles of dishes in the sink had gone unwashed
There had been no man there for years–at least it seemed so
She'd been married, but it hadn't worked out and he left her with the
baby
Rumor had it that he was living with some woman somewhere not too
far away
But he was far away
Far away enough
Far away . . .

Broken toys lay scattered on the floor, dolls with eyes missing, a
pink leg under the lopsided table, an armless pink torso with a
hideous hairless head in the corner by a broken chair, a broken
baby carriage, a book of nursery rhymes with its binding broken
pages torn out and flung across the rugged landscape of the
tortured couch with its insides piling out of it in places where
the glue of the adhesive tape had so aged that it no longer held

the skin of this once mighty beast together
From time to time a sharp spring would suddenly jut out full of
menace, like a scream in the night
It was painful to see how she lived
Here, within her apartment one could see the complex schematic of
Human hopelessness displayed like a stage set for some utterly
depressing drama
This was her private hell of shattered dreams
A world of fragmented yesterdays stagnant in a frozen world of
immovable distances existing beneath her skin like an itch she could
not scratch

Nothing ever stopped the child from crying
Nothing ever stopped the child from crying
Nothing ever stopped the child from crying
The child was born crying
While it lay lodged in her womb she could hear its unborn screams
Often she would confuse them with her own
and often she would wish that she were dead
Things had not changed much since those early days
What was once deep inside was now further out
Reality had become only more intense with the birth
Her belly once full with the budding of the child was now full of an
insatiable hunger that came close to the edge of an eternity into which
she would only sometimes glance
And then in a kind of startled madness she would fling her eyes back
across the abyss of her stomach's mind and frightfully they would scan
the abyss of her falling apartment and she would descend into
her familiar bed of depression and consider the comforts of suicide

The darkness increased
The darkness increased
The darkness increased and in the half-dark her eyes could make out
the time by the clock on the far wall which hung crookedly there
3:30 a.m.
It was always 3:30 a.m.
She gnawed her nails, and then the skin surrounding them until her
fingers bled
It was 3:30 a.m. and the child was crying
The will of the child's cry was stronger than the will of its body
to yield to sleep

It was stronger than the silence against which it struggled
It was stronger than her
It forced her into a troubled sleeplessness that only tempered her
hatred, exposing her naked soul to dangerous emotions over which
she lacked all control

Outside, the sky had shut itself
The wind prowled over the ground like a wounded animal
seeking shelter from the wind

She thought of making a cup of tea, but she decided to light
another cigarette instead while she hummed an old tune which she
could not name or place
And then her face fell off, tumbling into a strange oblivion
Mirroring the quality of her useless night in its searching despair
and its exaggerated terror that swept unnoticed with the wind against
the cracked panes of her windows out of which she never looked.

doi:10.1300/J135v06n02_01

Racism and Invisibility:
Race-Related Stress, Emotional Abuse
and Psychological Trauma
for People of Color

Anderson J. Franklin
Nancy Boyd-Franklin
Shalonda Kelly

SUMMARY. This article presents an overview of the complex experiences of racism and the invisibility syndrome as they relate to issues of race-related stress, emotional abuse, and psychological trauma for people of color. Racism, through domination, power, and White privilege, is manifested in its individual, institutional, and cultural forms. Race-related stress is discussed as an outcome of perceived racism creating emotional abuse and psychological trauma. Consequences of racism are considered for family and couple relationships. A case example is presented illustrating the issues of racism in the professional and personal development of a staff member in a mental health agency. Examples of

Address correspondence to: Anderson J. Franklin, Department of Psychology, The City College of The City University of New York, Convent Avenue at 138th Street, New York, NY 10031 (E-mail address: afranklin@ccny.cuny.edu).

The authors would like to express their appreciation to Reshma Stafford for her contribution to the research for this paper. The names and identifying information in the case example have all been changed in order to protect the confidentiality of those involved.

[Haworth co-indexing entry note]: "Racism and Invisibility: Race-Related Stress, Emotional Abuse and Psychological Trauma for People of Color." Franklin, Anderson J., Nancy Boyd-Franklin, and Shalonda Kelly. Co-published simultaneously in *Journal of Emotional Abuse* (The Haworth Maltreatment & Trauma Press, an imprint of The Haworth Press, Inc.) Vol. 6, No. 2/3, 2006, pp. 9-30; and: *Racism and Racial Identity: Reflections on Urban Practice in Mental Health and Social Services* (ed: Lisa V. Blitz, and Mary Pender Greene) The Haworth Maltreatment & Trauma Press, an imprint of The Haworth Press, Inc., 2006, pp. 9-30. Single or multiple copies of this article are available for a fee from The Haworth Document Delivery Service [1-800-HAWORTH, 9:00 a.m. - 5:00 p.m. (EST). E-mail address: docdelivery@haworthpress.com].

interventions to combat racism are given, such as identifying resilience and strengths of people of color, and the role of the antiracist movement. doi:10.1300/J135v6n02_02 *[Article copies available for a fee from The Haworth Document Delivery Service: 1-800-HAWORTH. E-mail address: <docdelivery@haworthpress.com> Website: <http://www.HaworthPress.com> © 2006 by The Haworth Press, Inc. All rights reserved.]*

KEYWORDS. Racism, White privilege, invisibility syndrome, micro-aggressions, race-related stress, antiracist movement

This article presents an overview of racism and its complexity. It focuses upon understanding the role that power and White privilege play in the treatment of people of color. The creation of an invisibility syndrome and the experience of emotional abuse and psychological trauma are also explored. Acquiring strategies of resilience and antiracist training are presented as a means of combating racism.

Racism is complex and not easily defined because of the different levels of meaning, beliefs, and acts associated with the concept. Based on erroneous principles of racial superiority, it bestows power and privilege on those who define, enforce, and establish the institutional mechanisms that maintain it. Jones (1997) argues that racism formalizes "the hierarchical domination of one racial group over another" (p. 11). It is an overarching orientation toward people and groups that creates attitudes and sanctions acts that express specific negative views of others. Racism is defined by Harrell (2000) as

A system of dominance, power, and privilege based on racial-group designations . . . where members of the dominant group create or accept their societal privilege by maintaining structures, ideology, values, and behavior that have the intent or effect of leaving nondominant-group members relatively excluded from power, esteem, status, and/or equal access to societal resources. (p. 43)

Jones (1997) disentangles the confusion in understanding the definition of racism by discussing the centrality of prejudice and discrimination to the concept. He defines prejudice as "a positive or negative attitude, judgment, or feeling about a person that is generalized from attitudes or beliefs held about the group to which the person belongs" (p. 10).

Implicit in prejudice is the tendency to attach one-dimensional attributes or stereotypes to the person at the expense of all other characteristics. This tendency to hold a fixed view of others results in a failure to see the diversity within groups or the individuality of its members. Moreover, the victim of prejudice often feels indignant because he or she has been classified into a category and not judged according to his/her own characteristics.

The consequences of prejudice become apparent only in exposing patterns of discrimination, which constitute another important facet of racism. Jones' (1997) definition of discrimination "consists of negative behavior toward a person based on negative attitudes one holds toward the group to which that person belongs, or, positive behavior toward a person based on positive attributes one holds toward the group to which that person belongs" (p. 11). The important element in discrimination is its conversion of prejudice into specific behaviors or acts. Those acts, resulting from narrow attitudes and feelings about a group, are an expression of the individual's personal prejudices. Acts can be legalized or organized forms of prejudice through institutional policies, laws, or other group practices. Segregation and inequities in housing or employment are examples. Racism therefore includes prejudice and discrimination as elements that help manifest it.

INDIVIDUAL, INSTITUTIONAL, AND CULTURAL RACISM

Jones (1997) identifies three different domains of racism, which are its individual, institutional, and cultural forms. *Individual racism* includes the attitudes and acts that express a person's prejudices. This form of racism is located in the individual's interpretation of his/her feelings about other people. People draw upon the prevailing attitude of their group toward others utilizing mechanisms within the larger society to support their individual beliefs, and to discriminate in accordance with those beliefs. *Institutional racism* is the process whereby individual racist beliefs, nurtured by convictions of power and authority, are converted into discriminatory policies and procedures of the institution. These policies manifest in the conscious or unconscious prejudicial feelings of the dominant group towards others. Through biased policies, institutions help maintain the advantages of one group and restrict the access of another group to valuable resources and opportunities. *Cultural racism* is the result of the privileged group's power to determine values, beliefs, attitudes, and practices so that they become legitimate expressions of its culture. It makes preferences and behaviors of the dominant group an intrinsic part of the social fabric, and sets the boundaries to be observed for acceptance or non-acceptance of others. Thus, cultural racism creates an environment that lets certain prejudices and discrimination appear natural and part of everyday behavior, as occurred with slavery in America and apartheid in South Africa. Individual, institutional, and cultural racism all breed White privilege.

WHITE PRIVILEGE

By the preeminence of cultural racism, White privilege becomes a presumed benefit of group membership. Since it is greatly determined by skin color, White privilege begins at birth and accrues benefits throughout the life span. White privilege therefore refers to unearned resources and/or power held by Whites. It results from acts of individual, institutional, and cultural racism that keep the advantage of Whites while marginalizing people of color. These unearned resources and power tend to be unacknowledged and bolstered by notions of superiority versus fairness. The disparities in advantage are only revealed, for example, when employment, educational, and health statuses of non-Whites are compared to Whites. McIntosh (1998) states that, "Whites are carefully taught not to recognize White privilege, as males are taught not to recognize male privilege" (p. 148). Similarly, Bowser and Hunt (1996) note that some Whites see racism as a "Black" problem, and thus they do not claim any personal ownership in the creation of the aforementioned disparities. The superiority of Whites, therefore, is often consciously, or unconsciously, assumed and promoted as their right. Since so many privileges are taken for granted, their expectation and benefits are often not stated explicitly and can easily be denied. Non-Whites, with less power and resources, are often put in the position of protesting unfair standards created by institutions controlled by Whites. Their protests are often dismissed as unworthy, or ignored because of the underlying challenge to White privilege. This process further excludes people of color from the privileges that Whites enjoy. When they are repeatedly placed in situations of this type, people of color can feel that their true talents and abilities are overlooked and undervalued as if they are invisible.

THE INVISIBILITY SYNDROME

Cumulative experiences of confronting race-related stress, emotional abuse, and the psychological trauma of racism can lead to the development of the invisibility syndrome (Franklin, 1999, 2004; Franklin & Boyd-Franklin, 2000). Symptoms of the syndrome are an outcome of psychological conditions produced when a person perceives that his or her talents and identity are not seen because of the dominance of preconceived attitudes and stereotypes. Persons of color experience this as a slight or microaggression (Franklin, 2004; Pierce, 1995). Unresolved psychological injury from slights can create debilitating symptoms. According to Franklin (2004), such debilitation from slights "limits the effective utilization of personal resources, the achievement of individual goals, the establishment of positive relationships, the satisfaction of family interactions, and the potential for life satisfaction" (p. 11).

Microaggressions and Everyday Racism

Slights are fundamental to the invisibility syndrome. They provoke indignation and emotional upset because they are acts based upon biased attitudes and beliefs. These acts are considered "microaggressions" (Pierce, 1995). Interpersonal interactions that take no genuine notice of the other person are unsettling, and can create disillusionment or confusion. Microaggressions, therefore, are acts of disregarding the person of color based on biased beliefs. Recipients of these acts of slight, as with other racist treatment, feel invisible in its rejection and disrespect of their personhood (Franklin & Boyd-Franklin, 2000; Pierce, 1995). People of color experience microaggressions as consistent with previous treatment of disrespect and injurious to their self-esteem. Repeated experiences of such slights, which come periodically but inevitably, require anger management and the resolution of the emotional upset from the incident. Inability to successfully resolve the upset from perceived recurring slights can cause mental health problems such as race-related stress, chronic indignation, depression, or substance abuse (Franklin, 2004).

Another problem related to such slights is internalized racism, wherein people of color begin to believe in their own inferiority and accept negative views disseminated in society about their racial group (Kelly, 2004). Kelly's data have shown that a variety of internalized racist views held by some African Americans are associated with increased symptoms of psychological distress.

Essed's (1991) research has further documented the experiences of "everyday racism" in the lives of people of color. On a daily basis, ethnic minorities must cope with overt as well as covert manifestations of racism on institutional, individual, and cultural levels (Jones, 1997). Overt and covert forms of everyday racism in the lives of people of color include ethnocentrism, harassment, humiliation, and institutional practices that restrain their goals and aspirations (Essed, 1991; Sanchez-Hucles, 1998). These constant experiences wear away at the psyche and can result in a cumulative experience of psychological trauma and emotional burnout over time.

PERCEIVED RACISM

Researchers and scholars have identified perceived racism as a major contributor to the race-related life stress experienced by people of color (Clark, Anderson, Clark, & Williams, 1999; Essed, 1991; Harrell, 2000; Jones, 1997; Sue, 2003; Thompson, 2002; Utsey, Chae, Brown, & Kelly, 2002). Harrell (2000) has indicated that these experiences with racism can be pervasive because they are embedded within the "interpersonal, collective, cultural-symbolic and sociopolitical contexts" (p. 44). As Jones (1997) points out, however, the vestiges of modern racism are often manifested on an institutional level and are so pervasive and entrenched within American society that they are essentially invisible to many White Americans. They are obscured by White privilege.

Clark et al. (1999) have demonstrated that the perception of racism is the most important aspect of its impact. They have defined perceived racism as the "subjective experience of prejudice or discrimination" (p. 809). The recognition that racism need not be proven "objectively" in order to produce stress was a very important step forward in research on this topic. Harrell (2000) has clarified the linkage between this subjectivity, perceived racism, and race-related stress:

> The subjective judgment of the individual is the critical point of analysis in understanding the impact of racism on well-being. However it is not uncommon for experiences of racism to be questioned or challenged by others. Such requests for "proof" can create a my-perception-against-yours dilemma that may include accusations of paranoia, hostility, oversensitivity, manipulation, self-serving motives, or having a chip on one's shoulder (Essed, 1991). Thus, the stress–and potential damage–of racism lies not

only in the specific incident, but also in the resistance of others to believing and validating the reality or significance of one's personal experience. (pp. 44-45)

RACE-RELATED STRESS

Harrell's (2000) research has identified six types of stress related to individual, institutional, and cultural racism. These stressors can lead to intense emotional and psychological reactions in people of color that might include anxiety, anger, a sense of vulnerability and sadness. *Racism-related life events* are significant life experiences with racism that often involve overt discrimination. *Vicarious racism experiences* may not occur directly to the individual but to friends or family members. They can also involve strangers, such as the 1998 dragging death of James Byrd, Jr., a Black man in Jasper, Texas. *Daily racism microstressors* are frequent reminders that one's race matters through little acts of slights or exclusion. Pierce (1995) and Franklin (1999, 2004), as previously noted, refer to this as microaggressions. *Chronic-contextual stress* is related to societal structural inequities and diminished opportunities for people of color. In addition, Harrell (2000) points out that the experience of being the "token" or "the only one" in predominantly White settings can lead to increased stress for people of color. *Collective experiences* involve perceptions of discrimination towards one's racial group as represented by ongoing disparities in the distribution of political power, wealth, and socioeconomic status. *Transgenerational transmission* is stress associated with the legacy of racism for many people of color. Harrell (2000) argues that one must understand the experience of each racial/ethnic group within the context of their history of treatment in America. Many researchers and scholars have documented that transgenerational traumas such as slavery, oppression, segregation, and discrimination can be transmitted through stories and "collective memory" (Crawford, Nobles, & Leary, 2003; Klonoff & Landrine, 1999; Marsella, Friedman, Gerrity, & Scurfield, 1996; Root, 1992).

Post-Traumatic Slave Syndrome

Some scholars believe the legacy of trauma from slavery transcends generations, creating residual effects that are manifested in present behavior. *Post-Traumatic Slave Syndrome* is a conceptual framework provided by Leary and colleagues (Crawford et al.,

2003; Leary, 2002) to describe the multigenerational trauma experienced by African Americans as a result of slavery and their past and present experiences of racism and discrimination. These injustices have created distinct psychosocial outcomes. Leary (2002) argues that these emotional and psychological traumas transmitted intergenerationally have never healed, and continue to have psychological consequences for African Americans. Some examples are a lack of self-esteem, or the anger and violence currently seen in some young African American males.

RACISM-RELATED EMOTIONAL ABUSE, PSYCHOLOGICAL TRAUMA, AND PTSD

Sanchez-Hucles (1998) clarifies that racism can be a form of emotional abuse and trauma for ethnic minorities because it involves negative, rejecting, and/or demeaning societal messages that undermine self-esteem. Building on the work of Hart, Germain, and Brassard (1983), Sanches-Hucles describes emotional abuse as "consisting of both acts of commission and omission that are psychologically damaging and can be perpetuated by groups or by individuals" (p. 73). Emotional abuses can adversely impact one's affective, behavioral, and cognitive functioning.

According to the *Diagnostic and Statistical Manual of Mental Disorders* (DSM-IV-TR; American Psychiatric Association, 2000), some instances of emotional abuse or psychological trauma can be justifiably diagnosed as Post Traumatic Stress Disorder (PTSD). The DSM-IV-TR discusses cultural aspects of PTSD in terms of immigrants' experiences of psychological trauma from abuse (e.g., torture) in their countries of origin. However, it does not discuss racism as a trauma despite the fact that racism can be extreme and catastrophic (Butts, 2002). Some argue that racism-related aspects of trauma may operate in ways that are different from classic PTSD (Marsella, Friedman, & Spain, 1996; Sanchez-Hucles, 1998). In particular, the DSM-IV-TR specifies that traumatic events must involve actual or witnessed "death, serious injury or threat to one's physical integrity" (American Psychiatric Association, 2000, p. 463). Yet Sanchez-Hucles (1998) notes that "the trauma and emotional abusiveness of racism is as likely to be due to chronic, systemic, and invisible assaults on the personhoods of ethnic minorities as a single catastrophic event" (p. 72).

A number of scholars, clinicians, and researchers have argued for expanding the definition of PTSD to include responses to racism by people of color (Allen, 1996; Butts, 2002; Marsella, Friedman, Gerrity et al., 1996; Root, 1992; Sanchez-Hucles, 1998). Root (1992) describes the trauma of racism as "insidious trauma." Sanchez-Hucles (1998) and Root (1992) both argue that current trauma theory and definitions of PTSD "fail to address the accumulated effects of devalued status for ethnic minorities that begins upon birth, persists through a lifetime, and carries threats to individuals' well-being even when actual violence is not acted out" (Sanchez-Hucles, 1998, pp. 78-79). Butts (2002) notes that the origins of trauma related to PTSD in the DSM-IV-TR are not inclusive enough. In his opinion, racial/ethnic discrimination experiences can result in symptoms associated with a diagnosis of PTSD.

Carter, Forsyth, Mazzula, and Williams (2004) have presented an important caution, however, against a blaming-the-victim approach to racism and PTSD. They clarify that the use of the term "disorder" locates the problem in the individual person of color. These researchers argue that "it is more accurate to assess the effects of racism (e.g., harassment and discrimination) as psychological and emotional injury than as mental disorder since the effects of racism come from the sociocultural environment, not from an abnormality that resides within the individual" (p. 12). They caution clinicians that diagnosing persons of color who have encountered race-related trauma with PTSD may lead to individual treatment strategies that may ignore the systemic, environmental, and institutional factors of racism.

Allen (1996) has established the link between racism, the trauma of urban community violence and PTSD. Hacker (1992) has argued that the persistent racism in America and its sociopolitical consequences have created a reality of trauma and deprivation in the lives of many persons of color, particularly those living in poverty. In fact, Hacker has referred to Black-on-Black violence as "self-inflicted genocide." Allen (1996) describes these experiences as "traumatogenic" (p. 216) and as major contributing factors in PTSD in inner-city, poor communities of color. He notes that the number of African American youth who have witnessed or experienced violence has added to the increase in violence in inner-city communities and to the increase in PTSD.

In this ongoing debate about racism and PTSD, it is important to note that the responses of people of color to racism-related trauma vary from person to person. Clearly, it would be unlikely that every person of color who experiences racism would also have PTSD. Other responses may include depression, anxiety, violence, problematic family and couple relationships, and medical symptoms. Many intervening variables may impact the extent of the psychological effects of racism, including the severity of the stressor. For example, the most at risk may be persons of color who have experienced or witnessed racial attacks or racial violence such as homicide, police brutality, or other events resulting in death or serious injury. It may also be helpful to explore the development of a new category such as "Reactions to Racism-Related Trauma" that would more broadly recognize the impact of racism without stigmatizing the victim. Risk factors such as poverty, mental illness, substance abuse, disabilities, and prolonged exposure to intense negative experiences with racism may all impact the response of a person of color. It is also important to recognize the impact of protective factors such as family and extended kinship networks, religion and spirituality, strong cultural values and racial identity, and personal strength and resiliency that may allow many people of color to rise above the debilitating, ongoing trauma of racism.

CONSEQUENCES OF RACISM

Effects on Mental and Physical Health

Clark et al. (1999) developed a biopsychosocial model demonstrating that when a person of color perceives an environmental stimulus as racist, it results in a sequelae of psychological and physiological stress responses that can seriously compromise both mental and physical health and well-being. A number of researchers have documented that racism is a unique source of stress impacting African Americans' mental health (Klonoff & Landrine, 1999; Utsey et al., 2002; Williams & Williams-Morris, 2000). Utsey et al. have shown that the stress of racism is associated with anxiety and major depression. African Americans report significantly more unfair treatment and chronic stress than Whites (Troxel, Matthews, Bromberger, & Sutton-Tyrell, 2003). The Surgeon General's Report entitled, *Mental Health: Culture, Race and Ethnicity: A Supplement to Mental Health: A Report of the Surgeon General,* has documented ethnic and racial disparities in mental health services (U.S. Department of Health and Human Services, 2001).

Experiences of racism and discrimination are also negatively associated with psychological and physical health (e.g., Bowen-Reid & Harrell, 2002; Carter et al., 2004; Jackson, Brown, Williams, Torres, Sellers, & Brown, 1996; Kwate, Valdimarsdottir, Guevarra, & Bovbjerg, 2003; Thompson, 2002; Troxel et al., 2003). There is a link between African Americans' racism-related stress and hypertension, heart disease, and poor functioning of the immune system (Brondolo, Rieppi, Kelly, & Guerin, 2003; Clark et al., 1999; Din-Dzietham, Nembhard, Collins, & Davis, 2004).

As a result of societal and institutional racism that has consistently led to inferior treatment for people of color by the medical field, disparities in health care have become a major health issue for the country (Allen, 1996). Johnson, Lee, Cook, Rowan, and Goldman (1993) compared African Americans and European Americans who presented with acute chest pain. Blacks in this study received a much lower rate of coronary bypass procedures than their White counterparts, irrespective of their socioeconomic level (Allen, 1996). Consistent with this finding, Kasiske et al. (1991), in their study of kidney, pancreas, and liver transplants, noted that fewer Black than White patients actually received these procedures (Allen, 1996). The AIDS epidemic is yet another example of these health care disparities (Allen, 1996; Boyd-Franklin, 2003; Hutchinson, 1992; Rockeymore, 2002; Smith, 1992). Allen (1996) and Smith (1992) describe AIDS as a devastating illness that is now the leading cause of death for Black men between the ages of 35 and 44. Boyd-Franklin (2003) and Rockeymore (2002) report that African Americans represent almost half (47%) of all U.S. AIDS cases while they comprise only 12% of the population. Hutchinson (1992) has indicated that the government's slow response to AIDS in minority communities is partly determined by racism (Allen, 1996).

The Effects of Racism and Poverty

The impact of racism contributes to conditions of poverty. Unemployment, underemployment, social and medical problems, and inequities in schools and financial lending institutions are as much consequences of racism as they are of poverty (Allen, 1996; Hacker, 1992). The unemployment rate in inner-city African American communities has had a devastating impact on the well-being of these individuals and their families (Allen, 1996; Wilson, 1996). Many of these chronically unemployed workers are no longer counted in national statistics and have become so discouraged that they have lost hope (Hacker, 1992). Such conditions have led some to become part of an underground illicit economy, such as selling drugs, in a desperate attempt to survive.

The statistics related to the disproportionate numbers of African American men in prison are staggering, and further represent the poverty dilemma. Allen (1996) considered this disproportional representation as a result of endemic societal racism and a source of ongoing psychological trauma for many African Americans. He discusses Hacker's (1992) research that demonstrated that the percentage of Black men in prison had doubled from 22% to 45%. Research also reveals that one-fourth of African American men aged 20 to 29 are either in prison, on probation, or on parole, and that more African American men are in prison than in college (Prothrow-Stith, 1991, as cited in Allen, 1996). Franklin (2004) notes that Black men continue to comprise 45% of male inmates in federal, state, or local prisons. Moreover, now close to a third of Black males have had some official contact with the justice system. They are also "overrepresented in all phases of the juvenile justice process. Blacks are more than six times as likely as Whites to be sentenced to prison by juvenile courts" (Franklin, 2004, pp. 155-156). The disproportional representation of adolescents of color in the juvenile justice system is in sharp contrast to their White counterparts, who are far more likely to be referred for mental health services (Boyd-Franklin, 2003).

The trauma of racism begins early in life for people of color as is evident in inner-city school systems. Racism, particularly for African American males, has contributed to low teacher expectations, heavy reliance on biased standardized tests, the overrepresentation of African American males in special education, and the disproportionally large numbers of children of color who are diagnosed with Attention Deficit Hyperactivity Disorder (ADHD) and placed on Ritalin (Boyd-Franklin, 2003; Boyd-Franklin, Franklin, & Toussaint, 2001). Allen (1996), Hacker (1992), and Kozol (1991) have documented hyper-segregation in the majority of American public schools. Kozol (1991) found chronic underfunding of inner city schools serving African American children. These are examples of patterns of societal and institutional racism.

As discussed by McGlade and Ackerman (this volume), the child welfare system is another arena in which the traumatic effects of institutional racism have been documented. Roberts (2002) in her book, *Shattered Bonds: The Color of Child Welfare*, has thoroughly researched the disproportionate representation of Black children in the foster care system. Roberts clearly describes the processes of racism and racial injustice that result in the removal of children from struggling, poor Black families, while keeping White families with similar presenting problems intact.

Consequences of Race-Related Stress and Trauma for Family and Couple Relationships

Racism clearly has an impact on family and couple relationships for people of color (Boyd-Franklin, 2003; Boyd-Franklin et al., 2001; Franklin, 2004; Kelly, 2003). Parents of color often report fear for their children, particularly their male children, when faced with such realities as racial profiling, police brutality, violence, and high homicide rates (Boyd-Franklin et al., 2001). African Americans and other parents of color have the challenge of developing positive racial identity in their children, while preparing them for the realities of racism in today's world (Stevenson & Davis, 2004). The additional challenge of this task is also cultivating in them a sense of efficacy and hopefulness in the midst of the continuing significance of racism across class levels.

Couple relationships are also profoundly affected by experiences of racism (Boyd-Franklin, 2003; Kelly, 2003). Racism and the invisibility syndrome of African American men affect the nature and quality of the couple's dynamics on all levels (Franklin, 1999, 2004). A number of researchers have discussed the relationship between experiences of racism, unemployment rates of Black men, the shortage of African American men, and the decline in marriage rates among African American couples (Taylor, Jackson, & Chatters, 1997; Tucker & Mitchell-Kernan, 1995). Racism has also influenced the racial identity dynamics in Black couples (Kelly & Floyd, 2001), the socialization of African American males and females, the complex and often contradictory gender messages that they receive, gender roles, and the dynamics of power in Black couples (Boyd-Franklin, 2003). All of these dynamics have major clinical implications for individual, family, couple and group treatment of African Americans and other people of color (Boyd-Franklin, 2003; Franklin, 1997, 1999, 2004; Kelly, 2003).

Racism and Middle Class People of Color

In the last 30 years, there has been a dramatic increase in the number of people of color who are middle class (Boyd-Franklin, 2003). Despite external manifestations of an improved lifestyle, however, many of these individuals and families still expressed that they felt a more subtle and covert form of individual and institutional racism that can be equally emotionally abusive and traumatic (Boyd-Franklin, 2003; Cose, 1993; Feagin & McKinney, 2003; Hill, 1999). Many of these individuals, although earning good incomes, feel a constant sense of vulnerability related to their own invisibility in the workplace (Franklin, 2004), the ongoing experience of the glass ceiling in terms of promotions and upper-level opportunities, and the continued experience of being the "last hired and first fired," particularly during times of economic hardship and downsizing (Boyd-Franklin, 2003; Cose, 1993; Feagin & McKinney, 2003; Hill, 1999).

Cose (1993), in his research on successful African Americans, discovered a tremendous amount of anger and rage about their daily encounters with multiple levels of racism. He reports the following types of experiences: the inability to fit in, low expectations by coworkers and supervisors, shattered hopes, faint praise, presumption of failure, coping fatigue, self-censorship and silence, and the fear of being forced to shed one's racial identity in order to succeed. Some of his respondents also reported feeling the pressure to keep quiet regarding the racist practices of their organizations.

Racism in the Mental Health Field

Although Cose (1993) addressed racism experienced by African Americans primarily in corporate America, many examples exist in other work environments, such as mental health and social service agencies (Markowitz, 1993; Rastogi & Wieling, 2004). The following example illustrates the experiences of a young African American social worker subjected to the subtleties of institutional and individual racism at work. (See Samuel-Young, this volume, for additional discussion of the impact of racism on helping professionals.)

Pamela: A Case of Race-Related Stress and Trauma

Pamela, a 27-year-old African American social worker and recent MSW graduate, began her first job in the field at a mental health agency in New Jersey. A well-trained clinician, she had received excellent evaluations in her graduate program and from her supervisors at her field placements. She had been pleased when she was offered this position because she knew that the clinic was in a poor, inner-city area. Her dream throughout her schooling had been to work with people of color in treatment. On her first day at the clinic, however, she was very surprised to learn that she was the only person of color on the social work and supervisory staff.

During her years with the agency, most of her White colleagues went out to lunch and socialized together but did not include her. Despite the fact that she was naturally friendly and often reached out to the other social work staff, they seemed polite but distant. As a consequence of these experiences, Pamela felt very isolated. These experiences are not unusual for persons of color in predominantly White institutions.

When Pamela changed her hair to "locks," an Afrocentric hairstyle, her supervisor commented that some of the staff had suggested that it was "inappropriate" and raised concerns about her ability to "fit in" at the agency. This was an example of cultural racism because the norms of the agency only accepted a more Eurocentric style and required her to behave in ways that were in conflict with her own cultural practice.

In supervision, Pamela often attempted to discuss the cultural issues related to the treatment of her clients of color, but her supervisor was dismissive. Staff meetings and case conferences were particularly difficult for her. The majority of the staff viewed cases and clients through a very White, Eurocentric lens and was not open to her attempts to discuss cultural dynamics and related issues of diagnosis and treatment. At one meeting, a staff member referred to their clients of color as "those people" and added that they are "all abusive of their children." When Pamela raised a concern about this use of racial stereotypes, she was told that she was "too sensitive." She would make comments in meetings that were ignored. Often, later in the meeting another staff member would raise exactly the same point and it would be welcomed and discussed favorably. Some of the other clinical staff would come to her privately and acknowledge her concerns about the treatment of clients, but they would remain silent during the meetings. Her supervisor began giving her feedback that she was "too assertive and outspoken" at meetings, and "too obsessed with cultural and racial issues." Over time, she felt silenced, invisible, and marginalized.

At the end of her second year, in response to a mandate from a funding source, the agency began instituting cultural competency training. Despite this training, her colleagues seemed oblivious to issues of White privilege and subtle forms of racism at their agency. For example, several of the young White social workers were being mentored by the director and were being given opportunities for training that were important to their career development and their ability to apply for supervisory positions in the future. They were given the opportunity to present at conferences with senior staff and supervisors and were encouraged to start a private practice. None of these opportunities for mentoring were ever offered to Pamela. She later learned that her salary was far less than many of the other social workers. The ability to find mentors and professional role models within our agencies is often a privilege that is unavailable to therapists of color.

As a benefit of the diversity training, the agency began a process of attempting to recruit other therapists of color. Pamela was often asked to be a part of the interviewing and recruitment of these candidates. A year later, when she raised the concern that very few persons of color were actually hired, she was told that they could not find "qualified" candidates, even though many were very qualified and had years of clinical experience. As a consequence of this institutional racism, she often felt like a "token," included only when the agency wanted to demonstrate its cultural sensitivity.

The cumulative effects of these microaggressions, everyday racism, experiences of invisibility, discrimination, institutional racism, and White privilege, were very traumatic for Pamela. Many of these experiences may have been unintentional on the part of her agency and her colleagues but the experience of racism led to increased stress and conflict for her. By the end of her third year, she began to feel depressed, overwhelmed, and burnt out. She was often angry. Although she loved her work with clients, she began to dread going into work. At night, she would often have nightmares about stressful work situations and would often relive the trauma during the day. Initially, she shared her experiences with her family and friends, who were sympathetic but had their own experiences of racism to share. She was so upset that she sought treatment to address this race-related stress and trauma. Despite her positive feelings for her clients and her sense that she was a good clinician, she began to look for another job and ultimately left the agency.

Pamela's experiences are very common among therapists of color in the mental health field and social service agencies. While the field has begun to address the issues of race-related stress, emotional abuse, and the trauma of racism related to the treatment of clients of color, the concerns of social workers, psychologists, child and family workers, and support staff of color have been largely ignored and "invisible" in the literature (Markowitz, 1993; Rastogi & Wieling, 2004). It is extremely important that their concerns be included in the dialogue if we are to create truly antiracist organizations.

STRATEGIES IN COMBATING RACISM

Resilience and Survival Skills in the Face of Racism

In combating the stress, emotional abuse, and psychological trauma caused by racism, invisibility, and discrimination, it is important to remember the inner strength, resilience, personal and collective determination, and spiritual faith that have allowed generations of people of color to develop effective coping mechanisms and to survive these traumas (Boyd-Franklin, 2003). Resilience as defined by Masten, Best, and Garmezy (1990) is the capacity for successful adaptation despite challenging or threatening risks. These "culturally constructed modes of adaptation, first learned in the family and at school, become the foundation for resilience across the years of childhood and adulthood" (Cohler, Scott, & Musick, 1995, p. 785). In his seminal research on Black families, Hill (1999) documents the legacy of strengths that have contributed to this survival: strong kinship bonds, spirituality and religious orientation, flexible roles, strong educational and work orientation. Mullings and Wali (2000) show how vital these practices and social networks are to African American women who remain resilient in spite of obstacles from racism in getting reproductive health care and the demands of raising young children in Harlem. Boyd-Franklin (2003) describes the ways in which African Americans utilize their blood and non-blood extended family and friendship networks as a buffer against these traumas. Similarly, spirituality and religious orientation have often provided an opportunity for healing the pain of emotional abuse and psychological trauma. Clinicians can learn to utilize strong kinship bonds and spiritual beliefs to help clients and families deal with the trauma of racism. Other aspects of resiliency and strengths- based interventions are discussed further in Edwards (this volume).

Antiracism: Developing an Antiracist Ideology

Scholars and community activists have identified a number of steps in the development of an antiracist ideology (Chisom & Washington, 1997; Jones, 1997; Sue, 2003). Many of these authors agree that the first step, particularly for concerned Whites, is to educate oneself through reading and discussions with persons of color about the nature of racism in its individual, institutional, and cultural forms. Knowledge of White privilege is equally important because it is so intrinsic to American life that deleterious outcomes are often unrecognized and unacknowledged by many White individuals (McIntosh, 1998). Sue (2003) addresses the role of White people and persons of color in the process of moving toward antiracism. He encourages White individuals to take responsibility for learning about racism directly from people of color. He points out that America is still very segregated along racial and ethnic lines, in terms of real, intimate contact between groups, and argues that this contact is necessary outside of the workplace if change is to occur. This involves sharing mutual goals and working with others toward antiracist social change. Sue clarifies that this involves learning from constant vigilance of one's own stereotypes, prejudices, biases, and fears. It also involves the willingness on the part of Whites to speak out about these injustices, particularly in terms of institutional racism, and to take the risks to work with people of color for social change. Blitz (this volume) and Kohl (this volume) offer suggestions for White workers for exploring these issues. One powerful aspect of White privilege is the ability to choose not to get involved. In the case of Pamela, described previously, she often sensed that her White colleagues agreed with her concerns about their clients of color. They would even verbalize their agreement privately. A major antiracist act for these clinicians would be to speak out against policies based on institutional racism as they impact their work with clients and compromise colleagues and staff of color.

Clinicians who are committed to this work may find it helpful to seek out trainings that offer them the opportunity to expand their understanding of racism and to explore their own cultural experiences and values, as well as their own prejudices, within a safe environment. It is also important to participate in trainings and conferences that provide clinicians with the opportunity to explore the ways in which racism, race-related stress, and trauma may impact the lives of clients of color and strategies for addressing these issues in treatment. Those interested in pursuing these opportunities are encouraged to contact their national and local professional organizations in the fields of social work, psychology, psychiatry, and family therapy for information on continuing education programs in areas such as multiculturalism, cultural diversity, and antiracism.

Chisom and Washington (1997) in their book, *Undoing Racism,* and their training by the same name, encourage concerned individuals who share these values to become a part of the antiracist movement toward social change and social justice. This requires that we move beyond the important discussion of individual racism and begin to confront institutional racism on the level of organizational change and social policy.

Sue (2003) and Chisom and Washington (1997) offer many concrete examples of ways in which White and ethnic minority practitioners can become actively involved in this work.

REFERENCES

Allen, I. M. (1996). PTSD among African Americans. In A. J. Marsella, M. J. Friedman, E. T. Gerrity, & R. M. Scurfield (Eds.), *Ethnocultural aspects of post-traumatic stress disorder: Issues, research and clinical applications* (pp. 209-238). Washington, DC: American Psychological Association.

American Psychiatric Association (2000). *Diagnostic and statistical manual of mental disorders* (4th ed., text revision). Washington, DC: Author.

Blitz, L. V. (2006). Owning whiteness: The reinvention of self and practice. *Journal of Emotional Abuse, 6*(2/3), 241-263.

Bowen-Reid, T. L., & Harrell, J. P. (2002). Racist experiences and health outcomes: An examination of spirituality as a buffer. *Journal of Black Psychology, 28*, 18-36.

Bowser, B. P., & Hunt, R. G. (Eds.) (1996). *Impact of racism on Whites* (2nd ed.). Thousand Oaks, CA: Sage.

Boyd-Franklin, N. (2003). *Black families in therapy: Understanding the African American experience* (2nd ed.). New York: Guilford.

Boyd-Franklin, N., Franklin, A. J., & Toussaint, P. (2001). *Boys into men: Raising our African American teenage sons.* New York: Plume.

Brondolo, E., Rieppi, R., Kelly, K. P., & Guerin, W. (2003). Perceived racism and blood pressure: A review of the literature and conceptual and methodological critique. *Annals of Behavioral Medicine, 25*, 55-65.

Butts, H. F. (2002). The Black mask of humanity: Racial/ethnic discrimination and post-traumatic stress disorder. *Journal of the American Academy of Psychiatry and the Law, 30*, 336-339.

Carter, R. T., Forsyth, J. M., Mazzula, S. L., & Williams, B. (2004, July). *Deconstructing racial discrimination: The intersection of psychology and the law.* Paper presented at the meeting of the American Psychological Association, Honolulu, Hawaii.

Chisom, R., & Washington, M. (1997). *Undoing racism: A philosophy of international social change.* New Orleans, LA: People's Institute Press.

Clark, R., Anderson, N. B., Clark, V. R., & Williams, D. R. (1999). Racism as a stressor for African Americans: A biopsychosocial model. *American Psychologist, 54*, 805-816.

Cohler, B. J., Scott, F. M., & Musick, J. S. (1995). Adversity, vulnerability, and resilience: Cultural and developmental perspectives. In D. Cicchetti & D. J. Cohen (Eds.), *Developmental psychopathology, Vol. 2: Risk, disorder and adaptation* (pp. 753-800). New York: John Wiley & Sons.

Cose, E. (1993). *The rage of a privileged class.* New York: Harper Collins.

Crawford, J., Nobles, W. W., & Leary, J. D. (2003). Reparations and health care for African Americans: Repairing the damage from the legacy of slavery. In R. T.

Winbush (Ed.), *Should America pay? Slavery and the raging debate on reparations* (pp. 251-281). New York: Amistad.

Din-Dzietham, R., Nembhard, W. N., Collins, R., & Davis, S. K. (2004). Perceived stress following race-related discrimination at work is associated with hypertension in African Americans. *Social Science & Medicine, 58*, 449-461.

Edwards, B. L. (2006). The impact of racism on social functioning: Is it skin deep? *Journal of Emotional Abuse, 6*(2/3), 31-46.

Essed, P. (1991). *Understanding everyday racism: An interdisciplinary theory.* Newbury Park, CA: Sage.

Feagin, J. R., & McKinney, K. D. (2003). *The many costs of racism.* Lantham, MD: Rowman & Littlefield, Publisher.

Franklin, A. J. (1997, Summer). Importance of friendship issues between African American men in a therapeutic support group. *Journal of African American Men, 3*, 29-43.

Franklin, A. J. (1999). Invisibility syndrome and racial identity development in psychotherapy and counseling African American men. *Counseling Psychologist, 27*, 761-793.

Franklin, A. J. (2004). *From brotherhood to manhood: How Black men rescue their relationships and dreams from the invisibility syndrome.* New Jersey: John Wiley.

Franklin, A. J., & Boyd-Franklin, N. (2000). Invisibility syndrome: A clinical model of the effects of racism on African-American males. *American Journal of Orthopsychiatry, 70*, 33-41.

Hacker, A. (1992). *Two nations: Black and White, separate, hostile and unequal.* New York: Charles Scribner & Sons.

Harrell, S. P. (2000). A multidimensional conceptualization of racism-related stress: Implications for the well-being of people of color. *American Journal of Orthopsychiatry, 70*, 42-57.

Hart, S., Germain, R., & Brassard, M. (Eds.). (1983). *Proceedings summary of the International Conference on Psychological Abuse of Children and Youth.* Indiana University: Office for the Study of the Psychological Rights of the Child.

Hill, R. (1999). *The strengths of African American families: Twenty-five years later.* Lanham, MD: University Press of America.

Hutchinson, J. (1992). AIDS and racism in America. *Journal of the National Medical Association, 84*, 119-124.

Jackson, J. S., Brown, T. N., Williams, D. R., Torres, M., Sellers, S. L., & Brown, K. (1996). Racism and the physical and mental health of African Americans: A thirteen year national panel study. *Ethnicity & Disease, 6*, 132-147.

Johnson, P. A., Lee, T. H., Cook, E. F., Rowan, G. W., & Goldman, L. (1993). Effects of race on the presentation and management of patients with acute chest pain. *Annals of Internal Medicine, 118*, 593-601.

Jones, J. M. (1997). *Prejudice and racism* (2nd ed.). New York: McGraw-Hill.

Kasiske, B. L., Neylan, J. F., Riggio, R. R., Danovich, G. M., Kahana, L., Alexander, S. R. et al. (1991). The effect of race on access and outcome in transplantation. *New England Journal of Medicine, 324*, 302-307.

Kelly, S. (2003). African American couples: Their importance to the stability of African American families and their mental health issues. In J. S. Mio & G. Y. Iwamasa (Eds.), *Culturally diverse mental health: The challenges of research and resistance* (pp. 141-157). New York: Taylor & Francis.

Kelly, S. (2004). Underlying components of scores assessing African Americans' racial perspectives. *Measurement and Evaluation in Counseling and Development, 37*, 28-40.

Kelly, S., & Floyd, F. J. (2001). The effects of negative racial stereotypes and Afrocentricity on Black couple relationships. *Journal of Family Psychology, 15*, 110-123.

Klonoff, E., & Landrine, H. (1999). Cross validation of the schedule of racist events. *The Journal of Black Psychology, 25*, 231-254.

Kohl, B. G. (2006). Can you feel me now? Worldview, empathy, and racial identity in a therapy dyad. *Journal of Emotional Abuse, 6*(2/3), 173-196.

Kozol, J. (1991). *Savage inequalities: Children in America's schools.* New York: Crown.

Kwate, N. O., Valdimarsdottir, H. B., Guevarra, J. S., & Bovbjerg, D. H. (2003). Experiences of racist events are associated with negative health consequences for African American women. *Journal of the National Medical Association, 95*, 450-460.

Leary, J. D. (2002, December 2). *Post traumatic slave syndrome.* Interview with Tavis Smiley. New York: National Public Radio.

Markowitz, L. (1993, July/August). Walking the walk: No refuge from racism. *The Family Therapy Networker, 17*(4), 19-31.

Marsella, A., Friedman, M. J., Gerrity, E. T., & Scurfield, R. M. (Eds.) (1996). *Ethnocultural aspects of post-traumatic stress disorder: Issues, research and clinical applications.* Washington, DC: American Psychological Association.

Marsella, A., Friedman, M. J., & Spain, E. H. (1996). Ethnocultural aspects of PTSD: An overview of issues and research directions. In A. J. Marsella, M. J. Friedman, E. T. Gerrity, & R. M. Scurfield (Eds.), *Ethnocultural aspects of post-traumatic stress disorder: Issues, research and clinical applications* (pp. 105-130). Washington, DC: American Psychological Association.

Masten, A. S., Best, K., & Garmezy, N. (1990). Resilience in development: Implications of the study of successful adaptation for developmental psychopathology. In D. Cicchetti (Ed.), *The emergence of a discipline: The Rochester Symposium on Developmental Psychopathology: 1* (pp. 261-294). Hillsdale: Erlbaum.

McGlade, K., & Ackerman, J. (2006). A hope for foster care: Agency executives in partnerships with parent leaders. *Journal of Emotional Abuse, 6*(2/3), 97-112.

McIntosh, P. (1998). White privilege: Unpacking the invisible knapsack. In M. McGoldrick (Ed.), *Re-visioning family therapy: Race, culture, and gender in clinical practice* (pp. 147-152). New York: Guilford Press.

Mullings, L., & Wali, A. (2000). *Stress and resilience: The social context of reproduction in central Harlem.* New York: Kluwer Academic/Plenum Publishers.

Pierce, C. M. (1995). Stress analogs of racism and sexism: Terrorism, torture, and disaster. In C. V. Willie, P. P. Reiker, B. M. Kramer, & B. S. Brown (Eds.), *Mental health, racism, and sexism* (pp. 277-293). Pittsburgh: University of Pittsburgh Press.

Prothrow-Stith, D. (1991). *Deadly consequences.* New York: Harper Perennial.

Rastogi, M., & Wieling, E. (Eds.) (2004). *The voices of color: First person accounts of ethnic minority therapists.* Thousand Oaks, CA: Sage.

Roberts, D. (2002). *Shattered bonds: The color of child welfare.* New York: Basic Civitas.

Rockeymoore, M. (2002). African Americans confront a pandemic: Assessing community impact, organization, and advocacy in the second decade of AIDS. In L. A. Daniels (Ed.), *The state of Black America 2002* (pp. 123-146). New York: National Urban League.

Root, M. P. P. (1992). Reconstructing the impact of trauma on personality. In M. Ballou & L. Brown (Eds.), *Theories of personality and psychopathology: Feminist reappraisal* (pp. 229-265). New York: Guilford Press.

Samuel-Young, L. (2006). Staying whole in a fragmented world: One Afro-Caribbean social worker's journey through wholeness–a psycho-spiritual perspective. *Journal of Emotional Abuse, 6*(2/3), 229-239.

Sanchez-Hucles, J. V. (1998). Racism: Emotional abusiveness and psychological trauma for ethnic minorities. *Journal of Emotional Abuse, 1,* 69-87.

Smith, D. K. (1992). HIV disease as a cause of death for African Americans in 1987 and 1990. *Journal of the National Medical Association, 84,* 481-487.

Stevenson, H. C., & Davis, G. Y. (2004). Racial socialization. In R. Jones (Ed.), *Black psychology* (4th ed., pp. 353-381). Hampton, VA: Cobb & Henry.

Sue, D. W. (2003). *Overcoming our racism: The journey to liberation.* San Francisco, CA: Jossey-Bass.

Taylor, R. J., Jackson, J. S., & Chatters, L. M. (1997). *Family life in Black America.* Thousand Oaks, CA: Sage.

Thompson, V. L. (2002). Racism: Perceptions of distress among African Americans. *Community Mental Health Journal, 38,* 111-122.

Troxel, W. M., Matthews, K. A., Bromberger, J. T., & Sutton-Tyrrell, K. (2003). Chronic stress burden, discrimination, and subclinical carotid artery disease in African American and Caucasian women. *Health Psychology, 22,* 300-309.

Tucker, M. B., & Mitchell-Kernan, C. (Eds.) (1995). *The decline in marriage among African Americans.* New York: Russell Sage Foundation.

U.S. Department of Health and Human Services (2001). *Mental health: Culture, race, and ethnicity–A supplement to mental health: A report of the Surgeon General.* Rockville, MD: SAMHSA.

Utsey, S. O., Chae, M. H., Brown, C. F., & Kelly, D. (2002). Effect of ethnic group membership on ethnic identity, race-related stress, and quality of life. *Cultural Diversity and Ethnic Minority Psychology, 8,* 366-377.

Williams, D. R., & Williams-Morris, R. (2000). Racism and mental health: The African American experience. *Ethnicity & Health, 5*(3/4), 243-268.

Wilson, W. J. (1996). *When the work disappears: The world of the new urban poor.* New York: Knopf.

doi:10.1300/J135v06n02_02

The Impact of Racism
on Social Functioning:
Is It Skin Deep?

Barbara L. Edwards

SUMMARY. The extent to which racism impacts social functioning is based on the recognition that those who are able to function adequately view the world and themselves with a sense of worth, independence, and self-determination. Racism adversely impacts oppressed people, manifesting in psychosocial and economic deprivations. Socially inflicted trauma, targeted marketing of commodities that harm health (e.g., alcohol and tobacco), availability of illicit drugs, food that lacks nutrition, and inadequate housing and medical care all impact social functioning. An examination of the onslaught of racism can help practitioners evaluate the extent to which oppression affects one's ability to handle various roles and responsibilities. Consideration will be given to the impact of racism on an individual's strengths and how racism exaggerates limitations. doi:10.1300/J135v06n02_03 *[Article copies available for a fee from The Haworth Document Delivery Service: 1-800-HAWORTH. E-mail address: <docdelivery@haworthpress.com> Website: <http://www.HaworthPress.com> © 2006 by The Haworth Press, Inc. All rights reserved.]*

KEYWORDS. Racism, social trauma, social functioning, resilience

---

Address correspondence to: Barbara L. Edwards, P.O. Box 629, Far Rockaway, NY 11691.

[Haworth co-indexing entry note]: "The Impact of Racism on Social Functioning: Is It Skin Deep?" Edwards, Barbara L. Co-published simultaneously in *Journal of Emotional Abuse* (The Haworth Maltreatment & Trauma Press, an imprint of The Haworth Press, Inc.) Vol. 6, No. 2/3, 2006, pp. 31-46; and: *Racism and Racial Identity: Reflections on Urban Practice in Mental Health and Social Services* (ed: Lisa V. Blitz, and Mary Pender Greene) The Haworth Maltreatment & Trauma Press, an imprint of The Haworth Press, Inc., 2006, pp. 31-46. Single or multiple copies of this article are available for a fee from The Haworth Document Delivery Service [1-800-HAWORTH, 9:00 a.m. - 5:00 p.m. (EST). E-mail address: docdelivery@haworthpress.com].

This article examines the extent to which social work practice with individuals from diverse racial groups might become more effective through the use of culturally competent strategies. Some of the working concepts highlighted include the strengths-based perspective in mental health service delivery and the benefits of fostering resiliency in those seeking intervention.

The elements of social work assessment are emphasized as an essential step in preparation for the development of a comprehensive service plan. The standards for the process of evaluation of adequate social functioning are reexamined against a deeply entrenched ideology and system of White dominance that compromises racial equity in social service policies, programs, and practices. A historical overview of the dynamics of unequal treatment is provided in order that one might better understand how the evolution of human distinctions and negative perceptions manifested into racism and prevails today.

HISTORICAL PERSPECTIVE

Cultural, political, economic, and religious differences have been the basis of human exploitation since the dawn of time. The reliance on racial and biological differences as a justification for human oppression is a product of more recent history. From the beginning of the 16th century to now, racism has been the most persistent element of oppression used to exploit human beings. This practice is a product of European expansionism throughout the globe and is the most socially impacting and psychologically dehumanizing dynamic of this period. Now, five hundred years later, racism not only lingers, but mutates and replicates itself crippling the social body of human society. If we seriously expect to eradicate the devastating impact of racism, it is important for us to analyze the cause and effect of this phenomenon.

Many Americans believe that racial discrimination is a thing of the past, as asserted by Brown et al. (2003). These researchers pointed out that it is also believed that any racial inequalities that persist–in wages, family income, access to housing or health care, can be attributed to the disadvantaged group's cultural, ethnic, and racial failures. While not denying the economic advances of Black Americans since the 1960s, these authors draw on new and compelling research to demonstrate the persistence of racism and the effects of organized racial disadvantages across many institutions in American society. The institutions include the labor market, the welfare system, the criminal justice system, schools, and universities. Looking beyond the stalled debate over current antidiscrimination policies, the authors also put forth fresh vision for achieving genuine racial equality of opportunity in a post-affirmative action world.

Racism remains a crushing force of oppression in our society, but the internal strength of individuals allows many people of color to achieve success and satisfaction in spite of it. It is from this point of view that I have become increasingly aware of the need for this positive potential, the strengths inherent in even the most vulnerable of people, to be activated in social work intervention–to work for social justice and individual emotional health.

Dimensions of Racism: Discrimination and White Privilege

What is racism? Racism is a system of structuring opportunity and assigning value that provides unfair advantage to some individuals while unfairly operating to disadvantage individuals of another group. This kind of advantage raises the issue of White privilege and a sense of White entitlement. While Whites enjoy greater advantages through the system of racism, it is undermining the realization of the potential of the whole society, because we are wasting the human potential of others. Thus, we are all adversely impacted by racism. Institutionalized racism manifests itself in terms of access to resources such as housing, education, employment, income, etc. Institutionalized racism also manifests in terms of access to power.

What is White privilege? White privilege is a favored state, either earned or conferred by birth, to establish dominance over others because of race. Racial discrimination has multiple manifestations. It can be experienced directly, vicariously, collectively, institutionally, and trans-generationally. However, it is the daily "micro stressors," such as being followed or observed in public places, that may be most detrimental to the psyche of African Americans in that the accumulative effects may increase their overall stress load. Social functioning impacted by racism and discrimination is likely to be affected by the coping strategies used. When coping strategies are actively engaged in an effort to resolve stressors, the outcome is usually a greater sense of self-efficacy and less distress. In contrast, the use of strategies that avoid stresses generally results in lower feelings of self-efficacy. However, the coping strategies used in response to racism and discrimination may have divergent effects on the oppressed person's adjustment and well-being given the ambiguity, power differential, unpredictability, and uncontrollability of unfair treatment. Many studies confirm that one of the cumulative outcomes of social inequities, systemic racial discrimination, poverty, and marginalization is the debilitating impact on social functioning, including the multidimensional impact of intersections of low levels of education, limited employment opportunities, and inadequate housing based on race (Cheung & Snowden, 1990).

The key element in understanding racism is to focus on the outward manifestation of an internal system of values deliberately designed to demean people of color and undergird belief systems out of which racist action emerges. This value system justifies power of position by placing negative meaning on perceived or actual biological factors that are different from the dominant White culture, such as skin color, texture of the hair, and other physical features. Cultural differences, such as language, religion, and ethnic traditions, are also given negative meaning that legitimizes treating others as inferior to the dominant White group. The result is unequal treatment, where people of color are consistently short-changed.

Many authors have explored the dimensions of racism and the manifestations of discrimination and White privilege, including Franklin, Boyd-Franklin, and Kelly (this volume). For example, Loury (2002) identifies racial stereotypes and racial stigma as fundamental causes of racial inequality in the United States. He points out that racial stigmatization plays a more important role than direct discrimination in producing racial inequality, by depriving people of color opportunities for development. He shares his observation that inequalities produced through intentional stigmatization become entrenched, perpetually reproducing negative impact on targeted people of color. Marable (2001) asserts that race is superimposed on people of color so that the national, religious, or ethnic differences are secondary to how they are racialized in an unfair way within society. Marable points out that the one thing that people of color have in common is a history of being denied basic citizenship, including political rights, in this country because of their race.

Hacker (1992) questioned why race remains America's deepest and most enduring division. He points out that despite efforts to increase understanding and expand opportunities, Black and White Americans still lead separate lives, continually marked by tension and hostilities. Hacker explains that racial disparities persist because of White people's need to hold on to privilege, social position, and resources. He uses updated statistical data to support the stark realities of unequal income, employment, education, political influence, and social justice. Hacker forecasts that race will continue to play a pivotal role in our society, unless or until we modify our value system.

No person of color has ever suffered discrimination simply because of the color of his or her skin, contend Oliner and Oliner (1995). If color were the only problem, then the solution would be a change in skin color. Axelson (1998) also argues that the problem is not skin color, but value systems that perpetuate evil against others and then justify that evil by focusing on outward differences. Outward differences, such as color, gender, language, or religion, contain no positive or negative value in and of themselves; they are merely biological or cultural factors. It is not skin color that forms the basis for discrimination, but the negative meaning and value given to the color of skin. The negative meaning is not inherent in the color nor the skin, but in the culture. This process of oppression justifies inequality by finding defects in the victims of inequality. The logical outcome of analyzing social problems in terms of the deficiencies of the victim is a simple formula for action. The uninformed social worker operates from the perspective of change the victim rather than one's value system. The more appropriate approach to a problem presented by a person of color necessitates a conceptual framework that enables the social worker to organize and accurately assess those factors interfering with adequate social functioning.

Effective social work practice with people of color requires consideration of the impact of adverse social, environmental, and political factors when assessing problems and designing interventions. Intervention strategies should match the client's level of need. Careful review of presenting problems will often include layered issues that will unfold based on the client's evaluation of the worker's level of empathy and genuine interest in providing help without prejudicial judgments. One might find a client's initial request for financial assistance as the first phase of a series of issues that will follow as the course of service delivery evolves. Many times ethnic clients phase in problem issues as they grow more comfortable with the social worker and evidence of acceptance becomes more apparent.

The kind of objectivity that is expected in the field of social work is too often colored by a practitioner's preconceived notions and stereotypes when clients from different cultures and races are encountered. Brooks (1983) argues that systemic, institutionalized racial discrimination is especially wrong and deserving of special rectification measures. Systemic, institutionalized racism generally refers to invisible dynamics within organizations and social structures that advantage Whites and make people of color more vulnerable to negative social factors such as poverty, unemployment/underemployment, or racial profiling. A society that maintains institutionalized racism, however, also creates a cultural milieu that produces a potential for outright violence and hate crimes. A key point of Brooks' argument concerns the ways group identities magnify the harms that are motivated by society's antipathy toward that group. For example, the terror of a racist lynching is experienced not just by the particular victim, but by everyone else in the group who is symbolically targeted by the lynching. By identifying with the victim, they feel the subhuman treatment vicariously and are therefore traumatized by the event. Thus, when clients reach out for help, they usually realize that they are not being evaluated on an individual basis, but on the perception of their race. The desired rapport for healthy dialogue and mutual respect in the helping relationship is heavy laden with doubt, mistrust, fear, and compromised engagement.

THE WEIGHT OF OPPRESSION ON SELF-CONFIDENCE AND SELF-IMAGE

The weight of racial oppression is an additional burden superimposed on the client who finds him or herself in need of social service. Oppression as a psychosocial process can be used to make one feel superior to others by making erroneous assumptions based on racial characteristics. There are three forms of oppression based on racism: individual, institutional, and cultural. The oppression of an individual may be a circular and reciprocal process; those perceived as inferior may internalize the other's perception as valid and behave accordingly (Henderson, 1999). The person perceived as inferior may develop a self-fulfilling prophecy in relation to this, until this cycle is broken. The effects of oppression on individuals include lowered self-esteem and inadequate self-concept. As an individual internalizes these negative ideas about him/herself, he/she may enact "The Pygmalion effect," a self-fulfilling prophecy where people conform to others' expectations regardless of their true abilities. If clients determine that their presenting problem will be addressed more quickly by diminishing their capacities, many will cater to the service provider's need to feel superior in order to have their basic needs met. Blitz and Illidge (this volume) discuss how internalized racial oppression can be enacted in staff dynamics and client relations.

Institutional forms of racism may include unemployment, inadequate housing and education, and other discriminatory practices that limit access to basic resources. Those people who are disadvantaged and relegated to a subdominant group because of their race face a devaluation that grows out of images that society uses to catalogue people. The catalogue need never be overtly taught since it is implied by all we see around us. These images are constantly reinforced by the kinds of people referenced in advertising, the movies, and media, which create an impression that people of color do not fare well. In many ways, these projections require no fueling from strong prejudice or stereotypes. The impact of these images expands the devaluation of people of color. They act as mental standards against which information about people of color is evaluated. This assessment fosters acceptance of images that fit devaluation. That which fits these images is accepted and that which contradicts them is suspect.

The client will often adapt a chameleon-like presence in an effort to find acceptance and problem resolution. Clients who have had demeaning experiences when seeking help opt to camouflage assets/strengths in order that they might become more eligible for services, withholding information or denying strengths. This has not always resulted in positive outcomes. In years past, families felt that they had to deny the presence of a father in the household so that they could be declared eligible for financial supplementation. This denial of an intact family was always up for scrutiny during a social worker's verification home visits. The man who had to vacate the premises and the mother who presented herself as a single head of household willingly masked their realities for the assurance of continued provision of basic human needs. These portrayals impact a healthy psyche over time and warp self-perception and self-worth. Such negative or stereotyping images do something else as well, something especially pernicious in the field of social work. They set up jeopardy of double devaluation for people of color, a jeopardy that does not apply to Whites.

Tragically, such devaluation can seem inescapable. Sooner or later it forces on its victims two painful realizations: the first is that society is preconditioned to see the worst in them; the second is that even if a person of color functions well, he or she will have to constantly disguise or prove themselves. Of course, individual characteristics that enhance one's value in society—skills, class, appearance, and success—can diminish the racial devaluation one faces. Sometimes the effort to prove oneself fuels achievement and boosts social functioning. Few individuals from any group, however, could hope to sustain so daunting and everlasting a struggle. Thus, too many people of color are left hopeless and deeply vulnerable. In significant part, the struggles experienced by people of color stem from the power of this vulnerability to undercut positive self-confidence and self-image, as discussed by McGann (this volume). Although racial vulnerability may undermine people of color, so many other factors seem to contribute, from the debilitation of poverty to the alleged dysfunction of culture.

A Need for Social Justice in Social Work Intervention

Erasing stigma improves the achievement of people of color and is the strongest evidence that this devaluation is what depresses adequate functioning. Poverty, social isolation, and poor preparation for negotiating hostile and racist systems may be substantially overcome in an atmosphere that reduces racial and other vulnerabilities. There is a basic expectation that people of color should assimilate to the dominant culture. It is often suggested to those members of a subdominant group that they may be helped to function adequately, if they master the culture and ways of the White American mainstream. This means that they are expected to give up many facets that are unique to them–styles of speech, appearance, value priorities, preferences–at least in mainstream settings. The offer of acceptance in return for assimilation carries a primal insult. It requires the most vulnerable among us to join in and identify with something that has made them invisible.

When social workers, or the overarching social service or mental health systems, encourage assimilation, this vulnerable population experiences the people they turn to for help as reinforcing how little they are valued more concertedly, persistently, and authoritatively than anywhere else in society. Clearly, no simple solution can fix this perception, but we now understand the basics of a corrective approach. Social work must focus more on reducing the social dynamics that contribute to vulnerabilities that block identification with achievement.

If what is meaningful and important to a social worker is to become meaningful and important to a client, the client must feel valued by the social worker for his/her potential and as a person. Among those who receive White privilege in our society, this relationship is often taken for granted. It is precisely the relationship between individuals that race can still undermine for people of color in American society. When clients bear race and class vulnerabilities, building this relationship is the first order of business. No social work modality or intervention, no matter how ingenious, can succeed without it. In keeping with the standard practice of social work, there is an expectation that practitioners will, regardless of ethnic/racial background, come to terms with how their own cultural background/experiences, attitudes, values, and biases influence their helping process. Social workers might routinely ask themselves, "Is it appropriate for me to view this client any differently than I would if they were from my own ethnic or cultural group?" An effective social worker's practice is enhanced when he or she respects a client's religious and/or spiritual beliefs and values, including attributions and taboos, since they affect worldview, psychosocial functioning, and expression of distress. Effective practice might also be aided by consultation with a practitioner relevant to the client's culture and belief systems.

ASSESSMENT OF SOCIAL FUNCTIONING AND STRENGTHS-BASED SERVICE PLANNING

Careful and diligent evaluation of a client's social functioning will always produce strengths as well as weaknesses. A full assessment will provide sufficient building blocks from which to structure an individualized service plan that incorporates a client's strengths. The challenge and the promise of personal fulfillment (for the client and the worker) should guide strengths-based treatment and service planning. The clients' present skills should be taken into account and they should be moved along at a pace that is demanding but doesn't defeat them. Their ambitions should never be scaled down, but should instead be guided to inspiring goals even when extraordinary dedication is required. Frustration will be less crippling when their potential is affirmed and they are credited with their achievement. A valuing social worker-client relationship will not progress without challenge, and challenge will always be resisted outside of a valuing relationship.

Racial and cultural competence is a useful element in assessment and treatment/service plan design. Cultural competence is defined as a set of congruent behaviors, attitudes, and policies that comes together in a system, agency, or among professionals and enables that system, agency, or those professionals to work effectively in cross-cultural situations (Cross, Bazron, Dennis, & Isaacs, 1989; Isaacs & Benjamin, 1991). Operationally defined, cultural competence is the integration and transformation of knowledge about individuals and groups of people into specific standards, policies, practices, and attitudes used in appropriate cultural settings to increase the quality of services, thereby producing better outcomes (Davis, 1997).

Cultural tunnel vision could be considered a form of racism. The word culture is used because it implies the integrated patterns of human

behavior that include thoughts, communications, actions, customs, beliefs, values, and institutions of racial, ethnic, religious, or social groups.
The word competence is used because it implies having the capacity to
function in a particular way: the capacity to function within the context of
culturally integrated patterns of human behavior defined by a group. Being competent in cross-cultural functioning means learning new patterns
of behavior and effectively applying them in the appropriate setting. For
example, a social worker with a group of African American children may
find that a certain look sufficiently quiets most of the group. Often African American adults use eye contact and facial expression to discipline
their children. However, this is not effective with all African Americans;
intra-group differences, such as geographic location or socioeconomic
background, require practitioners to avoid over-generalizing. With other
groups, one might have to use demanding tones, quiet non-threatening
language, or whatever is appropriate for the group members. The un-
knowing social worker might offend some group members and upset others by using the wrong words, tone, or body language. Being culturally
competent means having the capacity to function effectively in other cultural contexts.

There are five essential elements that contribute to a worker's ability
to become more culturally competent. The worker should (a) value diversity, (b) have the capacity for cultural self-assessment, (c) be conscious of the "dynamics" inherent when cultures interact, (d) increase
institutionalized cultural knowledge, and (e) develop adaptations to service delivery reflecting an understanding of diversity between and
within cultures. Further, these five elements must be manifested in every level of the service delivery system. They should be reflected in
attitudes, structures, polices, and services.

Many social workers operate under a framework of monocultural
tunnel vision. They are uncomfortable working with poor people or
people of color. They make implicit and explicit assessments that people of color are unresponsive to professional intervention due to a lack
of motivation to change or due to some form of resistance in seeking
professional help. These cultural assumptions show insensitivity to individual cultural differences, accept unreasoned conclusions with no
proof, do not evaluate other viewpoints, do not try to accommodate the
behavior of others, and are trapped in one way of thinking.

Historically, social work has focused on human weaknesses and
problems in its practice. This problems-focused approach has several
downsides and using a strengths perspective could be beneficial. When
helping people professionally, many practitioners focus mainly on their

client's problem in an effort toward solving it, but categorizing people does not necessarily reveal their real struggles. Plus, the problem is named in the professional's language, not the client's. Furthermore, if, for instance, alcoholism is the problem, the professional will seek specifically to help the client stop drinking. While seemingly logical, this approach actually draws the problem into the solution by making alcohol the center of the problem and the treatment. Concentrating on problems does not help people grow. Taking a strengths perspective involves asking clients questions that help them see their own resilience amongst conflict and recognize their own resources.

A strengths perspective focuses on helping people to see and appreciate their strengths. This approach is appropriate considering the mission of social work, which includes respecting everybody's worth and dignity. During the assessment process, it is important to focus on the client's strengths, potentials, and capabilities. One might ask, "what are strengths?" Strengths are what people have learned about themselves, others, and their world as they have struggled with life issues and situations. Strengths are qualities, talents, traits, and virtues that people possess and use in developing approaches to deal with obstacles, in rebounding from misfortune and hardship.

Focusing on a client's strengths fosters a helping relationship of collaboration, mutuality, and partnership. The essential element of strengths-based practice is the significant value emphasized in addressing, acknowledging, reexperiencing, and putting in perspective the social functioning issues of the client's life. A collaborative helping relationship utilizes five specific techniques: (a) accepting the client's definition of the problem, (b) identifying and building on existing strengths, (c) raising the client's awareness of issues of power imbalance, (d) teaching skills so that clients experience increased personal, interpersonal, and sociopolitical power, and (e) mobilizing resources or advocating for clients. The primary focus and purpose of strengths-based practice is always to look for the seeds of resilience and rebound. Bartle, Couchonnal, Canda, and Staker (2002) highlighted the importance of incorporating lessons learned from adversity–cultural, ethnic, and familial sources of adaptability.

The strengths perspective obligates workers to understand that however dysfunctional a client might be, they have survived (and in some cases even thrived). They have taken steps, summoned up resources, and coped. We need to know and reinforce what they have done, how they have done it, what they have learned from doing it, and what resources (internal and external) were available in their struggle to surmount their troubles. Clients are always attempting "to fix" their situation; as helpers we must tap into that work, elucidate it, find and build on its possibilities.

While we live in a multicultural society, it does not always reflect public sentiment or public policy supportive of a value for cultural diversity. Thus, social workers must incorporate knowledge of cultural norms and cultural variability with practices that respect and account for individual difference. Inherent in this combination is the need to understand the effects of oppression, discrimination, and a culturally sensitive explanation of human behavior. It is also necessary to understand the impact of unequal or restricted access to economic and political power, services, and resources.

The realization that culture permeates the ways in which people interpret and relate to others is significant for social workers in performing all their functions throughout the service delivery cycle. Becoming culturally competent is a developmental process, a journey that involves time, commitment, and a learning environment supportive of opportunities to safely share experiences and struggles when working with someone of a different culture. Education and training, through experiential and knowledge workshops, and consultation with members from diverse cultural groups are proactive methods of enriching cultural competency. Exposure in working with clients of different cultural groups along with cross-cultural supervision might also be helpful in this journey toward cultural competence.

Resiliency and the Process of Change

The concept of resiliency has deep roots in social work, and is defined as unpredicted or markedly successful adaptations to negative life events, trauma, stress, and other forms of risk. After years of focusing on pathology, social workers have begun the task of identifying strengths resources, and talents of individuals and families (Hawley & DeHaan, 1996; Rutter, 1987; Walsh, 1996). Resiliency has been defined as the ability to cultivate strengths (Smith, 1996), returning to "original form or position after being bent" (Valentine & Feinauer, 1993), and reparation of one's self after hardship (Wolin & Wolin, 1993). According to Walsh (1999), being resilient includes more than merely surviving and being a victim for life, it also encompasses the ability "to heal from painful wounds, take charge of their lives, and go on to live fully." Rutter (1987, p. 317) postulates that there are four main processes for developing resilience: "reduction of risk impact, reduction of negative chain reactions, establishment and maintenance of self-esteem and self-efficacy, and opening up opportunities. "If we can understand what helps some people to function well in the context of high adversity, we may be able to incorporate this knowledge into new practice strategies" (Fraser, Richman, & Galinsky, 1999, p. 133).

There are two key features to the process of change: resiliency and resistance. As noted by Franklin, Boyd-Franklin, and Kelly (this volume), resiliency is an important factor in how people of color resist racism. Human beings have a natural resilient nature, but it must be nurtured or it will be lost. Highly resilient people know how to bounce back and find a way to have things turn out well. They thrive in constant change because they are flexible, agile, creative, synergistic, and adapt quickly with the ability to learn from experience. When hit by major setbacks they often end up stronger and better than before. Integrating resiliency in social work practice provides a powerful intervention for moving from a narrow focus of risk, deficit, and pathology to a focus of strength and how it is brought to bear in promoting healing and health.

The assessment of strengths, and the acknowledgement that everyone has strengths and the capacity for transformation, gives clear direction, and informs us of "what works." Assessing strengths also helps us to move beyond risk identification or labeling pathology, practices that can harmfully label and stigmatize people of color and disadvantaged clients, their families, and their communities. Simply assessing for risk or diagnosis can perpetuate stereotyping and racism. Most importantly, the knowledge that everyone has innate resilience grounds practice in optimism and possibility, essential components in building motivation. Not only does this prevent the burnout of practitioners working with clients who present elements of dysfunction, but it provides one of the major facilitating factors required for effective social work and positive expectations. When the client and practitioner are of different races and share/internalize these expectations, they are more apt to become motivated and able to overcome adversity.

The major implication of integrating cultural competence and resiliency in social work practice is successful and measurable outcomes. If we hope to help people of color who are fragile and vulnerable to become socially competent and able to make life-affirming decisions, set goals, and believe in their future, then meeting their basic human needs for caring, connectedness, respect, challenge, power, and meaning must be the primary focus of any social work intervention. Fostering resilience, inclusion, and valuing difference can facilitate change at a deep structural, systemic, and human level. This change enhances mutuality in the helping relationship, embracing beliefs and opportunities for participation and power that are a part of every social interaction, every intervention no matter what the focus.

To be an effective social work professional who is able to create these safe, healing, and embracing relational experiences, one must first and foremost support his/her own resilience. Building community and creating a sense of belonging for our clients means we must also do this for ourselves. The need for community is universal. A sense of belonging, of continuity, of being connected to others and to ideas and values that are meaningful and significant is generally a desire of all people. Respectful relationships and opportunities to make decisions are important for the social work process in facilitating the goals and objectives of those we serve.

Modeling is a basic operating principle of resilience in our practice. It must be acknowledged that this is a major challenge for social workers given that we live in a society that does not place a high priority on those who are disadvantaged. This makes our work as providers not only a challenge but a vital necessity. Ultimately, integrating resiliency, cultural competence, and inclusion as a focus of our practice provides a mandate for social change. It is a clarion call for creating those relationships and opportunities in all human systems throughout the life span. Changing the status quo in our society means changing paradigms, both personally and professionally, from risk to resilience, from seeing clients as problems to seeing them as resources, from institution building to community building. For the personal development of the helping professional, fostering resilience is an inside-out, deep structure process of changing our own belief systems and working on the policy level for social and economic justice.

When we engage clients in a manner that invites their participation—their critical inquiry, dialogue, reflection, and action—we are creating the condition that allows for their innate potential for adequate social functioning, problem solving, sense of identity and efficacy. As adequate social functioning is sustained, hope for the future unfolds. In the process of fostering resiliency, cultural competence, and inclusion, we are building a critical mass of citizens who will recreate a social covenant grounded in social and economic justice, thereby moving toward the eradication of the negative impact of racism.

REFERENCES

Axelson, J. A. (1998). *Counseling and development in a multicultural society.* Belmont, CA: Wadsworth Publishing.

Bartle, E., Couchonnal, C., Canda, E., & Staker, M. (2002). Empowerment as a dynamically developing concept for practice: Lessons learned from organizational ethnography. *Social Work, 47,* 32-43.

Blitz, L. V., & Illidge, L. C. (2006). Not so black and white: Shades of gray and brown in anti-racist multicultural team building in a domestic violence shelter. *Journal of Emotional Abuse, 6*(2/3), 113-134.

Brooks, D. H. M. (1983). Why discrimination is especially wrong. In T. Mappes & J. Zembatyeds (Eds.), *Social ethics* (pp. 199-204). New York: McGraw-Hill.

Brown, M., Carnoy, M., Currie, E., Duster, T., Oppenheimer, D., Shultz, M. et al. (2003). *Whitewashing race: The myth of a colorblind society.* Los Angles: UC Press.

Cheung, F. K., & Snowden, L. R. (1990). Community mental health and ethnic minority populations. *Community Mental Health Journal, 26,* 277-291.

Cross T., Bazron, B., Dennis, K., & Isaacs, M. (1989). In Isaacs & Benjamin, 1991. *Towards a culturally competent system of care, Volume I.* Washington, DC: Georgetown University Child Development Center, CASSP Technical Assistance Center.

Davis, K. (1997). *Exploring the intersection between cultural competency and managed behavioral health care policy: Implication for state and county mental health agencies.* Alexandria, VA: National Technical Assistance Center for State Mental Health Planning.

Franklin, A. J., Boyd-Franklin, N., & Kelly, S. (2006). Racism and invisibility: Race-related stress, emotional abuse and psychological trauma for people of color. *Journal of Emotional Abuse, 6*(2/3), 9-30.

Fraser, M. W., Richman, J. M., & Galinsky, M. (1999). Risk, protection, and resilience: Toward a conceptual framework for social work practice. *Social Work Research, 23*(3), 131-143.

Hacker, A. (1992). *Two nations Black and White: Separate, hostile and unequal.* New York: Ballantine Books.

Hawley, D. R., & DeHaan, L. (1996). Toward a definition of family resilience: Integrating life-span and family perspectives. *Family Process, 35,* 283-298.

Henderson, N. (1999). Preface. In N. Henderson, B. Benard, & N. Sharp-Light (Eds.), *Resiliency in action: Practical ideas for overcoming risks and building strengths in youth, families, and communities* (pp. 172-180). San Diego, CA: Resiliency in Action, Inc.

Loury, G. (2002). *The anatomy of racial inequality.* Cambridge, MA: Harvard University Press.

Marable, M. (2001). *Race in America: Toward a truly pluralistic democracy. The Leadership Alliance.* Retrieved October 12, 2003 from, http://www.the leadership alliance.org

McGann, E. P. (2006). Color me beautiful: Racism, identity formation, and art therapy. *Journal of Emotional Abuse, 6*(2/3), 197-217.

Oliner, P. M., & Oliner, S. P. (1995). *Toward a caring society: Ideas into action.* Westport, CT: Praeger.

Rutter, M. (1987). *Psychosocial resilience and protective mechanisms.* American Orthopsychiatric Association, Inc., *57,* pp. 316-331.

Smith, H. Y. (1996). Building on the strengths of Black families: Self-help and empowerment. In S. L. Logan (Ed.), *The Black family: Strengths, self-help and positive change* (pp. 10-19). Lawrence, KS: Westview Press.

Valentine, L., & Feinauer, L. L. (1993). Resilience factors associated with female survivors of childhood sexual abuse. *American Journal of Family Therapy, 32,* 216-224.

Walsh, F. (1996). The concept of family resilience: Crisis and challenge. *Family Process,* 261-281.

Walsh, F. (1999). *Strengthening resilient families.* New York: Guilford Press.

Wolin, S. J., & Wolin, S. (1993). *The resilient self.* New York: Villard Press.

doi:10.1300/J135v06n02_03

SECTION II
CULTURE AND IDENTITY
IN THE CONTEXT OF RACISM

Immigrant West Indian Families and Their Struggles with Racism in America

Dadrene Hine-St. Hilaire

SUMMARY. Many questions arise in the struggle of West Indians to establish themselves in America, including the role that racism plays in their struggle to develop a community. Some West Indians object to being seen as Black Americans. Unlike White immigrants who may aspire to acculturate and become part of the dominant group, West Indian immigrants are forced to make decisions about their identification, and internalized racism plays a significant role in their ambivalence about fully assimilating into American culture. This article explores the role of internalized racism as it impacts their decisions regarding child rearing. Information from personal interviews of clients in the private psycho-

---

Address correspondence to: Dadrene Hine-St. Hilaire, P.O. Box 060280, Brooklyn, NY 11206 (E-mail: dhinesthilaire@jbfcs.org).

[Haworth co-indexing entry note]: "Immigrant West Indian Families and Their Struggles with Racism in America." Hine-St. Hilaire, Dadrene. Co-published simultaneously in *Journal of Emotional Abuse* (The Haworth Maltreatment & Trauma Press, an imprint of The Haworth Press, Inc.) Vol. 6, No. 2/3, 2006, pp. 47-60; and: *Racism and Racial Identity: Reflections on Urban Practice in Mental Health and Social Services* (ed: Lisa V. Blitz, and Mary Pender Greene) The Haworth Maltreatment & Trauma Press, an imprint of The Haworth Press, Inc., 2006, pp. 47-60. Single or multiple copies of this article are available for a fee from The Haworth Document Delivery Service [1-800-HAWORTH, 9:00 a.m. - 5:00 p.m. (EST). E-mail address: docdelivery@haworthpress.com].

Available online at http://jea.haworthpress.com
doi:10.1300/J135v06n02_04

therapy practice of the author is included as part of the source material for the article. doi:10.1300/J135v06n02_04 *[Article copies available for a fee from The Haworth Document Delivery Service: 1-800-HAWORTH. E-mail address: <docdelivery@haworthpress.com> Website: <http://www.HaworthPress.com> © 2006 by The Haworth Press, Inc. All rights reserved.]*

KEYWORDS. West Indian immigrants, Caribbean immigrants, internalized racism, assimilation, parenting, child rearing

This article represents an attempt to bring focus on the role that racism plays in the emotional struggles of West Indian immigrants in America and the effect that internalized racism has on the decision some West Indians make regarding assimilation into the American culture. The motivation to write this article comes from two sources: personal experience and professional relationships with clients of West Indian heritage. I am a West Indian female clinical social worker. In addition to my full-time position as director of a domestic violence shelter, I am also a psychotherapist in private practice. This paper draws upon concerns West Indian patients in my private practice have shared with me as we have explored issues of racial identity, the impact of racism, and their struggle to adapt to life in America and raise their children. The article refers to the West Indies collectively. It is important, however, to note that the West Indian islands and nations share many commonalities but each have their unique culture and history (also see Hargrove, this volume, and Madsen, this volume).

The West Indian Islands are a group of island nations scattered throughout the Caribbean Sea south of the United States. They are generally divided into three categories: the Bahamas, which consist of 3,000 individual islands and reefs, the Greater Antilles, and the Lesser Antilles. The Greater Antilles include the larger island nations of Cuba, Jamaica, Haiti, Dominican Republic, and Puerto Rico. The Lesser Antilles, a collection of smaller islands that run along the divide between the Atlantic Ocean and the Caribbean Sea, are further divided into the Leeward Islands and the Windward Islands. The Leeward Islands include: St. Kitts, Nevis, Antigua and Barbuda, Montserrat, Anguilla, and the British Virgin Islands. The Windward Islands include: St. Vincent and the Grenadines, St. Lucia, Dominica, Grenada, the Cayman Islands, Barbados, Trinidad and Tobago, French Guadeloupe, Martinique, St. Martin, Dutch St. Martin, Curacao, Buen Ayre, Aruba, St. Eustatius, Saba, Danish St. Thomas, St. John, and

St. Croix. Although they are not islands, Belize (formerly British Honduras) in Central America and Guyana (formerly British Guiana) in South America are also generally included because they share a parallel history of colonization and retain similar cultural traditions.

The population of the West Indies represents the original inhabitants of the land, as well as the people who colonized the area or were brought over as slaves or indentured servants. Their descendants have developed variations of habits and customs in their New World environment. They may be divided into six main groups: (a) White European immigrants (British, French, Spanish, and to a lesser degree, Dutch, Danish, and German) and West Indian born descendants of European immigrants; (b) African Blacks and West Indian born Blacks whose ancestors were from Africa (a fast-vanishing group); (c) biracial people who are a mixture of Europeans and Africans; (d) Indians recruited from India as laborers and West Indian born Indians; (e) Chinese; and (f) Aboriginal Indians descended from the original peoples of the Caribbean. Of these, the people of African blood are in a large majority, the "colored" race of mixed European and African blood being next in numerical importance.

The terms race and ethnicity are separate and distinct concepts within the discussion of race relations in the United States. Race, for the purpose of this article, refers to differential concentration of gene frequencies responsible for traits that are confined to physical manifestations such as skin color or hair form. Ethnicity refers to any social grouping that is defined or set off by religion, language, national origin, and cultural differences, or some combination of these categories. Some insights into the complexity of racism, racial inequality, and cultural identity are unfolded in an effort to address the experience of West Indian immigrants of African decent in the United States. Black immigrants in the United States are more often perceived as Blacks than as immigrants, thus suffering dual invisibility. They are excluded as contributors to the American culture and are subjected to degrees and forms of discrimination.

WEST INDIAN IMMIGRANTS

The West Indians who migrated to the United States in the 19th century faced some obstacles that many of their successors also faced well into the 20th century. As immigrants to America, two things about them were different: they spoke English and almost all of them were Black. The first difference was an advantage, but the second brought on many prejudices they had not experienced in their native countries. Most Whites in America saw the West Indian immigrants as only "Blacks" and not as Jamaicans, Barbadians, Trinidadians, or any West Indian native. West Indians were not readily accepted into the African American community and were constantly compared in performance and ability to African Americans. The West Indian immigrant discovered quickly that life in America was not like life in the West Indies (Brandon, 1994). In America, Blacks are a minority; in the West Indies, Blacks are the major racial group. It is customary to see Blacks as professionals and in leadership roles making important decisions. Therefore, most West Indians do not see themselves as not being able to attain goals they set for themselves. The West Indian immigrant in America finds him/herself in a different situation. Like the African American, they now belong to a minority racial group and find that they are denied the privileges and cultural status they enjoyed prior to migrating to America. This situation makes adjustment difficult for most West Indian immigrants.

The lives of Black people on the islands were strongly affected by slavery, which had an impact on stable relationships, as it did on American Blacks. Family members who were brought from Africa together were separated on the auction block and sold to different plantations, whose owners dictated who would mate with whom. There was no guarantee that the parent-child unit would stay together (Clarke, 1966).

Clarke's (1966) study of the West Indies explains that the dynamic that differentiated the situation in the West Indies from that in the southern United States was the fact that in the British West Indies, slaves could become upwardly mobile. The slave society in America was run under the assumption that African Americans were like children, needing constant supervision. Unlike American slaves, West Indian slaves were allowed to assume leadership roles during slavery. The slave owners did not live year round on their plantations. Unlike in America, where middle- and lower-class Whites were employed to monitor the slaves, in the West Indies other Blacks and "Mulattos" were given that responsibility (Brandon, 1994). West Indian Blacks developed skills needed to operate businesses and soon had business ventures of their own. With this history behind them, West Indians do not see themselves as "second class citizens" and find it difficult to assume this role.

In addition, it was the common practice among the owners and European plantation employees to take concubines from among the "better looking" of the female slaves (Brice-Baker, 1996). The Black landowners were the Black upper class. The illegitimate Black children of White plantation owners, the mulattos, formed the middle class. The two groups differ considerably in their attitudes toward the possibility of social mobility. They both have a strong desire to advance, but they disagree on the extent to which they can control their own destinies in a country that has a White majority. West Indians, as a result of having lived in a predominantly Black society, have had different experiences than African Americans. Even if they are not well-educated, they come to hope, and sometimes expect, that their children and grandchildren will achieve more. Because of their future orientation, they have been very thrifty and would sacrifice in the present in order to have something in the future.

The migration of West Indians to the United States dates back to the early 19th century. In the West Indies, the distribution of wealth is quite uneven with the upper class having extensively more resources than the lower classes (Brice-Baker, 1996). A great number of people who migrate to the United States do so to improve their economic status. Like most immigrants, the West Indian immigrant's decision to migrate to the United States is to take opportunity of the chance for a better life financially and socially. Unlike African Americans who were brought to the United States in slave ships and have a long history of negative experience here, West Indians have come to the United States voluntarily, looking for educational and occupational advancement.

Most West Indian immigrants come to the United States as skilled "laborers," yet most find themselves relegated to doing menial work well below their training and education. After the arrival of a substantial number of White working-class immigrants in the 19th century, Blacks were rarely hired as skilled laborers, and they were certainly not allowed into labor unions that might have given them an avenue to these positions. Many discovered that they were excluded from being hired for the very jobs they were qualified to do. West Indian Americans faced this racial prejudice by uniting against it. The West Indians kept their communities and their cultures separate from the American-born Blacks in an effort to distinguish themselves from the southern African Americans, whom they often considered inferior. They failed to realize that the educational opportunities they had were not open to African Americans in the rural South and only on a limited basis in the North (Brandon, 1994). West Indians soon discovered the limited freedom that African Americans faced.

Residential Segregation of West Indian Immigrants

West Indians, like African Americans, have limited access to safe neighborhoods in which to raise their children. Most West Indian immigrants, especially those of African decent, cannot freely move into communities equal in status to the communities where they lived prior to migrating to the United States. This is a concept with which West Indians were not familiar. Most West Indians coming to America are skilled or professional people accustomed to a higher level of living in their native countries. In order to gain entry and eventually permanent resident status, most West Indians enter the United States accepting jobs lower in status than those to which they are accustomed. Their plan is not to remain in these low-paying jobs but to begin working toward better paying jobs as soon as they become permanent residents. Along with better paying jobs, they plan to relocate to higher quality neighborhoods with better schools for their children.

To assess the relative role of race and ethnicity in shaping patterns of residential segregation, Crowder (1999) examined the residential patterns of West Indian Blacks in the greater New York City/New Jersey Metropolitan area. The socioeconomic characteristics of neighborhoods occupied by West Indian Blacks were also examined and compared to those occupied by African Americans. The results indicate that West Indians are largely denied access to residential areas predominantly occupied by Whites and are confined to areas of large black concentrations. The study also showed that West Indians appear to have carved out somewhat separate residential enclaves within these largely Black areas, and there is evidence to indicate that these areas are of somewhat higher quality than areas occupied by similar concentrations of African Americans. According to Crowder, these areas were formerly White neighborhoods with more affluent and highly educated occupants and higher rates of home ownership. Thus, West Indians are able to avoid relegation to the most depressed Black neighborhoods by accessing higher quality, racially changing neighborhoods and establishing ethnically distinct residential enclaves in these areas.

A substantial body of research has attempted to document and explain persistent patterns of residential segregation by race, with the bulk of research focusing on African Americans, the country's most residentially isolated racial group (Denton & Massey, 1988). There is a tendency to use economics as an explanation in an attempt to understand the persistent residential segregation of Blacks and other ethnic groups.

An overwhelmingly consistent finding of most segregation studies, however, is that black skin represents a substantial barrier to residential assimilation, which overshadows all other factors, including socioeconomic characteristics and ethnicity. Unlike the prevailing situation for Asian and Hispanic groups, metropolitan areas' levels of, and trends in, segregation of Blacks from Whites are apparently unrelated to the aggregate socioeconomic status and acculturation characteristics of group members in the area. Blacks appear less able than other groups to translate their human capital characteristics into access to higher quality neighborhoods and residences near Whites (Alba & Logan, 1993), with even relatively well-off Blacks often confined to racially isolated neighborhoods with less well-off Blacks. Overall, the segregation literature indicates that race represents a powerful master status by which residential patterns are determined, with Blacks in particular representing a substantial barrier to full spatial assimilation (Denton & Massey, 1993; Goldstein & White, 1985). According to Farley, Steeh, Krysan, Jackson, and Reeves (1994), race represents the primary basis for the stereotypes held by Whites. Real estate agents also share responsibility for racial segregation (Yinger, 1995).

Despite the apparent dual disadvantage of immigration and Black race, there is a common perception that West Indian immigrants have achieved greater socioeconomic success than their U.S.-born Black counterparts in America (Bryce-Laporte, 1979). The establishment of comparatively high-quality West Indian residential enclaves in formerly White areas points to the relative advantage of West Indian ancestry in altering the impact of race on residential patterns. The source of this advantage is in question. Foner (1985), Garcia (1986), and Kasinitz (1992) all present the possible explanation that West Indians face lower levels of discrimination than do African Americans. West Indians come from countries where Blacks make up a large part of the upper socioeconomic class. Therefore, this explanation, however plausible, is not comforting to West Indians. Any level of discrimination would mean delegation to a status of a lesser-class human being, a concept with which they are not familiar. Another more acceptable explanation is rooted in the combined effects of their somewhat higher average socioeconomic characteristics and their utilization of various ethnic resources (Crowder, 1999). Informal ethnically-based systems of capital pooling and rotating credit provided many West Indians access to the capital necessary to purchase homes and make other business adventures possible. The ability and tendency of West Indians to be thrifty, sacrificing in the present in order to have something in the future, gives them some advantage over African Americans (Brice-Baker, 1996).

Internalized Racism

Internalized racism can occur when a Black person is inundated with negative images of Blacks and comes to accept these images as true. This shame is internalized, which leads to self-hatred. Frazier (1957) asserts that the Black bourgeoisie are subject to self-hatred; in particular, Frazier points out that they are embarrassed by their African heritage and physical traits. Cross (1991) also states that Blacks harbor these feelings because they have internalized the negative stereotypes of Blacks. In my work with people of African heritage, racism has been the topic of many conversations as patients work on issues of self-esteem, self-image, and self-worth. West Indian patients have reported negative concepts of African Americans, which they learned through the media prior to their migration to the United States. One West Indian parent expressed concerns about her children being identified as African Americans. In her attempt to protect them, she responded by stating, "the more often they visit Trinidad the more likely that they will act less like Americans and more like Trinidadians. This will increase their chances of getting ahead." It is evident that this parent has internalized the negative stereotypes of Black people. Most of the West Indian parents who I have seen in my practice have voiced their concerns and fear that their children will be treated as poorly as they believe African American youths are treated. They agree that African Americans are not treated fairly, and most feel that these are racist acts. Some, however, have a difficult time identifying social or political reasons for what they see as the individual shortcomings of African Americans and blame them for their plight. Therefore, any opportunity to make a distinction between themselves and African Americans is readily taken.

The West Indies is a socially stratified community, composed of lower, middle, and upper classes. Class position is determined primarily by how much money one has and how readily he or she can get money when it is needed. A lower-class person is one who cannot meet his or her financial obligations and is dependent on some relationship with an upper-class person for survival. Middle-class persons are those who own or can afford to rent sufficient land to meet their obligations, are educated enough to obtain employment and save enough money to maintain their families, or who own and operate businesses. An upper-class person is one who does not exert any manual effort in the acquisition of food or money, but whose income derives from big businesses (Horowitz, 1971). In most West Indian communities, it is possible to improve one's class by working very hard. There is a conscious effort on most people's part to move upwards on the class rank. There is pride in ownership. One way to move upward is to acquire possessions, such as homes and businesses (Horowitz, 1971). Improving their children's education and participating in cultural activities are also very important steps to moving up the class rank. Therefore, one of the major foci of West Indian parents is their children's education. Children are encouraged to "keep company" with other children who are doing well academically. The perception, skewed by institutionalized racism in American culture, is often that African American children are less focused on education and by virtue of this would not be good peers for their children. Some West Indian children, especially those from small towns, often are conflicted as they are drawn to what appears to be glamour, for some sophistication, in the way some African American adolescents dress and present themselves. This attraction makes it difficult for them to keep their distance as their parents wish.

Attachment to Native Country

A number of West Indian-born and second-generation West Indian children spend their summers and other long periods out of school in the West Indies. Parents see this as a chance for them to maintain ties with their countries and strengthen their cultural awareness. Some children have maintained this attachment and others looked forward to this experience when they were younger but struggle with wanting to fit in with the American group. Most West Indian adolescents are proud of their heritage even if they do not physically separate themselves from African Americans. They wear or carry things that represent their native countries as a way of identification such as key chains, tee shirts, bags, jewelry, and other items that display aspects of their culture. This is quite noticeable during the West Indian Day Parade, a festive event displaying the many cultures of the West Indies, that is held in cities throughout the United States, Canada, and Great Britain and receives wide support from the West Indian community and others.

ETHNIC IDENTIFICATION OF SECOND-GENERATION WEST INDIANS

There has been substantial interest in the identity and affiliation of West Indian immigrants in the United States (Waters, 1994). However, very little research has been conducted on their children. The children of Black immigrants in the United States face a choice about whether to identify as American Blacks or to maintain an ethnic identity reflecting their parents' national origin. Second-generation West Indian immigrants in the United States will most often be seen by others merely as "Americans" and must actively work to assert their ethnic identities. First-generation Black immigrants in the United States tend to distance themselves from Black Americans, stressing their national origins and ethnic identities as Jamaicans, Haitians, Trinidadians, etc. However, they also face overwhelming pressure to identify only as Blacks (Kasinitz, 1992). According to Bryce-Laporte (1979), first-generation Black immigrants have been described as "invisible immigrants." Their ethnic identity is ignored as focus is placed on the color of their skin. Rather than being contrasted with other immigrants, they are compared with American Blacks. For example, Jamaican immigrants are not understood relative to Chinese immigrants, but are compared with African Americans who have been in this country for several generations and who are subject to very different social and economic pressures. This comparison seems to be based on race as opposed to immigrant status and accomplishments. This is not a fair comparison and will likely polarize the African American and West Indian groups. West Indians are one of several groups who came to the United States as immigrants with similar goals. If the attempt were to understand West Indian immigrants, it would seem that more information could be obtained by comparing them to other immigrants.

Unlike their parents, second-generation children (children born in the United States to West Indian parents) often lack a distinctive accent. Without a distinctive accent, it can be difficult to differentiate the second-generation West Indian children from other Black American children. Therefore, they can choose to be even more invisible, as ethnics, than their parents. A study of Haitian Americans conducted by Woldemikeal (1989) examined the self-identification of second-generation West Indian Blacks. He found that the second generation tends to identify as American Black while first generation stresses their differences from American Blacks. The second generation is pressured into adopting the dialect, speech, dress styles, and ways of behavior of Black American adolescents.

In-depth interviews conducted by Waters (1994) were used to explore the types of racial and ethnic identities of 83 adolescent second-generation immigrants from a number of West Indian islands. The individuals in the study were sorted into three types: identifying as Americans, identifying as ethnic Americans with some distance from American Blacks, or identifying as immigrants in a way that does not identify with American racial and ethnic categories. The result of this study revealed that 42% of the 83 respondents identified as Americans. These respondents do not see their ethnic identities as important to their self-esteem, and according to Waters (1994), disagree with their parents' criticism of Black Americans. Thirty percent of the respondents adopt a strong ethnic identity that involved considerable distancing from Black Americans. It is important to this group that they stress their ethnicity and that others recognize that they are not Black Americans in particular. The final 28% of respondents have an immigrant attitude toward their identities, as opposed to American-identified youth or ethnic-identified youth. Their accents, styles of dress, and behaviors clearly signaled to others that they are foreign-born and have strong West Indian identities. They did not evidence much distancing from Black Americans. Their identities were strongly linked to their experiences on the islands and they did not worry about how they were seen by Black or White Americans. The researchers felt that the type of identity the young people developed is influenced by such factors as the class background of their parents, the social network in which the parents are involved, the school the young people attend, and their family structure.

As I see in my practice, most West Indian immigrant parents encourage their children to preserve their culture. Many are comfortable with the idea of their children living in the West Indies for a prolonged period. Their desire is for their children to take full advantage of what both the United States and the West Indies have to offer. They feel that time spent in the West Indies will allow them exposure to the West Indian way of life. The general belief is that there are more people to care for them, the environment is safer, and the children can learn to live by West Indian values, described as "learning to live a community life," "to respect elders," and to "cooperate with others" (Justus, 1976). Attachment to their native country, culture, customs, and norms provides a structure in which adolescents and their families can operate.

The second-generation West Indian adolescents that I have seen in my practice show a strong identification with their culture. They often identify themselves as West Indians, especially if both of their parents are West Indians. These clients visit the islands of their parents' birth at

least once per year, usually during summer vacations. In some families,
the children spent considerable time in the West Indies with family during their latency years. Some of these adolescents present a different
opinion of racial issues than their parents. They, unlike their parents, believe that distancing themselves from African Americans has little effect on the way they are treated by Whites. Some share the same views
as those of some African American adolescents. Both groups believe
that the fact that they are not White is the basis for the discrimination
they experience, and both are very angry with the system as they feel
that they have little to no chance of getting ahead. This anger can result
in negative behaviors.

Racism and Racial Identity

My discussions with patients have revealed that some West Indians
object to being identified as African Americans because of a fear of racial prejudice. Some have bought into the concept that African Americans have not tried as hard as they could and therefore are at the mercy
of Whites. Most West Indians continue to believe that if they work
hard they can improve their financial situation, raise their class status,
and be less affected by racism. A White colleague shared with me a
conversation she had with another White colleague of hers. My colleague stated that, in conversation, the woman made the following
comment: "The problem with West Indians is that they do not know
that they are Black." West Indians of African decent have always
known that they are Black. The issue is that prior to migrating to the
United States, being Black was not a problem for most West Indians.

Although racism exists to some degree in the West Indies, being
poor and considered a member of the lower class is more the issue,
and is therefore the reason to migrate to the United States where
opportunities to improve class status are available. Being Black
became a problem for most West Indians when they migrated to
the United States, a problem that they were not prepared to handle.
Some West Indians question whether being Black is their problem
or the problem of Whites. Even those who are comfortable with
being Black have experienced the pain of racism. The negative
portrayal of African Americans by the media presents to the West
Indian immigrant preconceived ideas about this group of people
who resemble them. The struggle to keep separate from what is
considered a bad image, yet an image that so closely resembles
them, can only be described as emotionally draining and to no

avail. The challenge for West Indian immigrants lies in maintaining our unity and pride in our cultural heritage and racial identity, while finding harmony with our new identity as West Indian Americans.

REFERENCES

Alba, R., & Logan, J. R. (1993). Minority proximity to Whites in suburbs: An individual level-analysis of segregation. *American Journal of Sociology, 98*, 1388-1427.

Brandon, A. (1994). *West Indian Americans*. Toronto: Maxwell Macmillan International Publishers.

Brice-Baker, J. (1996). Jamaican families. In M. McGoldrick, J. Giordano, & J. K. Pierce (Eds.), *Ethnicity and family therapy* (2nd ed., pp. 123-133). New York: Guilford Press.

Bryce-Laporte, R. S. (1979). New York City and the new Caribbean immigrants: A contextual statement. *International Migration Review, 23*, 214-234.

Clarke, E. (1966). *My mother who fathered me*. London: Allen and Unwin.

Cross, W. E. (1991). *Shades of Black*. Philadelphia: Temple Press.

Crowder, K. D. (1999). Residential segregation of West Indians in the New York/New Jersey metropolitan area: The roles of race and ethnicity. *International Migration Review, 33*, 79-114.

Denton, N. A., & Massey, D. S. (1988). Residential segregation of Blacks, Hispanics, and Asians by socioeconomic status and generation. *Social Science Quarterly, 69*, 797-817.

Denton, N., & Massey, D. (1993). *American apartheid: Segregation and the making of the underclass*. Cambridge, MA: Harvard University Press.

Farley, R., Steeh, C., Krysan, M., Jackson, T., & Reeves, K. (1994). Stereotypes and segregation: Neighborhoods in the Detroit area. *American Journal of Sociology, 100*, 750-780.

Foner, N. (1985). The Jamaicans: Race and ethnicity among migrants in New York City. In N. Foner (Ed.), *New immigrants in New York* (pp. 131-158). New York: Columbia University Press.

Frazier, F. (1957). *Black bourgeoisie: The rise of a new middle class in the United States*. New York: The Free Press.

Garcia, J. A. (1986). Caribbean migration to the mainland: A review of adaptive experiences. *The Annals, AAPSS, 487*, 114-125.

Goldstein, I., & White, C. (1985). Residential segregation and color stratification among Hispanics in Philadelphia: Comment on Massey and Mullan. *American Journal of Sociology, 91*, 391-396.

Hargrove, P. (2006). Social work practice with Mexican clients: Service provision with illegal entrants to the United States. *Journal of Emotional Abuse, 6*(2/3), 61-76.

Horowitz, M. (1971). *Peoples and cultures of the Caribbean*. Garden City, NY: The American Museum of Natural History.

Justus, J. B. (1976). West Indians in Los Angeles: Community and identity. In R. S. Bryce-Laporte & D. M. Mortimer (Eds.), *Caribbean migration to the United States* (pp. 130-148). Washington, DC: Smithsonian Institution, Research Institute on Immigration and Ethnic Studies, Occasional Papers No. 1.

Kasinitz, P. (1992). *Caribbean New York: Black immigration and the politics of race.* Ithaca, NY: Cornell University Press.

Madsen, L. H. (2006). Coming together and falling apart: Looking at identity relationship. *Journal of Emotional Abuse, 6*(2/3), 155-172.

Waters, M. C. (1994). Ethnic and racial identities of second generation Black immigrants in New York City. *International Migration Review, 28*, 795-820.

Woldemikeal, T. M. (1989). *Becoming Black American: Haitians and American institutions in Evanston, Illinois.* New York: AMS Press.

Yinger, J. (1995). *Closed doors, opportunities lost: The continuing cost of housing discrimination.* New York: Sage.

doi:10.1300/J135v06n02_04

Social Work Practice with Mexican Clients: Service Provision with Illegal Entrants to the United States

Pia Hargrove

SUMMARY. This article surveys the history of Mexican-United States relations and discusses implications for social work practice engaging the undocumented Mexican population in treatment. Methods of service provision that seek to minimize clients' fear of obtaining social services are discussed. Factors considered include: self-awareness and cultural competency on the part of the worker, trauma symptoms arising from migration, and agency policy considerations that impact service delivery. Practitioners must be educated about immigration policies and public benefits and services available to illegal entrants. Agencies and social workers have to work to engage and empower Mexican clients to enjoy

Address correspondence to: Pia Hargrove, LMSW, Jewish Board of Family and Children's Services/Neptune Family Services, 63 Maple Street, Brooklyn, NY 11225 (E-mail: piahargrove@hotmail.com).

The author gives honor to God who is the head of her life. She would like to acknowledge the clients at Neptune Family Services for their self-determination and resilience in the face of adversity, and her colleagues for their advice and counsel. She thanks her mother, Myrna Blount, and uncle, Syl Williamson, posthumously for their support, and her aunt, Elzora Williamson, for providing her with insight in completing this project.

[Haworth co-indexing entry note]: "Social Work Practice with Mexican Clients: Service Provision with Illegal Entrants to the United States." Hargrove, Pia. Co-published simultaneously in *Journal of Emotional Abuse* (The Haworth Maltreatment & Trauma Press, an imprint of The Haworth Press, Inc.) Vol. 6, No. 2/3, 2006, pp. 61-76; and: *Racism and Racial Identity: Reflections on Urban Practice in Mental Health and Social Services* (ed: Lisa V. Blitz, and Mary Pender Greene) The Haworth Maltreatment & Trauma Press, an imprint of The Haworth Press, Inc., 2006, pp. 61-76. Single or multiple copies of this article are available for a fee from The Haworth Document Delivery Service [1-800-HAWORTH, 9:00 a.m. - 5:00 p.m. (EST). E-mail address: docdelivery@haworthpress.com].

Available online at http://jea.haworthpress.com
doi:10.1300/J135v06n02_05

their civil rights in the United States as they build families and flourish in this country. doi:10.1300/J135v06n02_05 *[Article copies available for a fee from The Haworth Document Delivery Service: 1-800-HAWORTH. E-mail address: <docdelivery@haworthpress.com> Website: <http://www.HaworthPress.com> © 2006 by The Haworth Press, Inc. All rights reserved.]*

KEYWORDS. Mexican, immigration, border patrol, illegal entrants, Mexico, trauma, racism, cultural competency

As an African American woman from Brooklyn, New York, I have always had an interest in social work in urban areas. New York City prides itself on being a beautiful mosaic tiled by a variety of races and ethnicities. It is evident, however, that many recent immigrants struggle socially and financially to survive. While my family is American, I was raised in an immigrant community. In pursuing social work practice, I made a conscious effort to learn Spanish. I now engage Spanish-speaking families who have migrated to Brooklyn from Mexico. In my work with this population, I have noticed that there is a gap in service provision to Mexican families in Brooklyn. Families present with a need for supportive counseling in adjustment to a new environment while simultaneously coping with family issues. Moreover, concrete material such as eligibility for public benefits and access to education and health care must be addressed.

CASE EXAMPLE

My interest in gaining a better understanding of the Mexican migration was sparked by my work with one case in particular. Miriam is a Spanish-speaking woman from Puebla, Mexico. She sought services from the agency where I worked to assist her with finding schools for her eight-year-old son and 10-year-old daughter who were born in the United States. Moreover, Miriam wanted help in applying for public benefits for her children. In reviewing this presenting problem, it was evident that many issues were at hand. This client did not seek traditional psychotherapy, nor did she even understand the concept. Miriam was fearful that by seeking help she might be deported for not having immigration status. It was clear that this client needed not only supportive counseling, but someone to advocate for her and her children in the system of public education and public benefits.

With time, Miriam revealed that she left her rural community in Puebla at 14 years old. Miriam's mother died of diabetic complications and malnutrition. With very little elementary education, Miriam decided to escape the home of her alcoholic, physically abusive father. Leaving nine siblings behind in their thatched roof home, Miriam rode a bus to Mexico City. There she sold flowers in the streets until she saved enough money to brave the travel to the United States. At 19 years old, Miriam paid a coyote (immigrant smuggler) $1,500 to get her illegally across the United States-Mexico border. Traveling in a small van with 15 passengers, Miriam survived the dangerous trip through Texas and across country. Miriam remembers having insufficient food and water for the trip and being afraid of border patrol agents who threatened to rape the women in the van if the driver did not give them money. She eventually arrived in Brooklyn, New York.

Miriam became involved in a relationship with a Mexican man who was an alcoholic and physically abusive toward her. She had her two children by him and looked to him for financial support because she had difficulty finding employment without immigration status. To escape the relationship, Miriam removed her children from their respective schools and went back to Mexico for a few years. When she returned to New York, she placed the children in school again but they were academically behind. She removed them again because she feared that they would feel badly about themselves for performing poorly.

I engaged Miriam about the importance of education and her children's right to receive additional services to help them with their weak points. I explained the legal obligation that she has to ensure that her children receive an education. It was important to be sensitive to her experience and her lack of knowledge about the services available. Through conducting home visits with Miriam in addition to office visits, she began to trust me as her therapist and advocate. Her fears of deportation subsided with reassurance that her children were entitled to education and health care. I accompanied Miriam to the local school and helped her to enroll her two children. We met with the committee for special education. Although her children did not have learning disabilities, they had missed significant amounts of school. After conferencing the case, both children received reading resource and attention in math. While the children were in school, I went with Miriam to the local office for public assistance to apply for benefits on behalf of the children. She now receives public assistance, food stamps, and a rent subsidy. Miriam took her children to the city hospital for their vaccinations, where she also received assistance in applying for Medicaid for her children.

Throughout the course of treatment, Miriam became empowered to seek service for herself and her children. She was able to begin learning English at classes offered at the local library. By learning her rights as a parent and her children's rights as citizens, she became more confident and better able to utilize community resources. My ability to visit her in her home and accompany her to other institutions allowed her to build her trust in me. With time, she was able to explore her feelings of loss about her mother and her family in Mexico. She expressed her hurt and anger toward her father and concerns about her own parenting. Together we discussed parenting styles and ways of encouraging and praising her children as they struggled in their new school. As the safety of treatment was established, Miriam expressed that she felt more comfortable with me because I am African American. She explained that she noticed how racism affects African Americans in her community and she admired my ability to be successful. Miriam felt that I could understand her fears in society because as an African American woman I experience racism similarly. She felt that I did not judge her according to her ethnicity and appreciated my acceptance of her and my willingness to help her stabilize her and her family.

OVERVIEW OF MEXICAN HISTORY

As discussed by other contributors to this volume (see Hine-St. Hilaire, this volume; Kohl, this volume; Madsen, this volume), to work effectively with clients who are immigrants to this country it is important to know something about their culture, country of origin, and immigration experience. In working with Mexican clients, clinicians must clearly examine personal views on immigration to the United States and, more importantly, their views toward Mexican immigration. Prejudicial attitudes toward this growing immigrant group may be projected during treatment. Clinicians must also begin to examine how individual culture, social values, and language affect work with the Mexican client. Clinicians are called to be aware of their ethnic identification and determine whether they assume societal privileges that others do not have.

The United States is a sanctuary to people worldwide, and those seeking refuge within our borders are representative of many nations, cultures, customs, languages, and religions. As of 2000, 10.4% of the total United States population was foreign born (Rein, 2002). The largest group of immigrants in the United States is from Mexico, representing 22% of the foreign born population (Padilla, 1997). Mexico shares a 2,000 mile border with the United States (Garcia, 2002; Salgado de Snyder, 2002). Five of the United States Southwestern states belonged to Mexico until the United States-Mexico War of 1845. There is a steady influx of Mexicans to many areas in the United States. Social service providers and mental health practitioners need a basic understanding of the historic interaction between the United States and Mexico to more comprehensively address the needs of Mexican clients.

For centuries, Mexico's social stratification has been plagued with discrimination based on skin color. The Spanish expedition of the Americas, led by Hernan Cortes in 1519, turned the course of Mexican history. The Spanish conquered Mexico (i.e., "New Spain") in 1521, garnishing the nation's wealth through silver and raw materials (Garcia, 2002). In usurping power from the Central American country, Spain gained economic and political strength above the other European countries of the epoch.

By the end of the 1500s, increasing numbers of Spaniards populated New Spain. There were two groups of Indian tribes inhabiting the country upon the Spanish conquest. Sedentary tribes had agrarian communities in towns and others lived in the desert. The second group of Indians was nomadic. The travelers were aggressive and looted their neighbors for survival (Garcia, 2002). Nonetheless, the two groups coexisted. The Spanish disdained these tribes and viewed them as inferior. With Spanish women absent from the expedition, the men raped and violated the natives (Gonzales, 1999). Their sexual violence left many women pregnant with a population who would come to be known as Mestizos. The word Mestizo is used to describe those people with mixed Spaniard and indigenous blood. Social stratification was built upon race, with the Spaniards (those born in Spain) at the top, followed by Peninsulares (Spaniards born in Mexico) who dominated the Mestizos; the most lowly were the indigenous people and the enslaved Africans (Garcia, 2002; Gonzales, 1999). This cultural superiority planted the seeds of racism that continue to flourish today.

At the beginning of the 1800s, there was growing animosity toward Spain's colonial rule. The social classes banded together against the Spaniard ruling class elite. The Mexican War for Independence was initially led by Miguel Hidalgo. The colony struggled to have autonomy from Spain. By 1821, New Spain gained its independence from Spain and called itself Mexico (Garcia, 2002). The post-bellum society had a democratic but weak government. Independent Mexico found difficulty in militarily protecting its borders and the Anglo immigration from the

United States posed a threat to security (Gonzales, 1999). In efforts to occupy the territory now known as Texas, the United States declared war against Mexico in 1845. Mexico surrendered in 1848. The United States and Mexico signed the Treaty of Guadalupe Hidalgo. The United States obtained Mexico's northwest, including Nevada, Utah, California, and Wyoming as well as parts of New Mexico, Arizona, and Colorado. The Gadsden Purchase of 1853 gave the United States the remaining parts of the aforementioned states (Garcia, 2002).

Many Mexicans remained in the southwestern states. Through the Treaty of Guadalupe Hidalgo, the United States agreed to honor Mexicans holding land titles in the area. As time progressed, however, Anglo-Americans took over the land. Like other countries of the world, Mexico was invaded by the United States and occupied militarily, but Mexico is the only country where the United Stated later annexed half its territory (Huntington, 2004). In the years following the Gadsden Purchase, Mexico continued to experience political and economic instability (Gonzales, 1999). There was much corruption, and discrimination against Mestizos and the indigenous people continued. An abundance of jobs in the Southwestern United States was–and is–a motivating factor for Mexicans to migrate in great numbers to the United States.

Mexicans and Migration

Like millions of others living in the United States today, Mexicans sought to live in the United States with hopes of improving their educational opportunity and increasing their earnings to create a better life. The agricultural industry then and now thrives with the hard work of undocumented Mexicans. Civil rights of Mexican laborers are often abused because they are not naturalized in the United States. While Mexicans account for the largest group of foreign born people in the United States, there is a low percentage of citizenship (Padilla, 1997). Studies indicate that the low percentage of naturalization is related to low educational and economic levels upon entrance to the United States (Garcia, 2002). Immigrants from other countries often come to the United States with more education and vocational skill. Moreover, other countries had historic ties with the United States that may have influenced Congress' decision to amend or develop immigration law to favor other groups. In some cases, Mexicans do not take steps to obtain naturalization because they often travel back and forth between the borders.

Anti-immigrant attitudes in the United States have continuously lashed out against Mexicans. In 1994, there was much controversy over Proposition 187 which was passed in California. Proposition 187 prohibited undocumented immigrants from receiving public social services, education, and public health services (Garcia, 2002). Moreover, employees of public agencies were obligated by law to report suspicion of undocumented workers. The proposition also made it a felony to print, use, or sell false citizenship documents. Proposition 187 was later overturned and declared unconstitutional. Rather than escaping discrimination through immigration, Mexicans experience it two-fold within American borders.

The United States Border Patrol was created in 1924 by the Department of Labor (Rotella, 1998). They aim to limit the number of Mexicans and other Central and South Americans who attempt to cross United States borders yearly. The patrol unit is equipped with attack dogs to assist them in controlling the thousands of Mexicans who attempt to cross into the United States each night (Rotella, 1998). Much of this amoebic border is the great expanse of the Sonoran Desert and the Rio Grande. To better define the borderlands, the United States has affixed steel walls, concrete channels, boundary markers, and morbidly festooned cattle fences and barbed wire (Barry, Browne, & Sims, 1994). If these indications of demarcation are not sufficient, the Border Patrol, known as "La Migra," is constantly on guard to capture Mexican migrants. If voyagers do not dehydrate in the desert, they may drown in the depths of the Rio Grande. Still others are victims of brutality at the hands of the Border Patrol.

For most illegal migrants, the sojourn across the border represents far more than a decided relocation. Leaving behind a home, family, culture, language, and custom is a rite of passage for young men (Barry et al., 1994). Each year many leave a Mexico robbed of its resources to come to a country anointed with economic plenty. The departure from Mexico represents an escape from the pitfalls of poverty to climb a ladder of success. Thousands leave behind educational disparity to find educational stimulation.

People risk their lives to journey to the United States. The Camino del Diablo is the 130-mile desert trail along the Sonoran Desert, one of the paths to the Southwestern United States. Historically, thousands of people have died in this path (Annerino, 1999). The temperature climbs above 100 degrees in the shade and canteens of water do not last long. Adults and children alike brave the scorching desert with only the clothes on their backs. Snakes and scorpions slither along the desert as migrants make their way across. As the heat and humidity become more tenacious, travelers will disrobe only to be seared by the intensity of the sun. Water supply is exhausted, throats are parched, and voyagers drink their urine through sun-blistered lips in attempts to escape delirium. Survivors of the trail will eventually crawl upon an Interstate highway and find their way to opportunity.

Others brave the border with the help of "coyotes." Coyotes are people who charge a fee to assist Mexicans in the dangerous journey past the Border Patrol into the United States. For the price of a month's wages in a California sweat shop, a Mexican can attempt to cross over into the United States with the help of a coyote (Annerino, 1999). Coyotes often drive overcrowded vans of Mexicans through paths laden with La Migra. If they are able to escape an automobile chase by the Border Patrol, they still may fall victim to murder, rape, or robbery by other Mexicans preying on travelers. People sell everything they have to make the journey and are usually carrying sums of money to come north (Rotella, 1998). Bandits along the borders prey on the van loads of Mexicans guided by coyotes. Some of the Border Patrol respond to crime at the border, but most migrants are left to survival of the fittest.

Immigration Law

Within the past decade there has been considerable change in United States immigration law. Illegal immigrants obtain jobs with significantly lower wages than American citizens. Many Americans felt that citizens were losing jobs to illegal immigrants who were willing to work for low wages. Moreover, illegal immigrants were continuously being exploited by employers. There was also controversy about whether illegal immigrants should have the same access to public assistance as citizens (Rein, 2002). Recent immigration law legalized segments of the undocumented population and penalized employers who intentionally hired illegal immigrants. Border enforcement units were implemented and increased to limit illegal entry into the United States. Since so many undocumented immigrants are exploited and abused by others, parts of the immigration law allow victims of domestic violence to self-petition for immigrant status (National Immigration Law Center, 2002; Rein, 2002). In recent years, priority has been given to employment-based immigration. Hence, there has been much upset over illegal immigrants receiving public benefits. The Welfare Reform Law of 1996 was designed to limit the eligibility of illegal immigrants to receiving public benefits. There was concern that public benefits in the United States may serve as an incentive for immigration.

SOCIAL WORK PRACTICE WITH MEXICAN CLIENTS

As the population of Mexicans without immigration status increases, so will their need for services. Practitioners will inevitably encounter Mexicans wishing to receive treatment. Practitioners in agencies have to gain a clear understanding of agency policy regarding treatment of clients without immigration status. Some social work settings require that clients provide their social security number and substantial documentation of their identity. These requirements would exclude illegal entrants from services. Practitioners must consider that Mexican clients may not have access to health care and may be unable to pay for clinical treatment. Practitioners must not only be aware of societal discrimination against Mexicans but must also examine personal areas of prejudice. Self-awareness is critical to engaging clients who may have distinctly different lives, experiences, values, customs, culture, and language.

Gathering an extensive social history of the client gives social work practitioners valuable information with which to begin a comprehensive clinical assessment. Open communication will assist in building a non-judgmental, trusting environment with the client. It is imperative that generalizations are not made about the client but rather clarity achieved on his or her specific migration experience. There is great diversity within immigrant families, and assessment of their experience should be done with caution (Gopaul-McNicol, 1995). With such information, mental health needs and concrete services can be addressed with the client.

In working with Mexicans who have recently migrated to the United States, one must acknowledge the social zeitgeist surrounding the topic of Mexican immigration. Hundreds of years later, avid discrimination remains as a social sentiment against Mexicans in this country. Some of the discrimination is based upon a sheer difference in culture, customs, and especially language. Furthermore, much discrimination is based upon race and is inextricably linked to socioeconomic status.

Ethnicity and Racism in Working with Mexican Clients

When social work practitioners are open to exploring internal feelings about race and class, these issues can be addressed with the client. Historically, the poorer Mexican citizens are those of indigenous and African descent, and poverty among these groups is prevalent today. Hence, many Mexicans who migrate to the United States are from these groups. It is pertinent for clinicians to explore the client's ethnic affiliation in Mexico and the region from which the client migrated. Many Mexicans who migrate to the United States are from the states of Jalisco, Michoacan, Guanajuato, Zacatecas, and San Luis Potosi (Salgado de Snyder, 2002). Social work practitioners should engage the client around discussion about their educational background and language skills in both Spanish and English. In conducting the social history, social workers can ask about family of origin and its attitudes toward migration. In exploring issues within the family of origin, one might ask about the client's birth order, age, gender role, and whether other members of the family have migrated to the United States. The socioeconomic and political factors involved in the premigratory period and departure are significant (Drachman, 1992). It is critical to explore with the client the reason for migration as perceived by the client and the reason as perceived by the family of origin. In addition to exploring the reason for migration, it is crucial to explore the method of migration.

Trauma of Illegal Migration

Engage the client around his mode of travel to the United States and immigration status. As discussed earlier, many Mexicans endure perilous conditions to make it to the United States. It is likely that travel under such strained conditions can have psychological impact on a person. One might explore how the client came to settle in a particular region of the United States. Some migrants may have support systems in place before travel; others may come to the United States completely isolated from what is familiar. Still others come to the United States assuming that a relative or family friend will supportively introduce them to American society, but rather find themselves exploited and abused by extended family.

Those who are successful in their journey to the United States may enter with tremendous trauma. Some may witness the death of others who were traveling with them, and others feel a threat to their lives. In certain circumstances, clients experience intense fear and helplessness. Miriam recounted an intensely difficult journey to the United States. She described her excitement as she packed bags of food and water for what was going to be a trip that would take days or even weeks. However, Miriam explained that as she and others like her walked through the desert, she shed all of her bags because of the unbearable heat. She remembered being unable to eat because of the diarrhea she suffered due to dehydration. At points, she was unable to walk. A traveler left behind on the trail, however, would indicate to the United States Border Patrol that coyotes were present. Miriam was tearful as she expressed that the coyotes threatened to kill those who gave up the trail. The sun-scorched skeletal bodies bore witness to those who had already died.

Clinicians must be cognizant that clients may demonstrate various symptoms of post traumatic stress disorder (PTSD). (See Blitz & Illidge, this volume; Franklin, Boyd-Franklin, & Kelly, this volume; and Peacock & Daniels, this volume, for further discussion on the combined impact of racism and trauma.) The symptoms can include intrusive thoughts of the event, recurrent dreams related to the event, and psychological reactivity to triggers that are symbolic of the events (American Psychiatric Association, 2000). The primary focus at the beginning of treatment with a client experiencing PTSD is establish-ing safety in the therapy. The therapist must begin to engage in a sup-portive relationship. Moreover, it is imperative to introduce educat-ional material regarding trauma and how it may affect one mentally and physically (Brandell, 1997). Clinicians must help clients to nor-malize their feelings about self and work through creating positive perspectives of self.

In working with the Mexican migrant who presents with PTSD as a re-sult of the border crossing, practitioners must identify the client's resilience and coping with an overwhelming situation (Berzoff, Flanagan, & Hertz, 1996). In the experiencing of a life threatening trauma, a client may have difficulty identifying mental strengths and acknowledging accom-plishments. The therapist should assist the client in identifying ways that the client's life has been affected by the traumatic experience of the crossing. Not all clients will be capable of expressing the trauma ver-bally. At times, unspeakable memories can be expressed through art, poetry, music, or other means (Brandell, 1997). Encouraging clients to explore other means of expression can sometimes be more healing than verbalization. In addition, the therapist needs to help the client recog-nize coping strategies that are characteristic of the client, to bear some of the losses that the client has endured.

My true admiration and respect for Miriam made it simple to ap-proach her from a strengths perspective. Miriam understood that she had experienced many traumas in her life. She was eager to explore her feelings about her experiences in efforts to impede any negative impact on her parenting. Miriam explained her unwillingness to allow her chil-dren to participate in any activities without her. She feared that without her protection they might somehow be exposed to some of the traumas that she experienced. With supportive counseling, Miriam was able to identify and take pride in her ability to provide for and protect her children in all circumstances, and place herself in safe environments.

In Miriam's case, her symptoms of PTSD appear to result not only from her border travel experience, but also from her travel in Mexico. During a home visit with Miriam, she decided to show me her skill at needlepoint. She explained that her mother taught her so that she could sell needlecraft items when she left for Mexico City at 14 years old. While showing me her artisan craft, she began to describe how her trauma had affected her. Miriam described having recurring nightmares in which she woke up crying. She described that in her dream she is a young girl running through the desert from her father who is chasing her. She explained that each time she had the dream, a different person would give her water. However, each time someone tries to save her with the water, her father would attack them and she would awake. Miriam reported having variations of the same dream for years. With greater exploration, Miriam expressed her guilt and shame for leaving her family behind in Mexico. She felt that her travel to the United States was a gamble between life and death. Miriam reports that she loves her life in the United States and her two children. However, she reports being haunted by the physical abuse that she suffered from her father. She also refused to journey the dangerous trail to visit her family in Mexico. She expressed that she is often terrorized by intrusive thoughts of the desert trail during her day. To reconcile some of her guilt and her fears, Miriam sends money home to her father and siblings in Mexico and tries to move forward with her life.

Clinician Self-Awareness and Countertransference

The therapist working with Mexican immigrant trauma survivors must be self-aware. Clinicians must work to identify countertransference and its function in the treatment. The worker must not contribute to the client's denial, avoidance, guilt, and shame (Brandell, 1997). Instead, the worker must fight the difficulties of countertransference. Clinicians must ensure that they receive support from peers and supervisors when working with trauma, particularly when it relates to personal experiences. It can be helpful to establish therapist support groups. Clinicians can explore how personal history affects work with clients and how to minimize the negative effects on treatment with clients. Moreover, practitioners working with trauma must identify personal coping strategies and maintain a balance of work, play, and rest to combat the emotional weariness of trauma work (Phillips, 2004).

My countertransference with Miriam was a positive one. For me, Miriam was an example of the many women who are disrespected and degraded. Miriam's resilience in the midst of adversity and her spirit of ambition was and is inspirational. Our rich therapeutic alliance developed as we shared a mutual respect and appreciation for one another. To cope with Miriam's trauma-laden descriptive history, I had the support of my colleagues. Weekly clinical meetings gave me the opportunity to share the treatment process with other practitioners. In addition, I had a strong relationship with one colleague in whom I could confide. I made a concerted effort to maintain a vibrant social life outside of work to distinguish my experience from the accounts of trauma that I heard during the course of the day.

RECOMMENDATIONS FOR SERVICE PROVISION

Despite the large numbers of Mexicans in the country, they remain unrepresented in service provision. Social work services have been underutilized by minority groups because traditional methods of services have been ineffective with minorities (Watkins & Gonzales, 1982). Practitioners must consider that many Mexicans have been discriminated against and are fearful of being deported. This fear may frequently interfere with the ability to create a trusting relationship.

Agencies wishing to increase service provision to Mexican clients may have to modify their methods of treatment. Agencies would have to make tremendous efforts to find a skilled worker who speaks both Spanish and English. If it is possible, the agency should consider the option of meeting with clients in their homes or in settings familiar to clients such as schools and community centers (Watkins & Gonzales, 1982). Service provision in a non-threatening environment can begin the engagement process with the client. Once clients feel that they can trust the worker, they may be inclined to conduct visits at the agency site.

Once clients are participating within the agency, administrators must consider additional services beyond counseling. Psychoeducational workshops and seminars can teach clients about their human rights despite their immigration status. Moreover, agencies may consider offering English classes to Mexican clients who are eager to acquire language skills. To conduct successful outreach within the Mexican community, an agency has to be dedicated to training its workers to the issues at hand for the clients.

Social workers must stay abreast of the agency policy of delivering services to clients without immigration status. Moreover, clinicians have to be educated about current immigration policy and the availability of public benefits for immigrants. Knowledge about immigration law is critical to having sensitivity to a client's fears surrounding their immigration status (Gopaul-McNicol, 1995). With this information, social workers can help clients to understand their eligibility for benefits. By exploring these issues in treatment, Mexican clients may feel more empowered to seek services if they are assured that they will not be penalized. Clinicians have to be willing to advocate on behalf of clients, particularly when language is a barrier. Moreover, practitioners need to become familiar with the legal services in the community. Many organizations provide free legal services for clients with immigration issues. Social workers can form a liaison with these legal service providers in efforts to assist clients. Helping clients to obtain lawful immigration status is the first step in helping them to be eligible for public benefits (Padilla, 1997).

Unfortunately, many clients may ignore their health problems for fear that if they seek medical assistance they may be deported. Clinicians must learn about the availability of health care to Mexican clients who do not have immigration status. As the therapeutic relationship continues to flourish, social workers must engage clients in discussions about their medical history. Social workers should be able to explain to clients the health-care options that are available to address their medical needs. Many public hospitals have outreach vans within the community to encourage people to have medical screenings. Workers may consider organizing a group of clients to utilize these services. Moreover, social workers must truly engage pregnant clients about receiving prenatal care.

Clinicians must also learn about policies regarding educational rights for children. Social workers might find that some of the Mexican children in a household may not be attending school. Parents, however, may not be aware that the child is allowed and expected to be in school. Unfortunately, if a family is undocumented, there might not be a way to monitor that children are in school. Once the therapeutic alliance is formed, therapists may inform clients about local education policy and expectations. Social workers must be willing to help clients navigate within the educational system to have their child in the appropriate learning environment. Clinicians must be aware that children may be discriminated against in the school system and placed in an inappropriate class-setting based on a child's limited English-speaking skill rather than cognitive ability. Social workers must be cognizant of parental rights in the education department and the availability of translation services to families who may have difficulty understanding.

Engaging Mexican clients without immigration status may mean extending oneself far beyond traditional therapy. It is not the ethnicity of the clinician that is most important, but rather willingness and ability to become involved with the client in all aspects of his or her experience. After establishing the therapeutic alliance, practitioners must fully explore the client's pre- and post-migratory experience. Social workers have to assess whether the client has experienced trauma and, if so, how it affects the client in the present. Supporting the client by emphasizing strengths and advocating on the client's behalf can be empowering. Clinicians must be aware of the different resources available to assist families in coping with the adjustment process.

While practitioners are to be supportive of their clients, they must also address their own needs. It is important to find an outlet where clinicians can share counter-transferencial experiences with others and also find that which is relaxing. With an open mind and clinical support, practitioners can engage Mexican clients in treatment. A brief understanding of the relationship between the United States and Mexico will allow the clinician to have a historical context for some of the current policy regarding Mexican immigration. The willingness to access community resources for immigrants and an eagerness to advocate on behalf of clients will build the foundation of treatment with clients without immigration status. The assessment of trauma and its effect is critical in the ability to help clients work through some of the emotional difficulty that they may experience in response to migration, trauma, and the many other adjustments that result in their relocation. Meeting the client where he or she is at physically and emotionally is at the root of the growth of the therapeutic alliance.

REFERENCES

American Psychiatric Association (2000). *Diagnostic and statistical manual of mental disorders* (4th ed., Text Revision). Washington DC: Author.

Annerino, J. (1999). *Dead in their tracks: Crossing America's desert borderlands.* New York: Four Walls Eight Windows.

Barry, T., Browne, H., & Sims, B. (1994). *Crossing the line: Immigrants, economic integration, and drug enforcement on the U.S.-Mexico border.* Albuquerque: The Resource Center Press.

Berzoff, J., Flanagan, L. M., & Hertz, P. (1996). *Inside out and outside in: Psychodynamic clinical theory and practice in contemporary multicultural contexts*. Northvale: Jason Aronson, Inc.

Blitz, V., & Illidge, C. (2006). Not so black and white: Shades of gray and brown in anti-racist multicultural team building in a domestic violence shelter. *Journal of Emotional Abuse, 6*(2/3), 113-134.

Brandell, J. R. (Ed.) (1997). *Theory and practice in clinical social work*. New York: The Free Press.

Drachman, D. (1992). A stage of migration framework for service to immigrant populations. *Social Work, 37*, 68-72.

Franklin, A. J., Boyd-Franklin, N., & Kelly, S. (2006). Racism and invisibility: Race-related stress, emotional abuse and psychological trauma for people of color. *Journal of Emotional Abuse, 6*(2/3), 9-30.

Garcia, A. M. (2002). *The Mexican Americans*. Westport: Greenwood Press.

Gonzales, M. G. (1999). *Mexicanos: A History of Mexicans in the United States*. Bloomington: Indiana University Press.

Gopaul-McNicol, S. A. (1995). Examining psychotherapeutic and psychosocial factors in working with immigrant families. *Journal of Social Distress and the Homeless, 4*, 143-156.

Hine-St. Hiliaire, D. (2006). Immigrant West Indian families and their struggles with racism in America. *Journal of Emotional Abuse, 6*(2/3), 47-60.

Huntington, S. (2004, March/April). The Hispanic challenge. *Foreign Policy*, 30-45.

Kohl, B. G., Jr. (2006). Can you feel me now? Worldview, empathy and racial identity in a therapy dyad. *Journal of Emotional Abuse, 6*(2/3), 173-196.

Madsen, L. H. (2006). Coming together and falling apart: Looking at racial identity relationship. *Journal of Emotional Abuse, 6*(2/3), 155-172.

National Immigration Law Center (2002). *Guide to immigrant eligibility*. Los Angeles: Author.

Padilla, Y. C. (1997). Immigrant policy: Issues for social work practice. *Social Work, 4*, 595-607.

Peacock, C., & Daniels, G. (2006). Applying an anti-racist framework to a residential treatment center: Sanctuary[R], a model for change. *Journal of Emotional Abuse, 6*(2/3), 135-154.

Phillips, S. B. (2004). *Counter-transference: Effects on the group therapist working with trauma*. Training presented at the Mental Health Association of New York City, Inc., New York, NY.

Rein, M. L. (2002). *Immigration and illegal aliens: Burden or blessing?* Farmington Hills: Gale Group.

Rotella, S. (1998). *Twilight on the line: Underworld and politics at the U.S.-Mexico border*. New York: W.W. Norton & Company, Inc.

Salgado de Snyder, V. N. (2002). Research and clinical perspectives on Mexican migration: Those who go, those who stay. *Journal of Multicultural Nursing &Health, 8*, 23-33.

Watkins, T. R., & Gonzales, R. (1982). Outreach to Mexican Americans. *Social Work, 27*(1), 68-73.

doi:10.1300/J135v06n02_05

Triple Trouble:
Battered Women of Color–
"Being Black, Being Battered
and Being Female . . .
I Ask Myself, Where Do I Begin?"

Janet A. Geller
Jacqueline Miller
Patricia Churchill

SUMMARY. A vast body of literature exists that illustrates the plight of women in a patriarchal society. Another equally vast body of literature discusses the difficulties of women who are caught in relationships where partner abuse exists. Much has also been written about the misfortunes of women of color in American society. Taken separately, each has obstacles to overcome; when these three intersect, the troubles of battered women of color often create insurmountable barriers to successful resolution. What follows is a description of the complicated impact of the interfacing of these factors and suggestions for improved conceptualization and delivery of services to battered women of color. doi:10.1300/J135v06n02_06 *[Article copies available for a fee from The Haworth Document Delivery Service:*

Address correspondence to: Janet A. Geller, JBFCS,120 West 57th Street–9th Floor, New York, NY 10019.

[Haworth co-indexing entry note]: "Triple Trouble: Battered Women of Color–"Being Black, Being Battered and Being Female . . . I Ask Myself, Where Do I Begin?" Geller, Janet A., Jacqueline Miller, and Patricia Churchill. Co-published simultaneously in *Journal of Emotional Abuse* (The Haworth Maltreatment & Trauma Press, an imprint of The Haworth Press, Inc.) Vol. 6, No. 2/3, 2006, pp. 77-96; and: *Racism and Racial Identity: Reflections on Urban Practice in Mental Health and Social Services* (ed: Lisa V. Blitz, and Mary Pender Greene) The Haworth Maltreatment & Trauma Press, an imprint of The Haworth Press, Inc., 2006, pp. 77-96. Single or multiple copies of this article are available for a fee from The Haworth Document Delivery Service [1-800-HAWORTH, 9:00 a.m. - 5:00 p.m. (EST). E-mail address: docdelivery@haworthpress.com].

Available online at http://jea.haworthpress.com
doi:10.1300/J135v06n02_06

KEYWORDS. Race, abuse, gender, women of color, domestic violence, battered women

At the Jewish Board of Family and Children's Services (JBFCS) in New York City, we administer a variety of non-sectarian programs for survivors of domestic violence and aim to provide services that are culturally relevant and useful. JBFCS is a very large mental health and social service agency that offers three emergency domestic violence shelters for 171 people. In addition, we run non-residential counseling, advocacy, and outreach services in the larger community.

Like many social service providers, it has been common for us to develop our domestic violence programs based on our beliefs about women's realities learned from our own experiences as women, feminists, and professionals. While JBFCS has long been conscious of providing services that are nondiscriminatory and accessible to all New Yorkers, as the agency moves toward incorporating an antiracist analysis of systems, we are looking at the relevance and appropriateness of the services we offer. We realize now that since White women were in positions of power at the genesis of these programs, the services were necessarily informed by a "White" perspective. We believe that this narrow frame may have impeded the development of truly responsive services for women of color who have survived abuse. Blitz and Illidge (this volume) give an in-depth analysis of how they are working against the dynamic of unconscious racism in one of our domestic violence shelters.

To determine how services in all our domestic violence programs might be improved, we went to the women themselves, both clients and the staff who work with them. To this end, we scheduled a series of community meetings at three shelters for battered women and at one of our programs offering non-residential domestic violence services in the North Bronx.

Our sites are located in New York City and therefore address a primarily urban, inner city population. The large majority of the women in these programs were African-American, with a smaller proportion of Latina and Afro-Caribbean females. In each of our programs, the staff and leadership are diverse and reflect the population of the women served. One of the authors of this paper is a survivor of domestic violence and professional social worker in one of the programs. As a person of color, she brings crucial expertise and perspective that inform the information we gathered.

JBFCS has been addressing issues of cultural diversity and individual/institutional racism. Through our relationship and training with the People's Institute for Survival and Beyond (Chisom & Washington, 1997), the staff at the programs are relatively comfortable with addressing the questions and concerns raised in our discussions. This seemed to help the women we interviewed to be as open and honest as they were. This article will look at the internal, familial, and external forces that form the context in which the battered women we interviewed live. We will conclude by making suggestions for improved conceptualization and delivery of services to battered women of color.

THE WOMEN'S MOVEMENT

In the United States, the 1960s and the 1970s gave rise to the Women's Movement, which raised consciousness about the United States culture as one that was ruled by patriarchy. For women of color, the issues raised by the Women's Movement were even more complicated: "Black women have had to confront and overcome double oppression–racism and sexism . . . in large measure the experience of African women in America has been conditioned by the patriarchal values of the system of male domination operative in Euro-American society" (Daniels, 2000, p. 1). A feminist philosophy or feminist theory framed within a sociopolitical construct arose that defined the issue (Brownmiller, 1975). While it is beyond the scope of this article to discuss the Women's Movement in depth, its influence on legislation, attitudes, and resources affecting women has been profound and bear relevance to our discussion.

Simultaneous with the Women's Movement in the 1970s, feminists' attention was drawn to women in abusive relationships as a result of the work of Erin Pizzey in England, who identified women who were living as victims of abuse at the hands their partners. Pizzey sought to help them escape these harmful relationships by opening Chiswick House, the first shelter for battered women (Pizzey, 1974). It was correctly postulated that American women might also be victims of partner abuse, like their English counterparts.

The focus on women living in abusive situations gave rise to the birth of the Battered Women's Movement. As an outgrowth of the Women's

Movement, the Battered Women's Movement adapted concepts from patriarchy. This Movement addressed the issue of partner abuse as the epitome of male domination over women. Statements such as: men abuse women because they can and battering of women is a power and control issue became hallmark phrases (Pizzey, 1974; Schecter, 1982; Walker, 1979). The lessons learned from the Women's Movement gave rise to advocacy efforts aimed at stopping abuse of women. Battering was viewed from a gender perspective, depicting men as the abusers and women as the victims, followed by a proliferation of data and statistics substantiating this viewpoint (Dobash & Dobash, 1979; Straus & Hotaling, 1980). The only solution freeing women from the abuse was for them to leave the relationship.

Paralleling the activities resulting from the Women's Movement, resources in the form of battered women's hotlines, shelters, and safe homes emerged. Legislative changes resulted in laws against domestic violence being enacted and enforced. Victims were educated by counselors and advocates about their legal rights and available resources. The premise was that women would leave husbands, lovers, and partners if they understood the patriarchal system, if there were resources to support and sustain them, and if abusers were punished by the criminal justice system. From the 1970s to the present, this position has remained the prevailing point of view and, as such, has defined both the nature of the problem and prescribed solutions (Mills, 2003).

THE "TROUBLE"

In analyzing the outcome of both the Women's Movement and the Battered Women's Movement today, similar circumstances prevail. Studies indicate that the problems the Women's Movement sought to solve still exist; at best, there has been a token response to issues of patriarchy and women earning less money than men (Mills, 2003). Women are still demeaned and undervalued in our society, as they were before the women's movement, and many women, then and now, feel alienated from feminism (Shah, 1995). For some women, their feminine ideal was to have a traditional relationship that defined them as successful (Goldner, Penn, Steinberg, & Walker, 1990).

Many women who aspired to the more traditional roles of caretakers and wives did not identify with the Women's Movement, with its emphasis on women's independence from men and career achievement (Steinem, 1983). The movement did not speak to them and sometimes even made them feel ashamed of their status as wives and mothers. Today, many women find feminism irrelevant (Baumgardner & Richards, 2000). Others have mixed feelings about calling themselves feminists (Saphier, 2004).

Nevertheless, domestic violence continues to threaten women. Nearly 31% of U.S. women report being abused by their male partner at some time in their lives (Carter, 2004). Advocates for battered women have been instrumental in very important ways, such as raising America's consciousness concerning battered women, advocating for and obtaining more effective legal and social policies in response to domestic violence, and affecting attitudes and societal responses. In the 30 plus years of their work, however, partner abuse has not been eradicated in America. In fact, Mills (2003) has stated that about half the women in abusive relationships stay, although she points out that there are no accurate statistics. Anecdotally, based on our experience in the field, it is a very small number of women who actually leave or even want to leave if given the opportunity to express their true wishes (Geller, 1992). The criminal justice system has not been a successful solution to battering as many abusers never go through the system. Punishment of abusers has not stopped abuse; some victims' level of abuse has increased as a result of criminal justice action and many victims recoil from criminal justice involvement. Many victims of abuse never access the resources available in society, finding the existing resources inadequate to their needs (Mills, 2003).

Many victims who leave abusive partners return, and the return to abusive partners is a complex issue. Based on the authors' experience, some women, for example, assert that single life is too hard or too alien; for others, the reasons relate to economics or other concrete reasons. Other victims want the abuse to stop, but their sense of love, commitment, religion, and family outweigh the impact of the rhetoric of the Battered Women's Movement.

Additionally, battered women of color were not significantly part of the Battered Women's Movement. Identified as a White movement, many women of color did not identify with the values of feminism or a perspective born and shaped from privilege and entitlement. "Because shelters are associated with the women's movement and many black women are estranged from women's politics, they may feel that only white women's interests are served in the shelters. [They are] . . . not to-

tally mistaken in this assumption" (Ammons, 1995, p. 3). What, then,
are the needs of women of color who are battered?

SELF-PERCEPTIONS IN A SOCIOPOLITICAL CONTEXT

In our interviews with 40 women in three shelters and one community program, there were mixed beliefs about how racism impacted their
experiences. The consensus was that during the actual violent episodes,
the experience of the victim is universal, regardless of race. Initially,
most of the women we interviewed felt that the situation was the same
in general for all women, or even all victims. As the women we interviewed focused more in depth on their perceptions of themselves as victims, they noted their own reluctance even to acknowledge the violent
experience as abuse. This discussion led to speculation that there might
be particular cultural and racial factors at work.

Traci West (1999), in her excellent book, *Wounds of the Spirit*,
speaks to the shame and self-blame that many victims of color experience in response to intimate violence: "Because shame has a psychic identity, it can readily merge with the social stigmas based on
race and gender that are usually already at work on black women's
psyches" (p. 67). Blitz and Illidge (this volume) also describe some
of the complicated issues faced by African-American women.

Without exception, the women of color we interviewed shared their
conviction that African-American women are "raised to be strong."
They described themselves as coming from a long history of matri-
archal families, where women were very often the head of the household. Traditionally, in our society, it has been much easier for women of
color to get work than for their male counterparts, and these women
grew up knowing that they would be called upon to be major partners in
supporting the family financially.

As one woman we interviewed said, "African-American women are
brought up to believe that they are the strong ones. No matter what happens in our life, we must persevere because it is our responsibility to
keep the family intact, to make sure the bills are paid . . ." The women
described being socialized from infancy to see themselves as strong and
resourceful. They heard their mothers and aunts talking endlessly about
their own strategies for managing the family, for keeping harmony in
the home, and supporting their men.

Throughout conversations and throughout the literature, the concept of "strong black women" is both a social construct and a reality to be maintained (West, 1999). Sometimes there were few reliable men around, and the environment was primarily female, with women assuming fiscal and administrative oversight of the homes. The support system was the community, with women developing networks of child care, socialization, and opportunities for sharing perceptions, concerns, and dreams about their men as they wished them to be.

Fighting Back

Some women we interviewed experienced their strength in their determination to fight back when attacked. One described her memory of her community: "the men in my neighborhood . . . were chasing their girlfriends up and down the block hitting them with belts (this was a game believe it or not), yelling at them . . . so getting into a relationship and yelling at one another and pushing one another and jumping into each other's faces was not a big deal to me–that is how you relate to one another!" She and the other women described how you have to try to "stand your ground" to show them that you are not going to take abuse from anyone. One woman spoke for many in saying that the determination to fight back meant that she was demanding respect despite the beating. What began as youthful playing evolved into serious fighting, and ultimately into terrible beatings. Before it became too violent, the women described themselves as holding their own and preserving valued, if tenuous, relationships with their men.

One worker in a shelter ventured her opinion that the Latina and Caucasian women do not fit this description. This worker's observation was that Latin and Caucasian women were less likely to defend themselves than the African-American residents. She attributed this to less emphasis on "strong, capable" women in these cultures. Whether Latina and Caucasian women are less likely than African-American women to defend themselves may be a question to further explore.

Part of fighting back involved wanting the children to see that Mommy was not going to be a victim: "my children were not going to see their mom get beat down." The women we interviewed described wanting their children to see that women could or should not be humiliated or physically abused, that they could fight back and defend themselves. They asserted that they wanted the kids to see that their mom could be a strong and passionate role model for self-protection. Many of them pointed to their own mothers' determination to defend themselves against unpredictable and aggressive men.

As the violence increased in each of these situations, however, it became impossible for the women to keep up this appearance. As a result, they typically were severely beaten by men who were often doubly enraged at the women's audacity to think they could challenge the men's authority. In those situations, the impact on the children was painful and poignant. As one woman stated, "they tend to think that they may have no one to protect them because their mom can't even protect herself." When the violence became chronic, the women we interviewed were torn between their desire to maintain a stable home, keep up appearances, avoid the embarrassment of a failed relationship, and the need to get help with a terrifying situation.

Women's Internal Conflicts

The women in our discussion groups also alluded to their own hesitation about acknowledging the abuse with which they lived. Many described their childhood experiences as characterized by families with much internal conflict and a constant sense of oppression by the society in which they live. One woman seemed to speak for the others by saying that she saw herself as "existing in a society where you know you are the minority, [and] oppression is something that we as African-Americans have had to deal with our entire lives."

Ammons (1995) highlights the plight for battered women of color who, in addition to the actual physical/emotional abuse, "suffer from the complex phenomenon of racism. The translation of racial oppression to [battered] women of color . . . stems from the basic assumption that people of color are inherently more violent" (p. 5). As a result, the battered women of color are left with "an overwhelming sense of hopelessness and low self-esteem" (p. 5).

The role of being subjugated in society, with unequal access to education, housing, and jobs was central to the life experience of the women we interviewed. In addition, the concept that familial violence was "normal" in their communities made the acknowledgement of the horror of the violence difficult to accept. Again, defining themselves as strong women prevented them from seeing the violence for what it was. As one woman with whom we spoke asserted, "I did not see myself as a victim of domestic violence because I fought back. . . . but I did know that beating up on each other was not what a relationship should be."

West (1999) addresses the phenomenon of self-doubt and self-blame:

Black women victim-survivors are sometimes held innately responsible for their racial subjugation in a fashion that mirrors and complements the self-blame induced by their experience of male violence. . . . Yet for the victim-survivor of intimate violence, what identifies her as guilty, that is, what can cause her to feel shame, is the very fact that she is beaten. . . . Said differently, the unequal treatment of blacks can become a convincing indicator of black inferiority that makes them feel ashamed, just as being beaten can make a woman shamefully decide that there is clearly something wrong with her because she continues to receive such treatment. These self-blaming phenomena can relentlessly echo off of each other, helping to deepen a woman's anguish. (pp. 72-73)

Family Values

Another factor that emerged repeatedly in our conversations was the women's belief that they needed to "take care of" their men. They understood our societal expectation that women in general are the caretakers in their families, and African-American women, in particular, are raised with this self-concept. In addition, they saw clearly how racism and oppression had "beaten them [the men] down," interfering with their opportunities for success educationally and professionally. As stated by West (1999), "Black women observe both the assault of white racism and the powerlessness of their men. They feel protective and responsible for assuaging the debilitating impact of white supremacist social violence upon the men" (p. 85).

The women we interviewed felt empathetic to their men; they understood their pain and suffering. Several women attributed the abuse to being the result of the men's "rough life," "tough childhood," or "troubled family history." They had entered the relationship believing and hoping that their love and concern could make the difference and enable the men to achieve their goals. They saw this in the context of a prejudiced society that denies men of color the same opportunities offered to White men.

If a man started using alcohol or drugs in addition to being abusive, they attributed it to depression about his frustrating life. They described how they kept feeling that if they could just do better and make him happy, the violence would stop. In between violent episodes, the men seemed needy and lovable. Many women expressed a desire to help empower their men by giving up their own status. The conflict between protecting themselves and protecting their men, therefore, is complex.

Most women in the group we interviewed described their conflicts in talking to their own mothers about the violence they were experiencing. In those relationships where the women were married, the familial pressure was strong to "hang on" to their men and to preserve a stable home to whatever extent possible. In some cases, the women reported that their mothers had urged them simply to "try harder" to do what the men wanted. Many of their mothers cited the men's requests for earlier dinner, quiet children, and constant sex as mere trifles that the women could give in pursuit of the goal of harmony.

Those women in our group who were married were seen by family members as moving out of the inner city, adopting middle-class and mainstream goals. They were viewed as buying into the American dream, and were therefore a credit to their families and communities. "Disappointing a family of origin who took pride in having a 'happy and successful' African-American woman daughter or sister places an especially heavy burden of shame . . . consequently [these women] are under pressure to keep the violence 'private' in order to disprove white assumptions of black inferiority" (West, 1999, pp. 87-88).

West (1999) goes on to talk about the married couples as embodying a "white" lifestyle, very different from their families of origin. She indicates that many parents are proud that the women had developed a lifestyle that defied stereotypes about inner-city families of color. When the violence became a factor, as described by the women in our group, their mothers were hesitant to acknowledge it, feeling saddened by their daughters' inability to hang on to what appeared to be a stable and upwardly mobile life. The parents also feared the increased financial and emotional dependence on them that might result from the break-up.

The men's role as provider was often cited by our women as the reason to stay in an abusive relationship. Their mothers reminded the women about the historic role of Black women as the strength and preservers of the family. They accused the women of being selfish and not thinking about the impact of this shame on the family and the community. Often, the family had good relationships with the men, seeing them as kind and caring providers. They also often accused their daughters of sabotaging what could be a ticket out of unhappiness and poverty.

The women we interviewed described themselves as totally alone with the pain, unsure where to turn when their own families were unwilling or unable to help. West (1999) suggests that with ". . . the pressure of trying to always be the strong woman and giving primacy to the support of black men, the mere admission of pain may seem shameful for victim-survivors. . . . We have women who are walking around, especially African-American women, with so much pain they don't even know they have because we have carried the weight of the world for so long that our attitude is 'get over it' " (pp. 84-85).

Role of the Community

The issue of the role of the community is complicated. On the one hand, women were raised to believe that, as one said, "the community will take care of you" if you are in trouble. There was no need to go to outside resources, such as counselors or police, because the caring community could be expected to step up to offer assistance. Where the communities were smaller and closer, in fact, this seemed to be true for the women in our discussion groups. Neighbors, clergy, even the authorities collaborated to offer support and often cautionary advice to the men. People knew that some guys were "tough on their women" or suffering from their own "demons," which "explained" the violence. Community members tried to stem the violence through their own personal relationships with the victims and the abusers.

In larger, less intimate communities, the women described feeling terribly alone and puzzled by the lack of response to the violence. Neighbors would ignore the screams and sounds of battle, acting as if it were not happening. Many of the women we interviewed described the prevailing attitude that this familial conflict was "normal" and that the close living situations made it necessary to preserve the illusion of privacy by not responding. This frequently led to a sense of "invisibility" in which the lack of response made victims question their own perceptions of the situation, indeed their own self-worth (West, 1999).

As indicated above, there was also a sense that boisterous play fighting, roughhousing, and light violence was part of most relationships. While some women saw this as a "normal" community response, others felt that it reflected hostility to women and permission for the violence. In either case, the role of the "community" as a reliable source of support for abused women was lost. This was exacerbated by the larger societal perception that inner-city communities are inherently more violent and less "worthy" of intervention or supports and therefore could be ignored.

Role of the Clergy

The clergy with whom the women consulted also typically advised them to stay in the relationships. Traditional religions in the black com-

munity often prescribe that women should obey their husbands. The
clergy of all faiths told the women with whom we spoke that they
should "try harder" to make the relationships work. They should understand that Black men have a hard and frustrating life as a result of the
lack of opportunities in our society, and that they can help them by
being more understanding.

Many evangelical and traditional churches preach that God wants
men and women to stay married regardless of what happens, and these
women described themselves as carrying out God's will by staying. The
church hierarchy and structure in communities of color are an enormously powerful force, which can sometimes impede the woman's efforts to seek help for the violence. Yet, many women found that their
belief in God was a sustaining factor during the times of violence. Faith
itself was regularly described as a powerful and positive resource in
abused women's lives. Even as they struggled to comprehend the meaning of the suffering they experienced, they found a fundamental sense of
support in the belief that God loves them and protects them (West,
1999).

Role of the Criminal Justice System

A constant issue impacting the disclosure of violence is the role and
expectation of the police in inner-city communities. Woman after woman
told of her reluctance to call the police and asserted that it is "common
knowledge" that Black men will be treated more harshly by the judicial
system and that they may be physically maltreated if taken to jail. The decision to alert authorities, therefore, is a larger consideration in the Black
community than it might be among White women. Women typically
want the violent episode to stop but they do not necessarily want the men
to be incarcerated where they will lose their income and standing in the
community.

Mills (2003) cites numerous incidents of women refusing to call the
police and staying in violent situations because of these factors. Once
the police are called, women described both the overreaction and the
underreaction of police officers. New York State has a felony mandatory arrest policy, which prescribes that abusers who commit a felony
must be arrested. As described above, some women are ambivalent
about mandatory arrest as they fear for the well-being and safety of their
men facing the court system.

On the other hand, numerous women recounted stories of the police not taking their complaint seriously, telling the abuser to "take a walk," and even refusing to come. The women we interviewed attributed this to "they think we will just take them back," "they don't care about poor people and people of color," or "they are identified with the abuser who is disciplining his woman." One woman alluded to her belief that the police response is largely determined by the officer's own history, personality, and attitudes toward women and/or people of color.

Women of color in our groups also described some of their horrific experiences with the court system. They perceived themselves as being the victims of racial and class discrimination within the judicial process. They were often made to confront their batterer and were interrogated with hostility by the defense lawyer. Little effort was made to ensure their safety within the courthouse or entering and leaving the building. They clearly experienced this as being a function of prejudice on the part of the largely White court system personnel. There appeared to them to be a stereotyping of them as "poor, black, battered women," which denied them their humanity. Having experienced this, as well as hearing about it repeatedly among their friends, many women were very hesitant to trust in the court system other than as a last resort.

Public Resources

Once the decision to separate from the abuser is made, a variety of considerations emerge. Many families of origin have neither the space nor the inclination to take in a woman and her children. Entering a shelter necessitates giving up virtually everything the woman has–her home, most of her clothes, furniture, and other possessions. The children have to be uprooted from their schools and often need to enroll in a school near the shelter, typically not in an excellent school district. The woman then needs to struggle with finding housing where she can afford to live and is safe. Once there, she needs to find employment and child care.

All of these endeavors are frequently more complicated if she is a person of color, since very often landlords, employers, and schools are less welcoming to people of color than they would be to a White person in the same situation. The sense of instability and disruption is pervasive and lasting. As Kanuha (1994) points out, "the sense of . . . limited options for battered women of color . . . is primarily related to the inaccessibility and racial insensitivity of existing social, psychological, and domestic violence services" (p. 441).

TOWARD A MORE RESPONSIVE SERVICE DELIVERY SYSTEM

Our conversations with the women in our shelters and other programs have confirmed that the combination of being battered, as well as being a woman and a person of color, is indeed a unique challenge, given the various intersecting layers of prejudice in our society. The advances of the feminist movement and the emphasis on White domestic violence victims have virtually ignored the particular plight of the battered women of color. Analyses of the origins of domestic violence that do not reflect understanding of the various subsets of populations necessarily skew our understanding about violence across all racial groups (Kanuha, 1994). Kanuha goes on to stress that most intervention strategies have evolved from the White, feminist movement and that the literature is scant regarding their impact on battered women of color.

Services, therefore, need to take the unique perspectives and challenges of battered women of color into account and need to be able to provide an open forum for discussion and resolution. It is crucial that service providers of all ethnicities be sensitized to the cultural issues for battered women of color. To this end, staff needs to be educated on institutional racism and its impact on all people, not just people of color. There are, for example, organizations available that specialize in raising awareness of institutional racism and can be called upon for education and training. As service providers become more aware of the factors impacting battered women of color, including the role of their own internalized racism, the hope is that they will be increasingly able to frame services specific to understanding and acknowledging the impact of institutionalized racism on battered women of color. This would be crucial to evolving more sensitive services.

Education and training on partner abuse should be offered to the most frequently used services in communities of color. These efforts can sensitize potential "helpers" and help them recognize and respond to the subtle and clear signs of abuse. Those to be trained include personnel in systems with which battered women of color must frequently come into contact. Generally, we are referring to the criminal justice system, the clergy, medical staff, and social service/mental health providers.

Criminal Justice System

Our services should reflect our understanding of "balanc[ing] the need for safety . . . with the real and perceived experiences of battered women of color that the very institutions mandated to help them such as the police and courts themselves have a legacy of violence toward men and women of color" (Kanuha, 1994, p. 447). With this understood as a genuine and real concern, advocating for culturally sensitive and anti-racist policies may improve the use of the criminal justice system by women of color. The challenges about identifying and reporting abuse in this community need to be understood and acknowledged by staff so that realistic options can be offered. Too often, personnel dismiss women of color's rejection of fully using the criminal justice system as an indication of their unwillingness to change. Similarly, women need education about the constraints relating to racism existing in the available services. To talk frankly, for instance, about what can be expected from systems defined by White rules can help prepare them for what may be encountered when accessing these resources. Role playing and written guidebooks are useful tools. Sensitizing everyone involved to issues of racism (the police, the judicial system, and the women themselves) can be helpful. Nancy Boyd-Franklin (personal communication, October 29, 2004) stated that understanding racism as endemic to U.S. society can universalize the issue and dilute the notion that negative or unhelpful attitudes are personal. Sharing this information with women of color would be empowering. Raising consciousness, sensitization, and advocacy for battered women have occurred. As this applies to women of color, however, we need to go further.

The Clergy

Education and outreach efforts to the clergy of all faiths are needed as the clergy promote the sanctity of family and family preservation. Many battered women of color have a strong connection to their church community. It would be important to dialogue with clergy concerning their needs when encountering battered women as well as to help sensitize them to the victims' needs. An experiential workshop on what it means to be a victim, for example, can help identify with the victim's plight. Outreach initiatives that are appropriate for each kind of congregation need to be developed. Very often, priests and pastors know very little about domestic violence and are unclear how or if to intervene. Biblical texts have been construed to support patriarchy and even oppression in their families. Service providers have a responsibility to meet with clergy, to educate and to offer tools for understanding and intervening. There are many videos depicting domestic violence that are powerful and drive home the message that can be shown to clergy. This training

initiative needs to be respectful of the unique cultural traditions of each
group in order to be successful. Former domestic violence victims may
be willing to talk about their experiences and share ideas about effective
responses.

A string of safe homes for members of the congregation could be developed and organized. Identifying individual parishioners who would
be willing to help "their own" may be more comfortable and familiar for
women of color, as it stays within the church community. Sermons de-
nouncing domestic violence would be a powerful intervention as well as
an invitation to seek out the clergy person for help. In tight-knit church
communities, members could be encouraged to be buddies to victims as
well as abusers, similar to the self-help 12-step model programs such as
Alcoholics Anonymous.

Medical Staff

In many emergency rooms today, staff is sensitized to the needs of
victims of domestic violence; therefore, we need not repeat what has
been effectively accomplished. What bears addressing, however, is covert attitudes and beliefs about people of color and the stereotypes that
follow, such as the idea that physical conflict is a normal part of life,
with women showing tolerance for abuse. Private medical personnel
would also benefit from education, sensitization, and procedures for
helping a patient who is a battered woman as they are less likely to be
aware of her needs.

Social Service and Mental Health Providers

Social service/mental health providers should take the lead in coordi-
nating outreach and sensitization efforts. While many are aware of issues of domestic violence and how to best address these issues, we
believe that the uniqueness of being a battered woman of color has not
been so well addressed. Forums, discussions, and other educational
venues focused on battered women of color can create the needed context. Recommendations suggested in this article apply to providers as
well. The authors of this article recommend candid discussions directly
with such clients. For us, this proved both enlightening and rewarding.
In pursuing these conversations, service provider and domestic violence
advocates need to be ever mindful of the unique and often unstated impact of racism, both personal and institutional, on our clients, on our
staff, and in the systems we use to help.

The Community

We prefer to see women's connections to their community as a fundamental resource that can give them strength. Offering education on community responsibility can occur through schools, houses of worship, and political leaders. Public figures known and identified with the community can be a powerful voice in advocating for the needs of women of color. The community can be an enormously powerful force in the reduction of violence. Strengthening community ties would be an important goal. "The combination of sanction and sanctuary is a powerful influence. . . . Where battering is absent [in a community or culture,] . . . . significant community level sanctions against battering [are] clearly demonstrated by active community and/or kin intervention when wife beating begins to escalate" (Campbell, 1992, p. 20).

Addressing Women's Needs

On the micro level, advocating for the traditional remedies offered to survivors of partner abuse is not sufficient and may not even be relevant. Thinking "out-of-the-box" to tailor services to the needs of battered women of color is called for. While sensitization is a beginning step toward change, policies and procedures concerning treatment need to be tailored to the differing needs of battered partners. Most social service and mental health programs of which we are aware have universal uniform policies that may prove unrealistic. Waiting lists might be a source of discouragement and do not address the need for immediacy that often accompanies crisis. Scheduled appointments as opposed to walk-in may be difficult to stick to considering the demands of family and employment. Closing cases of a client who has not been able to successfully juggle home and work demands with keeping appointments is a disservice and punitive. Sending her to different service providers for her concrete needs and only offering talk therapy might be overwhelming because of the difficulties already addressed that are attached to negotiating White systems. Very few agencies offer child care services, which is a deterrent to treatment. Setting up a system for child care seems like a manageable goal, whether staffed by volunteers or employees.

Family preservation in communities of color must be respected as an important value. Many survivors have told us that, while they want the abuse to stop, they do not want to terminate their relationship or resort to using the criminal justice system. Treating abusers thoughtfully and therapeutically, and when appropriate, not punitively, can give survivors what they want: an end to the abuse without an end to the relationship. Abusers can be treated effectively (Geller, 1992). The usual method for work with abusers is an educational group format, which does not go far enough. Mental health professionals are skilled in the theory and practice of therapeutic groups as one proven for the treatment of emotional/psychological problems (Yalom, 1985). The authors posit that people who abuse their partners are in need of mental health treatment as well as criminal justice or other interventions. We have spoken to women of color, and for the most part, they want their partners, and they want them healed from abusive behavior. Group treatment that focuses on the psychodynamics of abuse can deliver this service. The issue of couples counseling has misguidedly been censured as a viable method of intervention. Skillfully offered, combined with cognitive-behavioral techniques for the elimination of abuse and clear accountability for the batterer, it is an overlooked but effective method for meeting the needs and desires of battered women of color and their partners.

The Children

Another central service concern to address is the impact of domestic violence on the children. As indicated, the women we interviewed spoke of their impassioned efforts to hold their families together and present themselves as caring and strong parents. They were unaware that their children were being harmed by living in an abusive household. Research has shown that vicarious traumatization can occur by witnessing domestic violence. Carter (2004) cites a Simmons 25-year study of almost 400 Massachusetts residents indicating that "male teens exposed to family conflict and violence over the years were significantly more likely than other males to have suicidal thoughts, be depressed, have emotional and behavioral problems, be drug dependent or have post- traumatic stress disorder" (p. 2). The women in our discussion groups could barely acknowledge the impact on themselves and the actual pain they were experiencing, let alone their children. Educating mothers on the effect of domestic violence on their children and counseling services to help children understand and address their own traumatic experiences are essential.

Another crucial focus needs to be on developing strategies for preventing violence before it begins. We need to start with the children; for example, "teaching the next generation of boys that violence against women is always wrong; implementing dating violence education in schools and encouraging . . . adults to speak with children and teens about abuse" (Carter, 2004, p. 6). From day care on through high school, there needs to be increased consciousness about the negative impact of violence on families and children.

CONCLUSIONS

While by no means definitive, the authors see this article as a beginning step in furthering our understanding of what it means to be a woman of color who is battered. Further attention to this issue is needed as well as exploring whether similar differences in experience exist universally. For example, do rural as well as urban women of color have similar views to those held by the women in our New York City programs? Do regional differences play a role, are demographics significant, and so on?

Generally speaking, at this time in the history of our work with battered women, many of us understand what it means for our clients who are women and abused. The literature is filled with information on safety planning, advocacy, crisis intervention, and counseling; therefore, there is no need to repeat this here (Geller, 1992; Schecter, 1982; Walker, 1979). While many of the issues concerning battered women are the same whether a woman is a woman of color or White, we need to ask ourselves how culturally sensitive our services are and, as service providers, do we understand the unique challenges experienced by being a woman, being battered, and being a person of color.

REFERENCES

Ammons, L. (1995). Mules, madonnas, babies, bath water, racial imagery, and stereotypes: The African-American woman and the battered woman syndrome. *Wisconsin Law Review, 5,* 1003-1080.

Baumgardner, J., & Richards, A. (2000). *What is feminism? Manifesta: Young women, feminism, and the future.* Retrieved September 13, 2005 from, http://www.Feminist.com

Blitz, L. V., & Illidge, L. C. (2006). Not so black and white: Shades of gray and brown in anti-racist multicultural team building in a domestic violence shelter. *Journal of Emotional Abuse, 6*(2/3), 113-134.

Brownmiller, S. (1975). *Against our will.* New York: Simon and Schuster.

Campbell, J. (1992). Prevention of wife battering: Insights from cultural analysis. *Response to the Victimization of Women and Children, 14,* 18-24.

Carter, J. (2004, February). *Family violence cries out for prevention*. Retrieved September 13, 2005 from, http://www.womensenews.org/article.cfm/dyn/aid/1690

Chisom, R., & Washington, M. (1997). *Undoing racism: A philosophy of international social change*. New Orleans: The People's Institute Press.

Daniels, R. (2000, April 6-12). The struggle for women's equality in Black America. *Jackson Advocate Newspaper*, p. 1-2.

Dobash, R. E., & Dobash R. P. (1979). *Violence against wives: A case against patriarchy*. New York: The Free Press.

Geller, J. (1992). *Breaking destructive patterns: Multiple strategies for treating partner abuse*. New York: The Free Press.

Goldner, V., Penn, I., Steinberg, M., & Walker, G. (1990). Love and violence: Gender paradoxes in volatile attachments. *Family Process, 29*(4), 343-364.

Kanuha, V. (1994). Women of color in battering relationships. In L. Comos-Diaz & B. Greene (Eds.), *Women of color: Integrating ethnic and gender identities in psychotherapy* (pp. 428-454). New York: Guilford Press.

Mills, L. (2003). *Insult to injury*. Princeton, NJ: Princeton University Press.

Pizzey, E. (1974). *Scream quietly or the neighbors will hear you*. London: London Books.

Saphier, M. K. (2004, February 29). *Agony of patriarchy*. Sermon delivered at United First Parish Church, Quincy, MA. Available online from, http://server2.ufpc.org/sermons/saphier_20040229.pdf

Schecter, S. (1982). *Guidelines for mental health practitioners in domestic violence cases*. Washington, DC: National Coalition Against Domestic Violence.

Shah, S. (1995, July/August). *Race & gender. The co-optation of Asian American feminism*. Retrieved September 13, 2005 from, http://www.zmag.org/zmag/articles/july95shah.htm

Steinem, G. (1983). *Outrageous acts and everyday rebellions*. New York: Holt, Reinhart, and Winston.

Straus, M., & Hotaling, G. (1980). *The social causes of husband-wife violence*. Minneapolis: University of Minnesota Press.

Walker, L. (1979). *The battered woman*. New York: Harper and Row.

West, T. (1999). *Wounds of the spirit: Black women, violence and resistance*. New York: New York University Press.

Yalom, I. (1985). *Theory and practice of group psychotherapy*. New York: Basic Books.

doi:10.1300/J135v06n02_06

SECTION III
BUILDING ANTIRACIST SYSTEMS
IN SOCIAL SERVICES
AND MENTAL HEALTH

A Hope for Foster Care:
Agency Executives in Partnerships
with Parent Leaders

Kathleen McGlade
Joseph Ackerman

SUMMARY. Two foster care executives encourage agency and parent leaders to rethink their relationships to improve the lives of children in their shared custody. When mothers-of-color charged that white privilege harmed rather than helped children, the white executives connected the accusation to

---

Address correspondence to: Kathleen McGlade, PhD, Director of Corporate Compliance, Jewish Board of Family and Children's Services, 120 West 57th Street, New York, NY 10019 (E-mail: kmcglade@jbfcs.org).

The authors wish to acknowledge the work and contributions of Diana Pichardo-Henriquez; her example as a parent, a leader, and a colleague remains an inspiration.

[Haworth co-indexing entry note]: "A Hope for Foster Care: Agency Executives in Partnerships with Parent Leaders." McGlade, Kathleen and Joseph Ackerman. Co-published simultaneously in *Journal of Emotional Abuse* (The Haworth Maltreatment & Trauma Press, an imprint of The Haworth Press, Inc.) Vol. 6, No. 2/3, 2006, pp. 97-112; and: *Racism and Racial Identity: Reflections on Urban Practice in Mental Health and Social Services* (ed: Lisa V. Blitz, and Mary Pender Greene) The Haworth Maltreatment & Trauma Press, an imprint of The Haworth Press, Inc., 2006, pp. 97-112. Single or multiple copies of this article are available for a fee from The Haworth Document Delivery Service [1-800-HAWORTH, 9:00 a.m. - 5:00 p.m. (EST). E-mail address: docdelivery@haworthpress.com].

Available online at http://jea.haworthpress.com
doi:10.1300/J135v06n02_07

their experience as closeted gay leaders in a religiously-run organization. That unexpected insight became the sharper lens through which they saw some emotional damage caused by their decisions. The executives examined their behavior and transformed their adversarial relationship with parents into a partnership. Their suggestions are based on efforts with parents, mistakes with trustees, and hard lessons learned. doi:10.1300/J135v06n02_07 *[Article copies available for a fee from The Haworth Document Delivery Service: 1-800-HAWORTH. E-mail address: <docdelivery@haworthpress.com> Website: <http://www.HaworthPress.com> © 2006 by The Haworth Press, Inc. All rights reserved.]*

KEYWORDS. Foster care, parent partnerships, client voice, organizational insight, white privilege, queer eye

Children benefit from being separated from parents who brutalize them. Not so of children placed because mothers are mentally ill, victims of domestic violence, underemployed, or addicted. Therapy, shelters, job training, and recovery options are better alternatives for them. The emotional abuse of unnecessary separation of children from mothers is well documented; what is rare is foster care leaders' acknowledgements of their role in that abuse.

Emotional abuse occurs when leaders tell parents they want to help and then do not. It occurs at admission when agencies do not give parents the name and phone number of their child's care giver. It occurs during the multiple movements of children and is symbolized by the plastic garbage bags they are given to carry their belongings; how valuable can they be? Leaders contribute to emotional abuse by allowing staff to make false promises to parents: your children will go home if you take a parenting class, complete a recovery program, and find safe housing. The road to reunification has many more, often hidden detours.

If parent-child separation is unnecessary, agency participation in it is wrong. If the separation is related to leaders who have become numb and fail to employ competent staff, the separation may be neglectful. If the separation is related to executives forgetting their legal obligations to create permanency, it is neglectful. If the separation is related to corporate inefficiencies, absence of client feedback, unaddressed intra-agency communication blocks, or trustees who do not take seriously their oversight role, then a case can be made that agency leaders contribute to emotional abuse clinically and ethically, if not legally.

Substantive change in foster care is needed and more likely to happen when organizational leaders examine their roles. Change is likely to happen more quickly if executives ask parents what they think about agency behavior and beliefs. In New York City, where most of the children in foster care are children of color (Roberts, 2002), mothers-of-color have begun to organize. They want to be more than advocates who periodically tell their stories at board meetings (Child Welfare Organizing Project, 2004). They have begun to identify the executive's responsibility for their children and want executives of color to be hired. Mothers are redirecting their depression and rage and taking initiative to form or join parent organizations.

For two centuries, foster care agencies have survived on top-down management and relied on oversimplified, sometimes patronizing, missions to save good children from bad families. However unintended, they have contributed to unnecessary family disruptions. Some leaders want to change that and believe that consensus-building models that include parents can replace hierarchies and outmoded traditions (Fletcher, 1999; Lowe, 2002). They view parents as partners rather than problems and suggest agencies benefit from involving parents. They recognize agencies are resources, not replacements, for parents. The authors are two such leaders.

The following describes an experience that changed us. We offer our insights to encourage executives and parents to search for the energy that lies dormant in their tired and debilitating relationships. We recognize that ours is a New York story, yet we think it has relevance for other regions. We offer guidelines to agency and parent leaders, urging both to recognize that children's success depends on their alliance.

A PROFOUND EXPERIENCE

"You are no longer a leader if no one is following. If your decisions are predictable, you can be dangerous more than helpful. Because you are white, you should not be in charge of children of color." This was the powerful indictment handed to us by a group of mothers whose children were in our care; the shock jump-started us into deeper reflection and increased action.

We are two white professionals with advanced degrees in social work and years of clinical and community experience; we were senior executives in the same large child welfare agency. We are also gay and were closeted as the agency's religious affiliation made it unsafe to be out. Our relationship with parent leaders began one afternoon as we sat in a large auditorium with policy makers and administrators from other agencies. One by one, parents shared painful accounts of losing their children. From our seats in the back, we listened and felt badly. The distance made it easy for us just to feel bad. There was no face-to-face encounter to compel us to do anything. We had heard the pain before. We knew the system was unfair to women who were unemployed, of color, unschooled, and single. We were the good guys though; we came to show support. Then a slightly built 14-year-old white boy came to the microphone. His voice quivered. "I am gay," he said, "and I am afraid in foster care. Sometimes I get beat up. I always get made fun of and called names. I want the people in charge to know what my life is like."

We looked at each other, did not speak and did not move. Later we would tell each other that we wanted to stand with that courageous teenager to say that foster care is not safe for gay people. But we were not as brave as he was, and we feel shame every time we remember that moment. The prejudice of foster care hit home. We knew we were as different as he was, but we were safer because we were independent adults and knew how to hide. That young man pierced our armor and while we do not even know his name and can never find him to thank him and to ask his forgiveness, he changed the way we saw bias. He changed the way we saw ourselves.

After he spoke, a young Latina woman asked if we would meet with her. She was a parent leader and knew we were executives in an influential agency. We set an appointment and began a process that slowly peeled away our guard, made us understand our power and privilege, and helped us measure success by the layers of lies we would help destroy.

Marta was an inspiration. We were intellectually in sync with her message; the foster care system needed to stop taking children from mothers who were ill, beaten, unemployed, and undocumented. She was a community organizer who believed strongly that foster care was a racist system and no child of color was safe in it. Marta's children were with her at home, yet she had committed herself to helping other mothers get their children back.

During long walks and loud talks with Marta, her message took shape. Addiction, depression, rage, and violence were mothers' imperfect raw remedies against the bigotry of the powerful boards, family court, police, organized religion, landlords, and social workers who held them hostage and often took their children. Marta's words resonated with the words of the gay teenager. While eager to listen we were initially naïve, not realizing that Marta expected us to use our authority to make significant change rapidly.

We arranged for her to meet with the full executive staff and program directors. Anger exploded as she presented her point of view, essentially that agencies were complicit in destroying families and re-hurting children. Our colleagues reacted. "She's rude, why is she here? She seems unbalanced. She is too angry." A psychiatrist who had more insight and courage than most asked, "Who among us wouldn't be enraged at a world which wouldn't hire us, rent to us, help us stay safe, and then took our children away?"

Marta identified parent leaders who held "thunder sessions." We identified funds to help support them as they reached parents in ways social workers never could. For example, we observed one thunder session led by Diana, a talented, compassionate parent whose son was in our care. She was listening to an angry father rage that he wanted to blow up our building. She saw vulnerability where others could not. She helped him realize that he could never care for his sons but he could agree to an open adoption and continue a relationship. The session ended as he sobbed in Diana's arms, thanking her for helping him see a solution.

We held meetings to help supervisors behave differently towards mothers. Some supervisors responded to demands that children have more regular, private quality time with parents and siblings and agreed with mothers that visiting needed to be redefined. Parents did not want to just visit with their children; they wanted more time for more normal interaction. They wanted to play with their children, hold them, listen to their secrets, and get answers as to why a child's shirt was torn or his medication made him so drowsy. Some supervisors found parent leaders too demanding for insisting that case conferences be scheduled at times when they and all their children could be there, and for asking workers to stop judging their households as unfit because there were not enough separate beds. Parent leaders argued that lots of non-foster care families use a living room as a parent's bedroom and many do not have enough sheets or matching dishes. Some workers were angry as parents reminded them that "call back tomorrow" was no longer an acceptable response. When social workers used jargon, parents more regularly asked, "What do you mean?" Supervision became more challenging.

Parent leaders demanded that the agency recognize the love mothers and children share and charged that ignoring that love was abusive. While parents respected and praised foster mothers, they made clear that foster parents' roles were temporary. Parent leaders were fierce as they voiced the loss and anger mothers felt when children were encouraged to call foster mothers "mama." Parent leaders would not accept the terms biological or birth mother; they said they were mothers, they wanted no adjective. Adjectives were necessary only to clarify the roles of foster and adoptive parents. Parents are parents, and no adjectives are needed.

As leaders, we were faced with having to look at ourselves differently. As gay individuals fearful of being found out, we were in tune with the bias parents were expressing. We could relate to false assumptions, harming judgments, and demeaning behavior. We eventually shared with Marta that we were gay and she appreciated that our experience helped us understand parents. She said that it was easier for her to accept us even though we were white because other whites looked at us as damaged. That rejection helped her to trust us.

We also were moved by the compassion parent leaders demonstrated for mentally-ill, addicted, and non-English-speaking parents as well as the few white members in the group. The pain of losing their children created a strong bond no matter their differences. When the wound was foster care, the wounded treated each other with compassion and dignity.

Leaders require credibility. On one routine day, two strangers showed us we had lost ours. The courage of a gay teenager and the indictment of a parent leader shattered our false images and forced us face-to-face with the failure of our leadership. The lesson for us was that the bigotry we were ignoring in the foster care system was the same bigotry we were hiding from in our own lives. By being ourselves we could sense the lies we were managing. Parents were strong, not wrong; children were taken, not placed; decisions were arbitrary, not just.

SEEING THROUGH DIFFERENT LENSES

The unexpected and powerful indictment that our decisions were dangerous for children shocked us into reconsidering our motivations and behavior. We questioned our practices. Who were we leading? How had we become so numb to parents? We reasoned that our education, class, and race had provided us with the privilege and opportunity of leadership (see Blitz & Illidge; and Peacock & Daniels, this volume, for further discussion of white privilege in organizational settings). Parents made us realize not only were our degrees, social status, and skin color insufficient to make us foster care leaders, they could be obstacles keeping us from being effective. Although we were smart, we could not influence. Our economic status helped us keep our sexual orientation a secret, but pretending made us weak. Our skin color was a threat to many parents.

Clients who had been hiding in the shame of foster care seemed no longer willing to hide. Pretending politeness to mask rage was no longer an option for parents, and Marta admonished that it never should have been. She effectively argued that shame, anger, and fear are untapped assets that could be transformed into pride, competence, and action. We set a goal to create a parent-executive partnership. We defined our roles. Marta became a paid consultant. Diana was hired to implement the parent project. One of us (Joe) worked with her to establish the parent office and keep the social work supervisors engaged, while the other (Kathy) worked with the executive team and board to incorporate into policy this changing approach to parents.

The road was bumpy. One example shows how we stumbled forward less afraid. After teaching a financial management course to parents in a recovery program, Joe was asked by his students to be the graduation speaker. He wanted to demonstrate what the parents had inspired in him, that he was both teacher and learner. Although social work education and agency policy warned him not to, Joe decided to use his painful story of growing up gay to show his students he was significantly more connected to them than separated. He was teacher, male, sober, and not a parent. They were students, female, recovering, and mothers. Yet their willingness to look inside and let others see gave Joe confidence. As Joe thanked them for showing him how facing deep pain generates new life, the students also felt something new. They felt influential and they gave him a standing ovation, proud they had given a teacher something so valuable.

One woman, a powerful trustee, remained seated. Joe knew he would be called to account for saying out loud that he was gay. He was reminded that by being an out executive in a Catholic agency, he was no safer than mothers. The message was the same: "Do what you are told and you will get your children back." "Do what you are told and you will keep your job."

As we worked with parents to replace condescension and fear with authenticity and trust, the raw and rare honesty was both exhausting and intriguing. We had no guidance for deconstructing privileged positions (Ungar, 2004). We made mistakes. As we redefined boundaries while removing old barriers, insight deepened, awareness increased, and charged emotional energy rose. Parents were more assertive, employees had less control, and no one was satisfied. Mediation might have saved time, but we relied on the existing mutual motivation to create a breakthrough. The process was not perfect and the outcome not permanent; the lesson, however, seems important enough to share.

Intellectual lenses are neither right nor wrong, they are simply perspectives. Through lenses of client voice, white privilege, and queer eye we saw what we were not doing for parents. Parent leaders have a role in schools; why not agencies? Privileged-based power was not stopping unnecessary placements; why? Vulnerability kept people in place; at what price? The irony of vulnerability is that it generates both fear and strength. The lesson for us was that power to act on one's own behalf is never bestowed. Such power rests within an individual. Life's work is to find and develop it. As it emerges, a leader's work is to welcome and encourage it.

Many on our leadership team supported the parent partnership. However, several influential, conservative, and less experienced trustees began to argue that giving more voice to troubled clients and dissident employees was financially and legally risky. While we had anticipated some of the trustees' concerns, secret board maneuvers were not expected. We debated the pros and cons up front. We showed the consistency of our approach with changing public policy. We brought information directly to board members. We began to sense increased intolerance for differences from religious leaders and we worked to negotiate the growing divide. Eventually, each of us was confronted privately about being openly gay leaders in a Catholic agency. We and many other senior executives left the agency. We had lost control to a very few trustees who singularly focused on liability and corporate risk. They differed from the reformers who hired us expecting us to lead as they did, taking risks for children. We took our lessons about power with us, including the ones we were slow to learn.

DISCUSSION OF POWER AND PRIVILEGE

Foster care and child abuse literature lack any substantive discussion of executive-parent partnership. The literature implies a power differential between parents and executives, which becomes visible through an economic, race, and gender lens. This power differential is a factor that keeps children in care. Children come from families living in poverty and reflect the recent immigration patterns (Child Welfare League of America, 2002). Nationally, most children in care are white, while in large urban settings the predominant groups are African American and Latino (Roberts, 2002). In these urban settings, it is common for trustees and executives to be white and for organizations to be religiously affiliated (Administration for Children's Services, 2003; Child Welfare Watch, 2002).

While the economic lens points to poverty as the primary factor in out-of-home placements, that correlation is no longer sufficient to explain the complexities (Pelton, 1994). The lens of white privilege in child welfare dramatizes the hollow canyon between parents of color and white executives (Hyde, 2004; Nybell & Gray, 2004). Articulate voices for women (Kapp, 2004; Kurtz, 1990), youth (Whiting, 2003), gay youth (Hammelman, 1993; Mallon, 2000; Savin-Williams, 1994), and disabled children (Hayden & Abery, 1994) only whisper what should be shouted about unresponsive child welfare practices toward families.

Foster care leaders have a difficult time acknowledging white privilege (Child Welfare Watch, 2002), Nybell and Gray's (2004) discussion of it as the force of sanctioned white advantage is useful. White judges, executives, and legislators have lacked a collective resolve to ask why their work results in such a disproportionate number of children of color being placed (Child Welfare Watch, 2002; Eckenrode, 1988; U.S. Department of Health and Human Services, 1997). Child abuse has no one color and is often a subset of domestic violence, yet gender and race-biased practices disproportionately charge mothers of color with neglect, take custody of their children, and terminate their parental rights in accordance with the Adoption and Safe Families Act (1996), a public policy that caused organized parents of color in New York to refer to it as proof that foster care is the last vestige of child slavery (Child Welfare Organizing Project, 2004).

The Peoples' Institute for Survival and Beyond, a grassroots community organizing group that offers workshops on antiracism throughout the country, explains a concept of undoing racism (Chisom & Washington, 1997). They suggest that the social construct of racism can and should be undone rather than managed by laws and ethics. Their language describes success for the human spirit over institutionalized racism, one dyad and one conflict at a time. An objective for the foster care system would be to recognize the racial bias in assessing children at risk and remove race as a factor in placement. An antiracist effort in foster care would help to reduce the un-assessed but "just in case" mandated .reporting in public schools, hospitals, day-care centers, and mental health clinics. The myth that bruises and fears of white, higher-income children do not hurt also needs to be dispelled.

Once placed, racism becomes a concern in children's clinical care. Expressed rage should not be diagnosed quickly and simply as oppositional defiance; it is better viewed as a likely response to violence prior to or aggravated by separation. Therapists who say "Tell me about your anger" might shift to explain rage as a reaction to being violated, discounted, or demeaned, and let clients know they can help them redirect rage (Specht & Courtney, 1995).

Therapists working in foster care must understand that offering family-centered services means inviting parent anger to the surface and being prepared to deal with it. They can encourage therapeutic activism, a clinical intervention directed toward changing systems and challenging assumptions. Parent leaders and agency staff can teach parents to take appropriate actions when confronted with micro-aggressions of racism. Agency leaders and families would benefit by defining therapeutic activism, accepting it, and advocating for its use, as many staff need help identifying their internalized biases about race and the triggers that activate them.

Some experts forecast that racism will be undone by intermarriage (Better, 1998). One Pentecostal, Latino mother reminded us that if racism is ever undone in foster care, it may be revealed as but a symptom of stronger religious bigotry and economic policy. She admonished us as a Catholic agency, "If I had the $60,000 a year the state pays you to care for my son, I would not have lost him. I could have paid rent and be teaching him to pray to my God." To her, religious and economic biases were entwined with race but were more critical.

Rethinking Power as Leaders Examine Their Own Behavior

Parents and executives share responsibility to raise, protect, and educate children and to help children form loving and lasting relationships. Both sets of leaders come under heavy criticism for failing to keep children safe and prepare them for life. Children's success hinges on parents and agencies ending their adversarial positions and agreeing to examine how they behave with each other. If an earnest effort is made, foster care's stated goals might actually be achieved. Unnecessary separation of children from parents can stop. Temporary care can continue as a true safety net. Lasting relationships for every child can be developed.

Agency leaders can level the playing field by teaching parent leaders the regulations that govern agencies. They can make sure parents are told their rights and provide space and access to phones and copy machines so parents can organize, conduct meetings, and give feedback.

Organizations can encourage more open and substantive discussions among trustees and executives. Racism, sexual identity, spiritual beliefs, abortion rights, and bias-related rage are topics boards often ignore. Insurance companies, increasingly concerned about liability, suggest amending hiring or intake procedures to avoid dealing with specific higher-risk populations (New York Civil Liberties Union Foundation, 2004). Trustees can benefit from examining why they serve organizations whose client behaviors or characteristics make them uncomfortable. Beyond their role in monitoring risk and protecting assets, some trustees are honest enough to admit their personal preference to serve only those they consider worthy (Waken, 2004). Executives might encourage trustees to further examine this conflict by using the corporate approach of customer satisfaction. Begin by asking trustees if they view parents as customers. Many do not; many view children as the customer.

Parent leaders can help agencies succeed with their two primary goals: child safety and timely discharges. They can advise agency leaders on how parents experience the major foster care inconsistency: children in care are sometimes unsupervised and hurt. Parents can encourage executives to strengthen practices, including making sure parents know where their children are living and ensuring staff are prepared for service plan reviews and court. They can insist that parents' work and school obligations are considered when scheduling appointments.

Parent leaders can challenge agency leaders to correct false assumptions about parents. These false assumptions include thinking mothers are incompetent and immoral; fathers are cruel or missing; children adjust fairly easily to placement; and parents' anger signals a lack of gratitude. Parent leaders can create an effective lobbying force for systemic reform by adding credibility and volume to the up-to-now minimally effective voice of agency leaders.

Agency leaders who examine their role with parents may be more willing to move beyond the comfort of executive suites. Reflective leaders may be more willing than others to risk talking with parents. When willing to learn more, leaders accomplish more. Most leaders have not experienced success in preventing unnecessary placements, reducing length of stay, and achieving permanency for children. Some suggest they should be evaluated just on their efforts and their sense of mission. Leaders in partnership with parents will solve problems for families.

ESSENTIAL GUIDELINES FOR FORMING PARTNERSHIPS

The primary motivation for parent-agency partnerships is to advance the well-being of children. However, other motivations play a role. Foster care costs taxpayers between ten and one hundred thousand dollars a child per year (Center for Family Policy and Research, 2004). Unsuccessful foster care has a longer-term negative impact on the economy. Children who have extended stays are less likely to live stable lives and more likely to be underemployed and at-risk of adult institutional care for mental illness and criminal behavior (Center for Family Policy and Research, 2004). Competent agency and parent leaders will create economic arguments for investing in children, not bureaucracies, and will support their views with data, not anecdotes.

Motivation for partnering must also be personal. Foster care is difficult work and the idea of reframing the relationship requires executives to give up power and acknowledge their role in a failing system. Parent leaders also have to admit their limitations and work very hard to redirect their anger and teach others to do the same. Neither is effective without a deep personal commitment; neither will risk the exposure without a strong internal drive.

Both parties have to agree not to blame the other and to acknowledge their mutual distrust. A mediator can help develop written ground to manage communication amid the vast array of concerns and distractions. Conflict resolution skills are essential. Parent leaders will have to elevate the discussions and help parents stay focused on larger systemic issues. Agency leaders will have to listen to the details of pain as parents share their own stories. Both have to shift to using child time, time that moves more quickly than adult's let's-wait-until-tomorrow time. Parent-child bonds are irretrievably lost in postponements and wasted time.

Parents know they are judged as child abusers and executives know they are judged as money-makers for keeping children in care. Ground rules for partnership have to include demonstrating respect and encouragement. Leaders need courage to admit mistakes. The unevenness of power requires agency leaders do more initially. The process of becoming a partner with parents requires those in power to be in touch with their fears in much the same way that clients of foster care are expected to be in touch with their own fears in order to get their children back. Clinical experts refer to reachable and teachable moments. Leaders have such moments, too, but they do not occur in workshops, through reading, or in the company of like-minded individuals. These moments come during exposure to critics. Exposure is a brave, revitalizing act. By taking risks with each other, partners gain trust and children have hope.

Guidelines that help form parent-executive partnerships include:

- Express ideas and demonstrate a commitment to them and potential partners will find you;
- Understand the only behavior that can be changed is one's own;
- While radical systemic reform is not likely, radical reforming of relationships is at the core of foster care's work with families; keep in mind leaders can do what they expect clients to do;
- Write down in simple terms what parents can contribute to new relationships;
- Write down in simple terms what agency leaders can contribute to new relationships;
- Make a simple list of what a new partnership cannot achieve;
- Make a list of the priorities agencies and parents share;
- Make a simple list of anticipated obstacles and outline strategies to address them;
- Prepare constituents needed to make the partnership work: parents, staff, trustees, funders;
- Continually examine one's own behavior in the presence of critics;
- Do what's needed to sharpen insight;
- Identify specific roles, tasks, time frames, and agreed-upon communication processes;
- Assess efforts and achievements regularly;
- After setbacks, evaluate, modify, and keep going;
- Record and share pitfalls, mistakes, and progress.

Leaders need to be aware of what not to do as well. Leaders should not send out a meeting notice inviting anyone who wants to talk or work on building partnerships. Do not spend too much time planning or setting goals outside the presence of the other half of the partnership. Do not start by writing a proposal to ask for funding; if something is worth doing, demonstrate commitment by doing the required work with your time and energy. Do not behave as though you know everything—you only know what *you* need; do not assume you know what the other side of the partnership needs. And lastly, do not think you can choose a nice person to train to be a leader for the other side of the partnership. Partners choose each other. Be choose-able.

CONCLUSION

Foster care will continue to shrink as government cuts funding; however, it will not reform without the candid voice of parents. That voice has the potential to shock executives into examining the emotional abuse in which they collude. When face-to-face with parents, executives are more likely to find their conscience and remember their obligations.

The blurring of church-state boundary lines in faith-based organizations needs the attention of parents. Once public funds are accepted, boards cannot require clients and staff to practice the sponsors' religion. Parents have a right to have children raised in accordance with their own religion, and most parents and staff members recognize that the common ground of spirituality more than religion is a colorless and genderless path to wholeness in life.

Incorrect economic assumptions about clients need to be challenged. When trustees suggest that well-maintained long-term residential settings are therapeutic alternatives for disadvantaged children, they should be reminded that the unnecessary uprooting of poor children from their families is abusive and damaging. Leaders have to work with policymakers to remove the economic bias that faults parents for their poverty while paying agencies for unnecessary care. Wealthy trustees can be reminded that their business transactions with urban planners and investment bankers may create economic disadvantages for client communities.

As a result of a major shift in direction by the religious leaders of our board, we left the agency before being successful. Without executive partners, the three-year-old Parents-as-Partners project was dismantled. Parent leaders were discouraged, yet some joined the Child Welfare Organizing Project through which their work continues.

We documented what we learned to provide evidence of one hopeful step for parents. We never used the words but we learned to use the lenses of white privilege, client voice, and queer eye to examine the complexities of our relationship with parents. We gained a better understanding of our shared responsibility for the well-being of the same children. When we and parent leaders saw each other as partners more than adversaries, we realized it was possible to do together what had thus far eluded each of us alone: help children succeed.

As executives, we should have assessed our board more thoroughly and not assumed they would agree to this new partnership. Their strong objections sparked a more troubling debate over whether we had the authority to partner with parents. When power dynamics between the executives and parents started to shift, power dynamics between executives and trustees shifted as well. Not recognizing that interplay was a costly mistake for us and our parent partners.

We remain convinced that power is a resource rising or at rest within individuals, and effective organizations provide opportunities to benefit from its shared use. The power parents have begun to exercise is a gift to their children and to any agency that welcomes it. We currently work for a different mental health organization that provides some residential foster care. We are encouraged by trustees who more fully participate, a code of conduct that guides decisions, efforts to increase communication with parents, and an executive-led pursuit to understand how race impacts client services. There is hope.

REFERENCES

Administration for Children's Services (2003). *Foster care national statistics.* New York: City Limits Community Information Service, Inc.

Adoption and Safe Families Act, Public Law 105-89 (1996).

Better, S. J. (1998). *Institutional racism: Browning of America.* Unpublished monograph.

Blitz, L. V., & Illidge, L. C. (2006). Not so black and white: Shades of gray and brown in antiracist multicultural team building in a domestic violence shelter. *Journal of Emotional Abuse, 6*(2/3), 113-134.

Center for Family Policy and Research (2004). *The state of child welfare in America.* Columbia, MO: Author.

Child Welfare League of America (2002). *Children of color at a glance, 2002.* Available from http://ndas.cwla.org/research_info/specialtopic1a.asp

Child Welfare Organizing Project (2004). *Annual report.* Child Welfare Fund, New York City.

Child Welfare Watch (2002). *Who controls foster care?* City Limits Community Information Services, Inc.

Chisom, R., & Washington, M. (1997). *Undoing racism: A philosophy of international social change.* New Orleans: The People's Institute Press.

Eckenrode, J. (1988). Substantiation of child abuse and neglect reports. *Journal of Consulting and Clinical Psychology, 38,* 9-13.

Fletcher, J. K. (1999). *Disappearing acts: Gender, power and relational practices at work*. Cambridge, MA: MIT Press.

Hammelman, S. K. (1993). Gay and lesbian youth. *Journal of Gay and Lesbian Psychotherapy, 2*, 77-89.

Hayden, M. F., & Abery, B. (Eds.) (1994). *Challenges for a service system in transition*. Baltimore, MD: Paul H Brookes.

Hyde, C. (2004). Multicultural development in human service agencies: Challenge and solution. *Social Work, 49*, 7-16.

Kapp, S. (2004). The unheard voice: Assessing the satisfaction of parents of children in foster care. *Child and Family Social Work, 9*, 197-206.

Kurtz, L. F. (2004). The self help moment. *Social Work with Groups, 13*, 101-115.

Lowe, L. (2002). Gendering the silences. *Journal of Managerial Psychology, 17*, 422-434.

Mallon, G. P. (2000). Gay men and lesbians as adoptive parents. *Journal of Gay and Lesbian Social Services, 11*(4), 1-22.

New York Civil Liberties Union Foundation (2004). *Anne Lown Against the Salvation Army, Inc. Memorandum in law in opposition to defendants' motions to dismiss*. US District Court, Southern District of New York.

Nybell, L., & Gray, M. (2004). Race, place and space: Meaning of cultural competence in three child welfare agencies. *Social Work, 49*, 17-26.

Peacock, C., & Daniels, G. (2006). Applying an antiracist framework to a residential treatment center: Sanctuary®, a model for change. *Journal of Emotional Abuse, 6*(2/3), 135-154.

Pelton, L. H. (Ed.) (1994). Is poverty a key contributor to child maltreatment in child welfare? Yes. In E. Gambrill & T. J. Stein (Eds.), *Controversial issues in child welfare* (pp. 16- 22, 26- 28). Needham Heights, MA: Allyn and Bacon.

Roberts, D. (2002). *Racial disproportionality in the US child welfare system: Documentation, research on cases and promising practices*. Working Paper # 4 prepared for the Annie E. Casey Foundation, Northwestern University School of Law: Institute for Policy Research.

Savin-Williams, R. C. (1994). Verbal and physical abuse as stressors in the lives of lesbian, gay male and bisexual youth. *Journal of Consulting and Clinical Psychology, 62*, 261-269.

Specht, H., & Courtney, M. (1995). *Unfaithful angels*. New York: The Free Press.

Ungar, M. (2004). Surviving as a post modern social worker: Two Ps and three Rs of direct practice. *Social Work, 49*, 488-496.

U. S. Department of Health and Human Services (1997). *Children's Bureau National Study of Protection, Prevention and Reunification Services Delivered to Children and Families*. Washington DC: U.S. Government Printing Office.

Waken, D. (2004, February 2). A religious renewal at the Salvation Army raises the threat of church state dispute. *New York Times,* Metro Section, B1.

Whiting, J. B. (2003). Voices from the system: A qualitative study of foster children's stories. *Family Relation: Interdisciplinary Journal of Applied Family Studies, 52*, 288-295.

doi:10.1300/J135v06n02_07

Not So Black and White:
Shades of Gray and Brown
in Antiracist Multicultural Team Building
in a Domestic Violence Shelter

Lisa V. Blitz
Linda C. Illidge

SUMMARY. Racism is deeply entrenched in American culture and can be unintentionally perpetuated by the same social institutions that strive to help people overcome painful obstacles in their lives. Mental health professionals understand the need to address environmental and social forces when working with individuals and families. Unfortunately, the full meaning and impact of racism can be misunderstood or minimized by practitioners who are guided by "White-Centric" theories. The dynamics of oppression can inhibit the type of deep and honest discussion that can uncover racism embedded in the institution. This article explores the process of understanding and using an antiracist framework to inform staff team building in a domestic violence shelter in New York City. doi:10.1300/J135v06n02_08 *[Article copies available for a fee from The Haworth Document Delivery Service: 1-800-HAWORTH. E-mail address:*

Address correspondence to either author, Jewish Board of Family and Children's Services/Genesis Domestic Violence Shelter, P.O. Box 594, New York, NY 10018 (E-mail: lblitz@jbfcs.org; lillidge@jbfcs.org).

[Haworth co-indexing entry note]: "Not So Black and White: Shades of Gray and Brown in Antiracist Multicultural Team Building in a Domestic Violence Shelter." Blitz, Lisa V., and Linda C. Illidge. Co-published simultaneously in *Journal of Emotional Abuse* (The Haworth Maltreatment & Trauma Press, an imprint of The Haworth Press, Inc.) Vol. 6, No. 2/3, 2006, pp. 113-134; and: *Racism and Racial Identity: Reflections on Urban Practice in Mental Health and Social Services* (ed: Lisa V. Blitz, and Mary Pender Greene) The Haworth Maltreatment & Trauma Press, an imprint of The Haworth Press, Inc., 2006, pp. 113-134. Single or multiple copies of this article are available for a fee from The Haworth Document Delivery Service [1-800-HAWORTH, 9:00 a.m. - 5:00 p.m. (EST). E-mail address: docdelivery@haworthpress.com].

113

KEYWORDS. Multicultural, anti-racist, domestic violence shelter,
team building, racial identity

Domestic violence is the multi-layered, painful, life-altering experience of being beaten, raped, exploited, degraded, and threatened by an intimate partner that the victim once loved and trusted, and one to whom she may still be deeply bonded and dependent upon. Nearly 25% of all women in America have experienced domestic violence at some point in their lives (Tjaden & Thoennes, 2000), and for those who live in poverty the number rises to 65% (Josephson, 2005). Women who experience domestic violence are angry, ashamed, and frightened. None of them will have exactly the same story, or come away with the same scars or the same strengths. For many, the abuse does not stop; even after leaving the relationship, they may continue to be harassed or stalked by their abusive partners. In resisting racism, women of color face cultural violence daily, and those who live in poverty deal with the onslaught of community and state violence in their lives. The challenge for all these women is to become victors in the face of ongoing abuse.

As noted by Harris and Dewdney (1994), women need services to cope with and overcome the impact of violence in their lives; they don't need to be "fixed." The impact of the violence, however, can be profound. An understanding of the neurobiological, interpersonal, and psychosocial impact of violence is necessary to assess and respond to the complexity of the survivor's experience. Research has shown that trauma produces changes in the victim's neurobiological functioning that contributes to the symptoms of posttraumatic stress disorder (PTSD; van der Kolk, McFarlane, & Weisaeth, 1996). In a meta-analysis of research on PTSD and domestic violence, Jones, Hughes, and Unterstaller (2001) found that a substantial proportion of victimized women exhibit symptoms of PTSD, and that more severe abuse was associated with more severe symptoms. Women who were victimized multiple times in different relationships were at higher risk, as were women at domestic violence shelters, where PTSD symptoms were likely to be present in 40% to 84% of the residents.

Domestic violence is often understood as a pattern of coercive behavior designed to establish, demonstrate, and maintain power and control over the family, household members, or an intimate partner (Stark & Flitcraft, 1996). An understanding of gender inequality in our society is fundamental to this concept because it assumes that the dynamic of coercive control could not be effectively maintained if patriarchy was not culturally supported. Geller, Miller, and Churchill (this volume) expand on these ideas and give an overview of the history of the domestic violence movement. A social justice perspective is necessary to helping women move from victim to victor status because many of the dynamics that lead to abusive behavior and impact recovery from victimization are imbedded in cultural dynamics of dominance and oppression.

WOMEN IN DOMESTIC VIOLENCE SHELTERS

There are no national demographics on race or ethnicity of domestic violence shelter residents. It does seem clear, if not self-evident, that women use shelter when they need a safe place to go and have no other resources. Studies have shown strong links between poverty and the frequency and seriousness of domestic violence. It has been frequently noted that perpetrators of domestic violence will sabotage the woman's attempts to work or go to school to prevent them from becoming economically self sufficient (Plichta, 1996); thus, she is more likely to need public assistance. Women who receive temporary assistance to needy families (TANF or welfare benefits) are as much as three times more likely to have been victims of child abuse and/or domestic violence than women in the general population (Josephson, 2005). As of 1998, following "welfare reform," twice as many Black and Hispanic women as White women receive welfare benefits, although more White women received welfare benefits prior to this time (DeParle, 2004). Therefore, in large urban areas with significant populations of people of color, it is expected that shelter residents will often be financially poor women of color. In New York City, the number of women of color in shelter is highly disproportionate compared to White women, and in Genesis, the shelter to be discussed here, virtually all residents are women of color or women from marginalized ethnic groups.

RACIAL IDENTITY AND RACISM

Women of all races, ages, and socioeconomic backgrounds can become victims of domestic violence (Tjaden & Thoennes, 2000). Women who

have been victimized by domestic abuse are marginalized from the power
center of society both by their gender and by victim status. Women of
color, or those who belong to ethnic groups outside of mainstream White
America, and who are living in poverty, are further marginalized by race,
ethnicity, and economic status (Forcey & Nash, 1998; Sokoloff & Dupont,
2005). Since oppression and subjugation are common experiences among
people of color and many immigrants to this country, it is important that
helping professionals be knowledgeable about the dynamics of power and
powerlessness and understand how these forces operate in human functioning (Pinderhughes, 1995). Marginalization on multiple levels can inhibit the survivor's ability to envision herself as a strong, empowered
member of society, in charge of her own life. Advocacy, shelter, and healing interventions must be flexible and adaptive to the social and political
context of the survivor's life, in addition to addressing the deeply personal
injury of the abuse (Dietz, 2000).

Challenges, Loyalty, and Resistance for Women of Color
Dealing with Domestic Abuse

Geller et al. (this volume) discuss the challenges noted by the women
they interviewed, which are supported by discourse in the literature.
Historically, African-Americans and other people of color have used informal networks and seek support through family, prayer, personal spirituality, and religious organizations. The churches in communities of
color often serve as sources of strength and have historically been the
centers of social activism. In this context, women of color may be told
from the pulpit to protect their men because men of color are an endan-
gered species. Clergy who are unaware of the seriousness and complexities of domestic violence, however, may interpret the Bible's principles
of love, forgiveness, and submission in a way that unconsciously and
unwittingly reinforces sexism and subordination, which can be used to
justify abuse within the home (West, 1999). Some overzealous minis-
ters may overstate the value placed on suffering as a test from God
(Donnelly, Cook, van Ausdale, & Foley, 2005), a confusing message to
a vulnerable abused woman.

Women of color often face a loyalty trap and may be hesitant to seek
help because of conflicting race and gender loyalties. The antiviolence
movement has its roots in the early feminist movement, a White-dominated group where the unique needs and experiences of Black women
were ignored (Richie, 2005). African-American and other women of

color, suspicious of a gender analysis applied to their families, may view the violence in their home as being a result of racial oppression of men of color, not gender oppression working in their lives. Some women of color believe they become the object of their partner's rage because there is no other outlet in the greater society where he can enjoy such power and privilege.

The impact of political advocacy efforts has had a complex effect on women of color who are domestic violence victims. Some remedies that have been pursued (e.g., mandatory arrest laws for perpetrators) were thought to treat men and women as equals as they give women the same legal rights as any crime victim (Mills, 1996). Rather than reducing violence in the lives of women of color, however, these policies often have the effect of strengthening state violence in their community (Smith, 2005). In addition, cooperating with authorities in prosecuting her abusive partner may result in community abandonment or contempt because members of the community know that men of color are selectively penalized (Donnelly et al., 2005).

Women of color dealing with domestic violence are also faced with a lack of government support in the form of social services and public housing. Women may feel re-victimized by the intrusive and coercive control of state agencies such as the welfare system, which occur in ways that are racialized as well as gendered and classed (Sokoloff & Dupont, 2005). Black women also have to deal with the stereotype that their race predisposes them to engage in and enjoy violence. Women of color are more likely to be classified by domestic violence hotline workers as homeless or as substance abusers, rather than being victims of domestic violence. These stereotypes have contributed to their skepticism about seeking help, and when they do reach out, women of color are less likely to receive shelter and other services.

SOCIAL JUSTICE, CULTURAL COMPETENCY, AND THE SHELTER

As part of the healing process, the survivor of domestic violence is encouraged to develop a full appreciation of the broader context of her experience by looking at the dynamics of her family, her community, and the world at large. These explorations provide a natural context for discussions about racism, sexism, gender roles and expectations, and the dynamics of power and control. Domestic violence shelters are often run by and geared toward the needs and experiences of White;

non-immigrant, English-speaking women, however, and this is re-flected in the shelter rules and general culture (Donnelly et al., 2005). In this context, various forms of power and privilege associated with race, class, and formal education can be enacted covertly within the shelter, regardless of the race of the staff. It is vital, therefore, that discussions about social violence, in the form of misuses of power in a racist and pa-triarchal society, include openness to examining how these dynamics play out in the shelter.

Social justice begins with cultural competency. All members of the staff team must thoughtfully and honestly explore the forces of power and privilege in juxtaposition to marginalization and oppression within their organization and in individual relationships. A truly culturally competent helping professional, therefore, is one who has embarked on a process of *becoming multicultural* by developing awareness of her personal iden-tity, inherent assumptions and biases, and who is learning to appreciate different ways of being (Ronnau, 1994). It is also crucial that the helping professional have a well-articulated analysis of power that informs her thinking about stratifications based on race, socioeconomics, and gender, and then cultivate an understanding of the dynamics of difference.

People in the helping profession must examine their self-identity in depth, particularly as it relates to racial identity and the impact of exter-nal and internalized racial oppression or racial superiority (see Blitz, this volume; Chapman, this volume; Kohl, this volume). External op-pression refers to the unjust use of authority and power by one group over another. External oppression becomes internalized in people of color when they come to believe the negative messages from the domi-nant group. For Whites, racism becomes internalized when they be-lieve, often unconsciously, in their inherent superiority.

Internalized Oppression in People of Color

People of color sometimes begin to mistreat themselves and other members in their group in the same ways that they have been mistreated as targets of racism. In social service organizations, staff of color who are defensive in their racial identity may enact a dynamic of oppression by over-identifying with clients of color or by identifying with the op-pressor (Ridley, 2005). The dynamic of internalized racism has been handed down since the times of slavery. Historically, there were two kinds of slaves: the house Negro, who had more privileges and a higher standing, and the field Negro, who held a lesser status (Graham, 1999;

see Franklin, Boyd-Franklin, & Kelly, this volume). Slaves needed to be inducted into maintaining the race-based oppressive order because there were more Black slaves than White slave masters on Southern plantations. The slave master, therefore, upheld the illusion of the hierarchical differences between the groups as a way to maintain the system of slavery and order on the plantation. Remnants of this dynamic can be seen today as internalized racial inferiority. Internalized racism can be manifested when people of color join institutions, including social service or mental health organizations, that are unconsciously racist and carry out that institution's policies and practices against their own group.

People of color may feel disconnected from other members of their group and judge them harshly. Some people of color have divided or categorized each other by behavior or lifestyle, believing that some people are more deserving than others. In an effort to preserve some positive sense of self-worth, they may distance themselves from other members of their racial group, believing that what others do or experience is not part of their cultural norms. From this point of view, they hold the notion that the issue is one of class or education, detracting from the overarching issue of racism.

Internalized racial oppression can cloud the individual's judgment and can influence the way she thinks–or does not think–of herself. People of color may come to believe that they, and others like them, cannot be trusted, are disgusting and unworthy of respect, and deserve inhumane treatment. When the person who carries internalized racial oppression has hierarchical or gatekeeping power over others, the attitude of self-hatred gets projected out toward others of the same racial group. In a social services setting or shelter, this can result in the harsh attitude of staff towards clients. The attitude of internalized self-hatred can take the form of staff treating clients with suspicion, devaluing and disrespecting the people they are there to serve. In turn, the clients may feel re-victimized by the agency from which they sought help.

White Privilege and the Color-Blind Racist

White privilege maintains the social order of cultural and institutional racism by providing White people with unearned opportunities, advantages, and access to resources (McIntosh, 1988) and placing people of color at a disadvantage in these areas. White people, particularly those who consciously oppose racism, may want to see themselves as color-blind, believing that to notice race is to be a racist (Donnelly et al.,

2005). When race is not noticed, however, White culture becomes the norm and racism is perpetuated.

As they learn more about their racial identity and the meaning of race in our society, White people begin to understand how they benefit from and unintentionally participate in racism. For White helping professionals, this can cause serious dissonance, since they want to see themselves as helpful and caring (Ancis & Szymanski, 2001). Similar to internalized racial oppression of people of color, White people who remain unaware of their internalized racial superiority run the risk of enacting their unconscious racism against people of color. Enactments of unconscious racism include the dynamics mentioned above in the discussion of unconscious internalized oppression, such as devaluing people of color, blaming them for their problems, and treating them harshly. As part of the dominant culture, however, Whites potentially have even more power to do harm. Without an analysis of power and privilege that leads to an understanding of the longer-term and unintended impact of policy decisions, such as why "welfare reform" appears to be working for White women, but not women of color, or the link between the highly disproportionate number of children of color in foster care (McGlade & Ackerman, this volume) and residential treatment (Peacock & Daniels, this volume), internalized racial superiority becomes self-perpetuating. The victim of oppression is blamed for the result of being oppressed.

Self-Reflection and Understanding Power

Service providers need to understand the impact of internalized racial oppression and racial privilege to avoid the risk of unconsciously reinforcing systemic racism. Although White people are taught not to notice the ways in which they are hurt by participating in a racist society, being placed in the role of oppressor is also an injury to the integrity of being (Bowser & Hunt, 1996). Understanding the impact of racism on all members of our society helps move the discussion away from an effort to understand the "other" (Fine, 1997), and moves toward a discussion of a more inclusive *we* in the interpersonal multicultural/multiracial dynamic. In this process, all people are encouraged to identify the ways in which they are privileged by our society and the ways in which they are marginalized, and to explore ways in which they operate to dismantle racism, and at other times act in ways that perpetuate it (Thompson & Neville, 1999). An analysis of power and authority is vital to this process to recognize that power dynamics will be enacted unless thoughtfully deconstructed in a collective dialogue (Pinderhughes, 1989).

Uncovering Unintentional Racism

As Franklin et al. (this volume) discuss, racist assumptions are deeply entrenched in American culture and are woven into institutions, social structures, and relationships. All human nature and the organizations we create are both a process and product of social constructions (Newberg, 2001) where bias can become embedded and go unrecognized. The ability to deconstruct fundamental assumptions about culture and place the individual's experience in context is essential to fully appreciate the complexity and sometimes contradictory nature of social experience.

As facilitators of this process with clients, the staff must be engaged in personal explorations that reflect the quality and depth of discovery they hope their clients will achieve. To uncover racist or biased assumptions that may not be immediately obvious, members of an organization can engage in a process of deconstruction and debate to examine things they would normally take for granted (Cooper & Burrell, 1988). Deeper explorations will help uncover multiple meanings and bias in the organization's dynamics.

Racial dialogues (Miller & Donner, 2000) provide individuals with the opportunity to talk openly about their backgrounds and their assumptions relative to cultural differences and similarities. Dialogues about race and racial identity allow the organization's members to deconstruct assumptions about knowledge and power, and work towards personal and collective empowerment. Racial dialogues are a way to develop a genuine appreciation of self and other in a cultural context, which has been shown to lead to maximum productivity, self-efficacy among the team members, and creative applications in the work (Ely & Thomas, 2000).

As the group's discussions about race and culture evolve, it is important to encourage individuals to examine their language and the language of others, as the language itself acts upon social reality (Dowds, 1996; Miller & Donner, 2000). The words we use and the way we talk about ourselves and each other influence our thoughts, assumptions, opinions, self-esteem, and how we value others. The staff team must develop a high level of trust with each other in order to engage in discussion that involves risk-taking in personal disclosure. For people of color, experiences of oppression and victimization from racism can bring up painful personal memories and feelings. For White people, deeper recognition of their unintentional cooperation with racist systems, or confessions of more conscious participation in racial oppression, can bring up profound vulnerability and other feelings for all members of the group.

DEVELOPING AN ANTIRACIST FRAMEWORK AT GENESIS DOMESTIC VIOLENCE SHELTER

Antiracist work is very personal work. To do it effectively, professional boundaries must sometimes incorporate, not transcend or negate, personal boundaries. The authors of this article have been able to establish a trusting partnership that we renew daily to move the work forward. We began working together approximately three years ago, when Linda assumed the position of supervisor at the domestic violence shelter where Lisa is the director. Our conversations about race, racism, multiculturalism, and the intersections of privilege and marginalization began in our first meeting and have continued with increasing depth and complexity.

Linda is African American, in her 50s, has lived most of her life in New York City in a working-class blue collar section of Brooklyn, and comes to social work as a second career. Lisa is White, in her 40s, grew up in a White middle-class suburban area outside of Los Angeles, and has lived and worked as a social worker in New York City for 15 years. In spite of our obvious differences, we quickly discovered that we share similar ideas and values around race and racism, and most importantly, are in analogous stages of our racial identity development. Our similar world views are important factors in our ability to engage in difficult and sensitive conversations, and have helped us create an alliance in developing and implementing an antiracist framework for the shelter.

The Organic Whole: Viewing Shelter as Therapeutic Community

Domestic violence shelters typically offer safety planning, advocacy, and supportive counseling to help the survivor and her family heal from the abuse and plan for her future. Shelters can be conceptualized as therapeutic community settings because they offer environments where residents interact with each other and with staff throughout the day. Professional intervention can facilitate peer support, and group and individual therapy targeting posttraumatic stress and life adjustment issues can be offered on site and integrated into overall shelter services, completing the requisites for milieu therapy or therapeutic community.

The therapeutic community operates as a dynamic relational matrix that can be understood as consisting of multiple levels of parallel process, or organic whole, that include all members of the staff group and resident group (Bloom, 1997; Goldberg, 1988). The relational matrix of the milieu presupposes that the dynamics of one part of the system will have a direct effect on another part of the whole. All aspects of the relationships and interactions between staff and clients are part of the psychosocial interventions that lead to healing and growth in the residents. In addition to specific treatment or services they may provide, all staff members function as facilitators and role models.

The relationship among staff members is critical to the health of the milieu and the staff's function as role models for the residents (Madsen, Blitz, McCorkle, & Panzer, 2003). There is a fundamental assumption in milieu therapy that communication and quality of process between staff members translate directly to the client community, and act as a key component of the treatment. Therefore, to facilitate a healing environment that is safe and creatively rich, the staff team must achieve and maintain healthy relationships with one another. Staff members are encouraged to continually evaluate the quality of their communication and to work through difficulties that impede their relationships. Staff members, therefore, must have a strong ability to discuss differences in perspectives, resolve interpersonal conflict, and explore issues of authority and power.

Overview of the Genesis Shelter and Its Residents

Genesis is a domestic violence shelter for families in New York City. The shelter offers temporary safe haven and provides an array of services in the context of a non-violent therapeutic community. These services include crisis intervention, advocacy and support regarding legal, TANF, and housing issues, and counseling to address the impact of violence on both adults and children. Over the past six years, the shelter has been implementing Sanctuary® (Bloom, 1997), the same model used in the residential treatment center discussed by Peacock and Daniels (this volume). Whereas Peacock and Daniels discuss the use of Sanctuary® for implementing antiracist client services, we will focus on staff development.

The Genesis shelter operates as a therapeutic milieu, which offers counseling and other services geared to facilitate healing from the traumatic impact of abuse for all members of the family. Most new residents to the shelter initially respond positively to the support and caring they receive from staff. Once initial safety has been established, however, some become ambivalent about addressing the emotional impact of the abuse, and some may feel confined by the rules of the shelter. Many residents experience a continual tension in negotiating their responsibilities as autonomous adults and parents, their role as residents in a shared living situation, their dependency upon shelter resources, and their readiness to face the impact of trauma (Madsen et al., 2003). In response to shelter rules and expected standards of behavior, the tensions of oppression and control also become activated, and the dynamic of racism intertwines in ways that are both obvious and covert.

The Staff Team

The staff of Genesis is multidisciplinary, multiracial, and multicultural, and includes administrative staff, clinicians, case managers, direct care workers, and maintenance workers. All 24 shelter staff members at this time are female, ranging in age from early 20s to mid-60s. The shelter director is White, the supervisor is African-American, and they function together as the team leaders. The rest of the staff includes women from the West Indies, Puerto Rico, Columbia, Mexico, Gambia, and South Africa, as well as Black and White Americans. The management and clinical staff hold master's level educational degrees, the case managers typically hold bachelor's degrees, and the direct care and maintenance staff have a high-school diploma or some college. Several members bring personal experience and practice wisdom from 12-step recovery programs, personal psychotherapy, and personal experience with domestic violence, and some have had advanced training in clinical theory and application.

The cultural diversity also extends to include team members who are Jewish, Muslim, and Christian, observant and secular, and those of other faiths, including those with non-defined spiritual beliefs. The diversity of the team includes sexual orientation, marital status, parental status, personality style, socio-economic background, and dissimilar life experiences. A basic tenet of the team's composition is that just about any new resident who comes through the door should be able to find at least one staff member that she can identify as being "like me" in some fundamental way.

Flattened Hierarchy

A hierarchical, top-down communication and relational style in organizations tends to promulgate the dominant culture with little opportunity for experiential or relational encounters that demand an appreciation of conflicting points of view. Hierarchy can then become a foundation for oppression, if only in the perceptions of the people at the lower part of the structure. Since the dominant cultural norm in America is White, once an oppressive dynamic is enacted, it becomes racist in result, if not intent.

The Sanctuary® therapeutic milieu emphasizes a flattened hierarchical structure, the articulation of shared assumptions about the work, and close teamwork among staff members. Optimally, the staff group becomes a living enactment of sound decision-making, conflict resolution, support, and negotiation of power (Goldberg, 1988). Each individual within the staff team is equally valued and work load is shared among members according to specialization and role (Bloom, 1997). Management and supervisory staff retain some hierarchical authority, but all staff members participate in a shared decision-making process in most aspects of shelter functioning. All staff members are empowered to exercise authority commensurate with the responsibility of their role, and variety of opinions is encouraged in team discussion.

From an antiracist framework, flattening of the hierarchy requires a complex understanding of staff dynamics and the interplay of issues of diversity, power, and privilege that become activated in the staff group dynamic. Dynamics of power, privilege, and assumptions about the value of certain types of knowledge, however, can inhibit the individual's ability to trust that her voice will be heard and respected (Karakowsky & McBey, 2001; Pinderhughes, 1989). Open acknowledgment of the power and authority issues that become activated in the milieu, and an examination of how they relate to race, racism, and racial identity, are crucial factors in how the Genesis team struggles with these issues.

Multiple Perspectives

The presence of multiple perspectives brings the challenge and opportunity to maintain a flexible position that includes a spectrum of ideas and avoids an "either/or" stance. The fact that staff members come from different cultural backgrounds and have had different educational and other life experiences provides a foundation for exploring different points of view. Beyond these naturally occurring differences, the team can practice flexibility by explicitly exploring additional views. For instance, staff members are encouraged to interject any idea *not* being expressed in the discussion, even if it is not congruent with their personal opinion, as a way of challenging the group to look at the situation from a different angle. By rotating which team members take leadership in voicing the alternative view, all members practice flexibility in thinking and reinforce creativity in problem-solving. Practicing flexibility in team discussions helps the staff combat the tendency to see issues or circumstances as concretely one way or the other.

Most decisions are made collectively and each member of the team is asked to voice an opinion. Initially, several members of the team, typically those with the least formal education who were also women of color, would remain quiet and not participate. Their lack of contribution was repeatedly challenged by the team leaders, who would use a combination of support and confrontation to encourage the participation of all team members. Eventually, the quietest members were able to express that they did not believe that their opinions would be valued or that their ideas would be respected. The team discussed the origins of these assumptions by placing them in the context of our understanding of racism and oppression. Additionally, we used our tradition of asking that one person in any discussion take an opposing view on a topic to remind people that there are no "right" or "wrong" ideas, and that any idea may be accepted or rejected depending on the broader context of the discussion. Over time, all team members have become increasingly comfortable expressing their views, although some are still more hesitant than others.

Teaching About Privilege, Oppression, and Racism

Education in the mental health field is a career-long process extending far beyond the years the professional spends in school. Additionally, many treatment settings such as Genesis rely on contributions from mental health or direct care staff who may not have received any formal post-secondary education. It is essential, therefore, that the educational process extends into the workplace through supervision, training, and experiential learning. If agencies are to become the center of intercultural learning, as suggested by Matthews (1996), it becomes crucial that the administrators, supervisors, and practitioners take leadership in using educational opportunities at the agency to promote antiracism in social service practice. At Genesis, we use a combination of opportunities in our staff team meetings, which are held three times a week, informal discussions among staff, and weekly group supervision that we call TREAT: Trauma Recovery Education and Treatment.

TREAT is facilitated by the shelter supervisor, and twice a month a clinical consultant with an expertise in trauma recovery treatment attends to co-facilitate the sessions. During TREAT, the group discusses an array of issues from the framework of psychosocial, family systems, and trauma recovery theories. Discussions often include the intersections of domestic violence victimization, patriarchy, racism, and trauma, and the client's ability to access supportive resources, work toward future goals, develop a positive sense of self and secure attachments with others. The team leaders and clinical consultant are equally invested in discussing multiculturalism and social justice issues openly, and examining ourselves and our work with clients. The mutual investment of the team leaders is necessary and a vital part of bringing about change in the organizational system. Our discussions about institutional and internalized racism, and concerns about how these dynamics may have been getting expressed in the shelter milieu, led us to conclude that we needed to begin a training program on systemic racism for the shelter staff. We decided to use the TREAT meetings to begin the process, and then expanded our discussion to the general team meetings.

To stimulate discussion, the team first watched a video that addressed the issues of racism, White privilege, and internalized oppression. This very provocative film stimulated a great deal of feeling in the group participants and heightened the team's sense of urgency to learn more about racism and racial identity. The second step was to provide a sociopolitical definition of racism. We gave the staff a historical overview of how race was invented and the ways in which ideas about racial superiority and inferiority have been embedded into our culture (see Blitz, this volume).

In the third step, the team leaders developed a simple tool (see Table 1) to guide staff in a discussion of their own racial and cultural identity to help deepen their self-awareness. The group participants used the tool to discuss their family, cultural life experiences, and their exposure to individuals of other cultural, ethnic, and racial groups. The team was able to have open conversations about culture, class, sexual orientation, race, and ethnicity, and explore the ways in which these factors have influenced their worldviews. The fourth step was to teach the Helm's (1995) Models of Racial Identity Development for Whites and People of Color to discuss the implications for our understanding of our residents and their needs (see Blitz, this

TABLE 1. Cultural and Racial Identity Exploration Tool

Issues related to culture:	Issues related to racial identity:
What is culture?	Share some memories of your first encounters with someone who is different from your cultural, ethnic or racial group.
How does your family identify their: a. Race? b. Ethnicity? c. Culture?	What are some words or ideas that you associate with people of your own racial group? When you think of power and authority, are you likely to think of people like you? Discuss this.
How are cultural rituals incorporated in your daily life?	Who are your heroes? Why do you look up to them? What racial/cultural group do they belong to?

volume, and Kohl, this volume). We use the Helm's Models because we have found them to be clear and accessible to staff with a range of formal education.

The discussions were also an opportunity to share experiences of racism, prejudice, and discrimination from the points of view of the oppressor and the oppressed. The sincerity and honesty with which the staff engaged in these discussions heightened trust and empathy between members. The stronger relationships between staff members translated into more honest and straightforward discussions about client services and began to facilitate change in how the staff talked about and responded to shelter residents. The team continues to be engaged in a process of learning from each other and moving toward a deeper appreciation of differences as a way of celebrating individuality and culture.

Mission Statement

The discussions about racial identity and racism led the team to conclude that we needed to ensure that a clear antiracist framework was informing our approach to all clinical interventions and service delivery. We revised our Mission Statement to provide us with a structure and outline of our professional ideals. Our previous Mission Statement had included a sentence regarding the importance of non-discriminatory practices, noting that no client would be turned away based on race, ethnicity, or cultural origin. The team's growing appreciation of cultural and institutional racism, however, made us aware that we could still be practicing in a way that perpetuated systemic racism even if we were inclusive in our intake and admissions policies and provided services without prejudice. The process of developing the Mission Statement together allowed us to explore how antiracist practice could be embedded in our general approach to our work. See Table 2 for an example of our revised Mission Statement.

"Safety" in the Dialogue on Race and Racism

Both the director and supervisor at Genesis encourage staff members to have ongoing discussions about race and racism during staff team meetings, individual supervisory sessions, and during informal discussions with their peers. We openly maintain the stance that racial identity development and a commitment to antiracism in all aspects of social service delivery and therapy are vital factors in professional development. One of the ways this is done is through modeling, where the team leaders take advantage of opportunities to talk about the impact of racism on themselves as individuals, and also as people of color and Whites as groups. We remain sensitive to the timing of discussions and, although we rarely avoid commenting on an underlying racist dynamic, we will not always challenge the staff to explore the issue more deeply in the moment.

TABLE 2. Genesis Domestic Violence Shelter Mission Statement

Mission	Genesis provides emergency shelter to families who are in immediate danger due to domestic violence. Assistance in finding permanent housing, schools for the children, education and/or vocational training programs for parents, therapy for all family members, emotional support, and parenting support are offered while we help our residents heal from the effects of violence.
Vision	We are a therapeutic community that offers respite from domestic violence. We offer quality services that promote living and coping skills, empowerment, confidence, and self-reliance in our residents. We see the whole family as being impacted by the violence in their home and able to benefit from services and support to heal from the injury of abuse.
Values	Safety is our highest value. To work towards ensuring that all members of the Genesis community feel emotionally, psychologically, and morally safe we work from an antiracist/social justice framework. We are a culturally competent staff who work toward undoing social factors, such as racism, classism, sexism, and poverty, that contribute to the impact of family violence trauma. Genesis staff value open communication, believing that this is the best way to build trust, form healthy relationships, and make informed choices. We also value hard work (for staff and clients), a healthy community, and access to resources. Staff is learning and being trained in trauma recovery theory and milieu therapy to develop skills and share knowledge with each other, our clients, and other professionals. We run as a flattened hierarchy where we emphasize individual role, boundary, and authority, rather than hierarchical power. We make decisions as a team to reflect our values of shared responsibility, accountability, and multiple perspectives.

We acknowledge how difficult it is to have these discussions, because the issues of oppression, race, prejudice, and privilege arouse deep feelings for all people. Initially, most discussions with staff began with questions about safety, both psychological and emotional safety as well as practical safety, regarding how self-disclosure will be used in decisions regarding promotion, requests for flexibility, or disciplinary action. While the agency's non-discrimination policies offer some layer of protection, we also acknowledged that there is no completely "safe" way to discuss deeply personal issues. We also acknowledged that people of color rarely feel "safe" when discussing race and racism. It was crucial that the White people on the team developed an understanding that their desire for emotional safety was an enactment of White privilege. Safety for all members is something we eventually earned and built together, but it could not be promised or granted at the beginning of the dialogue.

Teachable Moments–Racial Identity Development

In addition to discussion in formal team meetings, it is important to take advantage of teachable moments, impromptu dialogues that provide an opportunity to explore issues of racial identity or racism. An example of a teachable moment came when a White team member was talking in informal conversation with other staff about an experience she had with a long-time friend over the weekend. She and this friend had clashed over issues of understanding racism, and the staff member expressed that she felt as though she was evolving in a way that was making it significantly harder to tolerate ignorance about racism in others. The other staff present listened supportively, and one of the team leaders was able to use the conversation as an opportunity to review racial identity development theory, using the Helms (1995) model in a practical context. By looking at the model's stages of racial identity development, each team member present was able to identify where they see themselves in their development and begin to understand how their social relationships are impacted by their growth. Later discussions tied this into professional service delivery and psychosocial understanding of shelter clients and our relationships with them.

Humbling Moments–Internalized Racial Inferiority and White Privilege

In a formal staff discussion, two Black team members disclosed that they had grown up believing "White people have all the brains" and that this influenced several areas of their life, including early decisions that limited their professional ambition. Neither recalled ever actually being told this, but said that it was the assumption they acquired because those messages were "all around" and nobody specifically gave them positive messages to counter the negative ideas. As other members of the discussion group reacted to this, all the group members experienced varying degrees of anger and sadness as they connected to the pain of the women who had disclosed. One of the White women in the group became tearful, stating that she felt guilty for not realizing how many of her advantages were tied to her race. She stated she now recognized that White privilege gave her ability to take fundamental concepts of self-worth and self-image for granted, never fully realizing that all intelligent, caring women did not share the same self-assumptions. She made it clear that although she was crying she did not expect the group to take care of her, which was a very important message to the women of color in the room. She also added that she felt inhibited about talking about the topic because she was not sure what words to use to properly convey her feelings, and she did not want to add insult to injury by saying the wrong thing. The people of color in the meeting thanked her for being respectful and reassured her that her honesty and sincerity negated any clumsy language.

The conversation evolved into looking at how this internalized sense of racial inferiority impacted how the Black staff members interact with the clients, who are almost exclusively women of color. We also examined how the clients may carry a similar sense of internalized racism that may trigger unconscious internalized racial superiority in the White staff members. For example, we have noticed that clients sometimes treat the White staff with a greater degree of formality and politeness than they do staff members who are women of color. In response, the White staff may develop a more favorable and empathic rapport with the client, but underlying this they are rewarding a subservient position in the relationship, reinforcing racism and creating a barrier to genuine intimacy. At the same time, the Black and brown staff members may be more suspicious of the client's motives and behavior and be less able to connect empathically with her vulnerability, also creating a barrier to genuine intimacy.

CONCLUSION

In spite of the arousal of painful feelings, the staff continues to have an open dialogue on race and racism resulting in a positive outcome.

Staff members have frequently verbalized how productive these discussions have been. They feel secure enough to talk about their personal experiences and assumptions, and to ask questions about cultures and ways of being that are different from their own. Our ability to move beyond cultural competency and begin an evolution towards an antiracist framework has enriched our shelter milieu and positively impacted the individuals who participate in it. The staff is committed to continuing the open dialogue on race and racism to further build on the antiracist framework.

REFERENCES

Ancis, J. R., & Szymanski, D. M. (2001). Awareness of White privilege among White counseling trainees. *The Counseling Psychologist, 219*, 548-569.

Blitz, L. V. (2006). Owning whiteness: The reinvention of self and practice. *Journal of Emotional Abuse, 6*(2/3), 241-263.

Bloom, S. (1997). *Creating sanctuary: Toward the evolution of sane societies.* New York: Routledge.

Bowser, B. P., & Hunt, R. G. (1996). *Impacts of racism on White Americans.* Thousand Oaks, CA: Sage Publications.

Chapman, R. T. (2006). Internalized racism of the clinician and the treatment dynamic. *Journal of Emotional Abuse, 6*(2/3), 219-228.

Cooper, R., & Burrell, G. (1988). Modernism, postmodernism, and organizational analysis: An introduction. *Organization Studies, 9*, 91-112.

DeParle, J. (2004). *American dream: Three women, ten kids, and a nation's drive to end welfare.* New York: Penguin Books.

Dietz, C. A. (2000). Reshaping clinical practice for the new millennium. *Journal of Social Work Education, 36*, 503-520.

Donnelly, D. A., Cook, K. J., van Ausdale, D., & Foley, L. (2005). White privilege, colorblindness, and services to battered women. *Violence Against Women, 11*, 6-37.

Dowds, M. W. (1996). Paranoia in an ethnically diverse population: The role of group work. *Social Work with Groups, 19*, 67-77.

Ely, R., & Thomas, D. (2000). *Cultural diversity at work: The moderating effects of work group perspectives on diversity.* Unpublished manuscript.

Fine, M. (1997). Witnessing whiteness. In M. Fine, L. Weis, L. C. Powell, & L. M. Wong (Eds.), *Off White: Readings on race, power, and society* (pp. 57-65). New York: Routledge.

Forcey, L. R., & Nash, M. (1998). Rethinking feminist theory and social work therapy. *Women and Therapy, 21*, 85-99.

Franklin, A. J., Boyd-Franklin, N., & Kelly, S. (2006). Racism and invisibility: Race-related stress, emotional abuse and psychological trauma for people of color. *Journal of Emotional Abuse, 6*(2/3), 9-30.

Geller, J., Miller, J., & Churchill, P. (2006). Triple trouble: Battered women of color–"Being black, being battered and being female . . . I ask myself, where do I begin?" *Journal of Emotional Abuse, 6*(2/3), 77-96.

Goldberg, K. (1988). The quilt-work theory: A milieu approach. *New Directions for Mental Health, 38*, 5-21.

Graham, L. O. (1999). *Our kind of people: Inside America's Black upper class.* New York: HarperCollins.

Harris, R. M., & Dewdney, P. (1994). *Barriers to information: How formal helping systems fail battered women.* Westport, CT: Greenwood Press.

Helms, J. E. (1995). An update of Helm's White and People of Color racial identity models. In J. G. Ponteroto, J. M. Casas, L. A. Suzuki, & C. M. Alexander (Eds.), *Handbook of multicultural counseling* (pp. 181-198). Thousand Oaks: Sage Publications.

Jones, L., Hughes M., & Unterstaller, U. (2001). Posttraumatic stress disorder (PTSD) in victims of domestic violence. *Trauma, Violence, & Abuse, 2*, 99-119.

Josephson, J. (2005). The intersectionality of domestic violence and welfare in the lives of poor women. In N. J. Sokoloff with C. Pratt (Eds.), *Domestic violence at the margins: Readings on race, class, gender, and culture* (pp. 83-101). New Brunswick, NJ: Rutgers University Press.

Karakowsky, L., & McBey, K. (2001). Do my contributions matter? The influence of imputed expertise on member involvement and self-evaluations in the work group. *Group and Organization Management, 26*, 70-92.

Kohl, B. G., Jr. (2006). Can you feel me now? Worldview, empathy and racial identity in a therapy dyad. *Journal of Emotional Abuse, 6*(2/3), 173-196.

Madsen, L. H., Blitz, L. V., McCorkle, D., & Panzer, P. G. (2003). Sanctuary in a domestic violence shelter: A team approach to healing. *Psychiatric Quarterly, 74*, 155-171.

Matthews, L. (1996). Culturally competent models in human services organizations. *Journal of Multicultural Social Work, 4*, 131-135.

McGlade, K., & Ackerman, J. (2006). A hope for foster care: Agency executives in partnerships with parent leaders. *Journal of Emotional Abuse, 6*(2/3), 97-112.

McIntosh, P. (1988). *White privilege and male privilege: A personal account of coming to see the correspondences through work in women's studies.* Wellesley, MA: Center for Research on Women.

Miller, J., & Donner, S. (2000). More than just talk: The use of racial dialogues to combat racism. *Social Work with Groups, 23*, 31-53.

Mills, L. (1996). Empowering battered women transnationally: The case for postmodern interventions. *Social Work, 41*, 261-268.

Newberg, D. (2001). Postmodernism: Implications for organization theory? In R. T. Golembiewski (Ed.), *Handbook of organizational behavior* (2nd ed., rev. & exp., pp. 525-545). New York: Marcel Dekker, Inc.

Peacock, C., & Daniels, G. (2006). Applying an antiracist framework to a residential treatment center: Sanctuary®, a model for change. *Journal of Emotional Abuse, 6*(2/3), 135-154.

Pinderhughes, E. (1989). *Understanding race, ethnicity, and power: The key to efficacy in clinical practice.* New York: The Free Press.

Pinderhughes, E. (1995). Empowering diverse populations: Family practice in the 21st century. *Families in Society, 76*, 131-140.

Plichta, S. (1996). Violence and abuse: Implications for women's health. In *Women's Health: The Commonwealth Fund Survey.* Baltimore: Johns Hopkins University Press.

Richie, B. E. (2005). A Black feminist reflection on the antiviolence movement. In N. J. Sokoloff with C. Pratt (Eds.), *Domestic violence at the margins: Readings on race, class, gender, and culture* (pp. 50-55). New Brunswick, NJ: Rutgers University Press.

Ridley, C. R. (2005). *Overcoming unintentional racism in counseling and therapy: A practitioner's guide to intentional intervention* (2nd ed.). Thousand Oaks: Sage.

Ronnau, J. P. (1994). Teaching cultural competence: Practical ideas for social work educators. *Journal of Multicultural Social Work, 3,* 29-42.

Smith, A. (2005). Looking to the future: Domestic violence, women of color, the State, and social change. In N. J. Sokoloff with C. Pratt (Eds.), *Domestic violence at the margins: Readings on race, class, gender, and culture* (pp. 416-434). New Brunswick, NJ: Rutgers University Press.

Sokoloff, N. J., & Dupont, I. (2005). Domestic violence at the intersections of race, class, and gender. *Violence Against Women, 11,* 38-64.

Stark, E., & Flitcraft, A. (1996). *Women at risk: Domestic violence and women's health.* Thousand Oaks, CA: Sage Publications.

Thompson, C. E., & Neville, H. A. (1999). Racism, mental health, and mental health practice. *The Counseling Psychologist, 27,* 155-223.

Tjaden, P., & Thoennes, N. (2000). Extent, nature, and consequences of intimate partner violence. *National Institute of Justice and Centers for Disease Control and Prevention.* Retrieved May 27, 2004 from http://www.ojp.usdoj.gov

van der Kolk, B. A., McFarlane, A. C., & Weisaeth, L. (1996). *Traumatic stress: The effects of overwhelming experience on mind, body, and society.* New York: The Guilford Press.

West, T. (1999). *Wounds of the spirit: Black women, violence and resistance ethics.* New York: New York University Press.

doi:10.1300/J135v06n02_08

Applying an Antiracist Framework to a Residential Treatment Center: Sanctuary®, a Model for Change

Caroline Peacock

George Daniels

SUMMARY. This article addresses the impact of systemic racism and White privilege in a residential treatment center for children who are referred by the child welfare and juvenile justice systems. The chosen treatment approach, the Sanctuary® Model, addresses all forms of oppression through the core concepts of therapeutic community, safety, and trauma theory. doi:10.1300/J135v06n02_09 *[Article copies available for a fee from The Haworth Document Delivery Service: 1-800-HAWORTH. E-mail address: <docdelivery@haworthpress.com> Website: <http://www.HaworthPress.com> © 2006 by The Haworth Press, Inc. All rights reserved.]*

KEYWORDS. Racism, residential treatment, White privilege, Sanctuary® Model, milieu treatment, therapeutic community

Address correspondence to either author, JBFCS, Hawthorne Cedar Knolls, 226 Linda Avenue, Administration Building, Hawthorne, NY 10532 (E-mail for Caroline Peacock: cpeacock@jbfcs.org; E-mail for George Daniels: gdaniels@jbfcs.org.)

[Haworth co-indexing entry note]: "Applying an Antiracist Framework to a Residential Treatment Center: Sanctuary®, a Model for Change." Peacock, Caroline and George Daniels. Co-published simultaneously in *Journal of Emotional Abuse* (The Haworth Maltreatment & Trauma Press, an imprint of The Haworth Press, Inc.) Vol. 6, No. 2/3, 2006, pp. 135-154; and: *Racism and Racial Identity: Reflections on Urban Practice in Mental Health and Social Services* (ed: Lisa V. Blitz, and Mary Pender Greene) The Haworth Maltreatment & Trauma Press, an imprint of The Haworth Press, Inc., 2006, pp. 135-154. Single or multiple copies of this article are available for a fee from The Haworth Document Delivery Service [1-800-HAWORTH, 9:00 a.m. - 5:00 p.m. (EST). E-mail address: docdelivery@haworthpress.com].

Available online at http://jea.haworthpress.com
© 2006 by The Haworth Press, Inc. All rights reserved.
doi:10.1300/J135v06n02_09

Nationwide, children of color are disproportionately represented in the child welfare and juvenile justice systems (Gibbs & Huang, 2003). They are more likely to be overrepresented in child maltreatment reports than White youths, based on general population estimates. African American children represent 28% of substantiated allegations of abuse or neglect, and they represent 41% of the child welfare population, despite being only 15% of the general U.S. population (Petit & Curtis, 1997). African American youths are more likely to be detained by police authorities than White youths. Youths of color are more likely to encounter the juvenile justice system because of living in neighborhoods with higher crime rates and harsher police practices (Petit & Curtis, 1997). White youths who commit crimes are more likely to receive probation than youths of color, who disproportionately receive out-of-home placements (Snyder & Sickmund, 1999), while White youth are given more opportunity to stay with their families. The National Mental Health Association (2004a) reports that African American youths between the ages of 10 and 17 make up 32% of delinquency referrals to juvenile court, 46% of juveniles committed to secure institutions, and 52% of juveniles transferred to adult criminal court.

Children in the juvenile justice system have higher rates of mental disorder than in the general population (National Mental Health Association, 2004b). Despite the high rates of mental disorder, children do not receive adequate mental health screening upon entrance to the juvenile justice system. Since youths of color are more likely than White youths to become involved in the juvenile justice system, they are also more likely to have their needs under-identified. Their access to adequate mental health screening is lacking, despite the prevalence of mental disorders.

Among the reasons why youth of color are more often involved in the juvenile justice system than White youths are racial profiling and racial bias in the system (Gibbs & Huang, 2003). White youths who commit crimes are more likely to be referred to mental health systems for treatment than to juvenile justice placements. The population in residential treatment centers (RTC) for youth mirrors the adult prison system in that nationwide, African Americans make up almost half the prison population, yet only 12% of the general population (National Association for the Advancement of Colored People, 2005).

INVISIBILITY SYNDROME: SEEKING TO BE SEEN

Children of color are often expected to live amicably in a racist system, in which their voices are not heard and their playful behavior is viewed as threatening or deviant. Franklin (2004) describes the conflict that African American families experience when balancing keeping their children safe and allowing them to be kids: "Our safety is connected to how and when we make ourselves visible, particularly outside of the community. It is such a powerful concern that when African American boys want to engage in normal, innocent risk-taking behavior–boys will do–they get caught in a protective net of community vigilance" (p. 80). His example refers to children who are still in their communities and not in the juvenile justice or child welfare systems. Parents attempt to protect their African American children from the unfair standards and expectations placed upon them by a racist society. Within a residential treatment setting, the children are either temporarily or permanently parentless. They have experienced such pervasive trauma that their ability to take guidance from caring adults is compromised. Without a thoughtful parent in the picture, a child may behave recklessly, without concern for consequences. This often translates into behavior that is seen as deviant: stealing, fighting, disrespecting adults, truancy, self-harm, and drug and alcohol abuse. All children, particularly adolescents, are looking to find a solid sense of self. They seek attention and validation in ways that may unfairly create more personal problems.

Children Living with Constant Racism

Franklin (2004; Franklin, Boyd-Franklin, & Kelly, this volume) discusses the signs and symptoms that African American boys and men display as a result of persistent micro-aggressions or racial slights. He lists the following: frustration, increased awareness of perceived slights, chronic indignation, pervasive discontent and disgruntlement, anger, immobilization or increasing inability to get things done, questioning one's worthiness, disillusionment and confusion, feeling trapped, conflicted racial identity, internalized rage, depression, substance abuse, and loss of hope. These signs and symptoms describe many of the children in residential treatment. Not surprisingly, these symptoms are also some common post-traumatic reactions. There is a link between racism and chronic stress, and the shared reactions they create.

Racism and Post-Traumatic Reactions

"The chronic, institutional stresses of poverty and racism are examples of social forces that can be termed traumatogenic in that they breed interpersonal traumatic acts" (Bloom & Reichart, 1997, p. 37). When people are under constant stress from multiple directions, interpersonal violence is an increasing threat. Additionally, a person living in an environment of constant violence and stress is less likely to develop interpersonal trust, thereby reducing the development of healthy attachments. Many children in residential treatment have difficulty forming healthy attachments with adults because of the stressful environments in which they were raised. This limits their ability to relate to others empathically and makes anti-social behavior more likely, leading to negative consequences. When a child has been traumatized in the past, her current functioning is impacted. Some common adolescent expressions of post-traumatic reactions are drug and alcohol abuse, self-harm, and aggressive and violent behavior. Children with these behaviors are easily considered as "bad" or "delinquent" by society.

Traumatic reminders may trigger reactions that seem confusing to those who do not know the child's trauma history. Existence of ongoing stress, such as institutional racism, can exacerbate a person's post-traumatic reactions. Therefore, it is essential to work from a lens based in trauma theory, which acknowledges forms of oppression, such as racism and poverty. The lens must also include methods by which oppression is not perpetuated. Effective intervention must acknowledge impact of trauma and recognize racism and poverty as potential sources of traumatic injury. Furthermore, residential treatment must not itself be a source of trauma, including the trauma of racism and oppression.

RACISM AND WHITE PRIVILEGE WITHIN CHILDREN'S RESIDENTIAL TREATMENT

Racism is race prejudice plus power. It is not about individual acts of meanness or prejudice, but refers to a systemic power arrangement which permeates every institution in American society (Chisom & Washington, 1997). Pinderhughes (1989) explains that the problem of racism is not caused by a single entity, but by the complex interlocking of policies and institutions that reinforce one another. She states, "Belief in superiority of Whites and the inferiority of people-of-color based on racial differences is legitimized by societal arrangements that exclude the latter from resources and power and then blame them for their failures, which are due to lack of access" (p. 89). This excerpt pointedly describes the situation of children and families held hostage by the child welfare and juvenile justice system. Although many White individuals within American society would not describe themselves as racist, they allow for the perpetuation of the "social arrangements" that hold captive millions of people of color in the adult and child judicial and welfare systems. But where is the justice and where is the welfare?

Abramovitz and Bloom (2003) describe the historical trends of treatment of youths in residential treatment settings. Post World War II, many treatment settings applied psychoanalytically-informed individual therapy, group therapy, and milieu therapy. The emphasis on psychoanalytic theory placed the blame of bad behavior on the child, rather than considering the external stressors, such as systemic racism and poverty. The emergence of social psychiatry of the 1960s and the creation of the PTSD diagnosis in the 1980s were efforts to consider external factors that may contribute to delinquent behavior. It is important for residential treatment programs to be aware of cultural and race bias embedded in psychological theories, which may be applied in individual psychotherapy, created by Whites in a White-dominant culture. In a milieu treatment setting, all modalities–individual, group, case management, advocacy, skills training, etc.–are considered equally important in healing.

Antiracist Framework

As discussed in Blitz and Illidge (this volume), working within an antiracist framework requires that all people, staff, and residents must have the opportunity to develop a healthy and well-integrated racial identity. Developing such an identity is extremely challenging for children of color in residential treatment when racism has so profoundly impacted their lives, and continues to impact them through their living in an environment in which people of color are lower paid with less access to training and education. In residential treatment, people of color may be more likely to hold lower-paying front-line jobs that do not require advanced formal education, as will be described below.

No RTC is exempt from the dynamics of institutional racism and unearned White privilege. One way of addressing the "systemic process of racism" (Pinderhughes, 1989, p. 90) is by looking at one institution in which racism and White privilege exist by virtue of being a part of the larger interlocking institutions described above. In order to work toward an antiracist system, it is necessary to define the areas in which racism and White privilege are present. Unless an organization is intentionally antiracist, everything it does will disproportionately benefit White people and disseminate racism.

In *Why Are All the Black Kids Sitting Together in the Cafeteria*, Tatum (1997) eloquently describes what it means to a passive participant in .racism:

> I sometimes visualize the ongoing cycle of racism as a moving walkway at the airport. Active racist behavior is equivalent to walking fast on the conveyor belt. The person engaged in active racist behavior has identified with the ideology of White supremacy and is moving with it. Passive racist behavior is equivalent to standing still on the walkway. No overt effort is being made, but the conveyor belt moves the bystanders along to the same destination as those who are actively walking. Some of the bystanders may feel the motion of the conveyor belt, see the active racist ahead of them, and choose to turn around, unwilling to go to the same destination as the White supremacists. But unless they are walking actively in the opposite direction at a speed faster than the conveyor belt–unless they are actively antiracist–they will find themselves carried along with the others. (pp. 11-12)

Walking or running in the opposite direction is necessary to work from an antiracist perspective. To some extent, all White people are beneficiaries of unearned White privilege, and all people of color are affected by racism. Some people may wonder why it is necessary to change the status quo if they are benefiting from the situation of White privilege. In reality, the entire society suffers from the oppression of people of color due to "the loss of human potential, lowered productivity, and a rising tide of fear and violence in our society" (Tatum, 1997, p. 200).

The following sections will provide a view of one RTC from an antiracist lens, highlighting the relationship between power, privilege, and race in that system. The analysis is in no way a critique of individuals, but rather a snapshot of a large system informed by the greater society, in which racism and White privilege are dominant.

A word about the authors: one author, George, is a Black heterosexual male director of the RTC, who has worked in residential treatment for 25 years. George has experienced the negative effects of interpersonal, institutional, and societal racism, and has been the beneficiary of male privilege. The other author, Caroline, is a White lesbian administrator for a trauma-based model of care on the campus and has been working in social service settings for six years. Caroline has been the recipient of unearned White privilege in educational, professional, and everyday situations. She has experienced the negative effects of inter-personal, institutional, and societal homophobia and heterosexism, which have made her more sensitive to social and institutional preju-dice. George and Caroline began discussions together about racism and White privilege when given the task of writing this article. George has been personally mindful of racism and White privilege for many more years than Caroline. Throughout the process of writing this article, new ideas have been developed while thinking about racism and White privilege on the campus.

THE FACILITY

In New York State, RTCs care for children referred by the child wel-fare and juvenile justice systems. Similar facilities exist throughout the United States, although they may have different names. This article will describe one such facility, located in the suburbs north of New York City. The residents, girls and boys, range in age from 10 to 18, and come mainly from the boroughs of New York City. The children are grouped by age and gender in cottages on a central campus. The initiating event for entering the child welfare or juvenile justice system can range from being the victim of abuse to being the perpetrator of petty or more seri-ous crimes. The children can either be removed from their home of ori-gin by child protective services, or their families can request removal based on difficulty in disciplining or managing the child.

Description of Staff

At the RTC, children receive a variety of forms of treatment: psycho-therapy (individual, group, and family therapy), milieu, recreational, and drug and alcohol treatment. The RTC is staffed by 161 employees, including milieu counselors, social workers, administrators, mainte-nance workers, nurses, and psychiatrists. The position of milieu coun-selor requires a high-school diploma, although many have some college credits or college degrees. Social workers are required to have a mas-ter's degree, and must have or be working toward state licensure. Ad-ministrators have a variety of educational backgrounds based on the discipline. Maintenance workers are required to have a high-school di-ploma or GED. Nurses are required to be licensed by the State, and psy-chiatrists must have a medical degree and be licensed in the State. At this RTC, 93% of milieu counselors are people of color and 7% are

White. Fifty-six percent of administrative staff members, including assistant unit directors, unit directors, and administrative supervisors, are people of color and 44% are White. Twenty-two percent of social workers are people of color and 78% are White.

Description of Clients

Children who have been involved in the child welfare system may have had numerous unsuccessful foster care placements (e.g., for having behaved in ways that the foster parents could not manage). Some who come to the RTC have been in as many as 11 different foster care placements. As their emotional distress and behavioral difficulties increased, they have been placed in an RTC, which is a more restrictive and highly supervised environment. Some children who have been placed at the RTC through the juvenile justice system have been given a "last chance" to straighten up before being remanded to a detention facility. The children in the RTC are often seen by court judges as "bad kids" because their behavior may include fighting, stealing, truancy, and other difficult-to-manage conduct. Many have parents who are themselves survivors of the child welfare and juvenile justice systems. Some have parents who are incarcerated or engaged in their own drug and alcohol treatment. The common denominator for the majority of the children in the program is traumatic exposure, usually of a pervasive and interpersonal nature.

The children in the RTC are predominately from families of color. Ninety-six percent of the children are people of color and 4% are White. Many come from impoverished neighborhoods, low or no-income households, in which access to adequate food, health care, shelter, and education is lacking. Most of the children are far below grade level in their education and many are illiterate.

Professional and Paraprofessional

The milieu counselors provide the essentials: supervision of residents, food, and rules for the living environment. They are the temporary parents of the children in this residential setting. The milieu counselors spend their time "on the unit" and are available to the residents at any time. Milieu counselors are always there: nights, weekends, and holidays. When there is one child left on the unit on Christmas day, a milieu counselor is there providing supervision, food, and care. For our setting, this means that the people who spend the most amount of time with the children are of the same race and sometimes ethnicity.

The social workers and psychiatrists provide therapy, case management services and psychotropic medication, when necessary. They have private offices in the clinic wing, where individual treatment sessions can take place with the child. The physical setting differentiates the type of treatment the child receives in the milieu as compared to in the clinic wing. The clinical treatment has traditionally been referred to as "professional," while the milieu treatment is called "paraprofessional." Referring to one discipline as "professional" and another as "paraprofessional" assumes that one position is less legitimate. On the contrary, the position of milieu counselor requires extreme patience, excellent people skills, crisis management knowledge, and flexibility, to name a few attributes. The system could not function without milieu counselors. They are very much "professional."

The clinic wing is often locked and only accessible by those who have a key, which does not include all of the milieu staff. The residents' case records are located in the clinic wing, and based on the previously mentioned fact regarding the locked door, are primarily accessible to clinical staff only, creating an inequity in accessibility to important treatment information. This is what Tatum (1997) refers to as "passive racism." The lack of access is not directly communicated as a racial issue, but because it primarily limits people of color from obtaining information that will assist in their work, it is a racial issue.

Behavior Management and Treatment

The clinicians are thought to be responsible for the *treatment* of the residents, while the milieu staff handles the *management* of the children. When a resident is "in crisis" the team of milieu counselors and clinicians works to calm her down. When she becomes a physical danger to herself or others, a therapeutic restraint is used as the last resort. If there is a crisis on the unit and the clinician is present, she has the option of retreating to the clinic wing. The milieu counselors are required to stay and *manage* the situation. Staff members of all disciplines are trained in the techniques of therapeutic restraints, but the clinicians rarely take part. The restraints are almost exclusively made by milieu staff; the clinician does not have to participate in the activity. McIntosh (1988) explains that Whites are regularly given the option of staying comfortable and confident, while people of color are made to take part in violence and hostility. In this situation, people of color are made to physically express dominance over children of color for the goal of safety.

Training and Education

From a baseline, there is a higher level of education among White employees than people of color. This mirrors the image of the general population, with higher-level positions being held by Whites and lower-level positions by people of color. Within our RTC, staff members of all disciplines receive training. Social work staff is required to complete 180 hours of in-service training to enhance their clinical skills. Milieu counselors attend a child-care "professionalization" institute, which reinforces that their position is not professional. Milieu counselors have to work overtime to attend training, as it is not built into the regular work schedule. Throughout the year, there are other training opportunities that are only made available to clinical staff, creating a distinction between what is referred to as "professional" and "paraprofessional" staff.

Child-Rearing Techniques

Child rearing techniques are an important aspect of milieu treatment because milieu counselors are in the role of parents on the unit. Boyd-Franklin (2003) explains that many African American families may choose physical discipline over other forms of discipline. She suggests that therapists might try to understand the "protective posture" of families who choose corporal punishment, meaning that it may be used as a way to protect children from future and possibly harsher punishment for "bad" behavior. Based on racial differences, the child-rearing techniques of the milieu counselors may differ from those of the clinical staff. Despite some of the cultural similarities between the children and the milieu counselors, the clinical approaches may be viewed as superior by the institution. As a result, there may be a cultural distinction between the approaches that milieu counselors and clinicians may have experienced or used in their own families. The authors are not arguing one case over another, but merely acknowledging the potential racial difference in approaching discipline. The National Mental Health Association (2003) has goals and principles for providing culturally-competent practice, which is one form of developing an antiracist framework. One principle is that major differences in worldviews may exist in cross-cultural relationships between providers and consumers. The difference in worldviews also exists between providers and providers. The National Mental Health Association recommends addressing and discussing these differences.

The Message the Children Receive

Children are keenly aware of the unspoken messages among the adults around them. They see the power dynamics among clinical and milieu staff. They know who the "professionals" are and who are not. They know who the gatekeepers to their discharge are: not the milieu counselors, but the social workers, supervisors, and administrators. Chestang (1972) describes the concept of "social inconsistency" as "the institutional disparity between word and deed. It is the social immorality perpetrated on the oppressed group by the manners, morals, and traditions of the majority group" (p. 42). At the RTC, as in most institutional settings, there is a social inconsistency in word and deed. We support the concepts of cultural competency and antiracist practice, and yet there are disparities in the application. In our setting, the children become active players in the institutional racism and White privilege that is maintained by the outside and inside systems.

OUR APPROACH: THE SANCTUARY®MODEL

Over the past six years, the RTC has been implementing Sanctuary®, the same model used in the domestic violence shelter discussed by Blitz and Illidge (this volume). Whereas Blitz and Illidge focus on discussing the use of Sanctuary® for antiracist staff development, we will focus its impact on clients. The process is supported through the agency's Center for Trauma Program Innovation (CTPI), whose mission is to enhance trauma-related services throughout the agency and community. This model was adopted in an effort to create a consistent method of working with traumatized children and to address the impact of chronic stress and trauma on the lives of clients, staff, and the system.

Sanctuary® is a trauma-based model that uses therapeutic community to create a safe environment in which people can heal from traumatic experiences. Sanctuary® was co-created by Sandra Bloom and colleagues in a short-term acute inpatient psychiatric setting. The book *Creating Sanctuary* (Bloom, 1997) describes the work over many years. Over the past two decades, Sanctuary® has been modified and implemented in a variety of settings to match the population, including this RTC. Although Sanctuary®

is not explicitly an antiracist model, it inherently addresses the effects of all forms of oppression through core anti-oppression and humanistic concepts. More than a product or a model of care, Sanctuary® is a process. The process of creating Sanctuary® includes the collective development of a shared vision. In the shared vision, multiple perspectives are honored through a flattening of the hierarchical structures and a commitment to democratic practices. Sanctuary® places an emphasis on open communication between and among different disciplines, creating an atmosphere in which the traditionally oppressed or devalued voice is heard and becomes an important part of the decision-making process. The Sanctuary® Model rests on a foundation of shared assumptions by which all staff approach working with the children and with each other. The shared assumptions were co-created by an original Sanctuary® team and have been slightly adapted to apply to the clients in the RTC. At the RTC, five main assumptions have been adopted as guidelines for creation of a safe and therapeutic community. All five assumptions implicitly address the impact of racism and offer a guideline by which to confront it.

SHARED ASSUMPTIONS

#1: Safety and Non-Violence Are the Cornerstones of a Sanctuary® Unit

"The first value to be established, goal to be set, and practice to be formulated is that of safety. Regardless of whether we are referring to an individual victim of violence, a small group, or an entire community, healing cannot advance unless there is an environment of safety for all community members" (Bloom, 1997, p. 228). Creating a safe environment is a tall order in residential treatment. The children, staff, and system need to feel physically, emotionally, socially, and morally safe in order for healing to take place. The concepts of safety and non-violence are taught to the staff and residents through the teachings of Rev. Martin Luther King, Jr. and Mahatma Gandhi. Role models who are people of color are essential applications of this assumption. On a systems and personal level, racism and White privilege are inherently unsafe for all parties. Although the White individual or system may prosper due to the unbalanced power structure, it is only committing violence against itself through the oppression of others.

One way that children and staff maintain personal and community safety is through use of Safety Plans. Every staff person and resident has a card on which she has identified five options for staying safe when feeling overwhelmed by feelings or difficult situations. The Safety Plans are designed to be used at any time, in any situation within the RTC community or while visiting family. Because it is a self-monitoring tool, the Safety Plan places the power of recovery in the hands of the child. While staff offer consultation and support, the child develops her own plan and owns her choices. Self-monitoring is inherently antiracist because the power is in the hands of the client.

#2: Children in Residential Treatment Are Not Sick or Bad, but Hurt and Injured

It is easy to attend to only the behavior of children who end up in residential treatment. If a child in this system were only defined by his behavior, it would be difficult to have empathy. The Sanctuary® Model requires and supports understanding the current behavior in relation to the trauma history. Here is a case example:

> Michael is refusing to stay in his room at night. He keeps his roommate awake, disturbs the milieu staff, and says that he is "not tired." Michael is frequently agitated in the mornings, and tends to fall asleep in school. After reviewing his trauma history, the staff understands that Michael's behavior is related to his history. He was removed from his family in the early morning, and his disruptive behavior around sleeping comes from his fear of the danger that morning can bring.

One way the assumption that children in residential treatment are not sick or bad, but hurt and injured is actualized is through the protocol for case conferences. Every conference begins with a review of the child's trauma history, followed by a discussion of the current behavior in relation to the history. In Michael's case, the team will link his current behavior with his trauma history. They understand his needs and can create a treatment plan that focuses on recovery from the trauma of removal. One possible intervention would be for an evening milieu counselor to reassure Michael before bed that in the morning a particular staff person will be there to wake him and be a support. This treatment plan addresses Michael's avoidance and hyperarousal symptoms in relation to his trauma history. It also engages milieu counselors in a critical part of treatment. They are providing treatment, rather than managing his behavior.

Another expression of this assumption is through the Sanctuary®
question: "What happened?" Whenever there is a crisis or a child is upset, staff begin by asking "What happened?" rather than, "What is
wrong with you?" or "What did you do wrong?" The approach of viewing the child through a trauma lens is not a free pass for bad behavior.
The child is still held responsible, but when the staff and child have an
understanding of the events that led to a negative occurrence, the path to
better decision-making is more accessible. With a societal predisposi-
tion of viewing youth of color as "bad," this concept of children as "hurt
and injured" provides a framework to look at each child individually
and to avoid racially-based assumptions.

#3: Leveling of Hierarchy

Leveling of hierarchy means that every individual in a system is
equally important. It does not mean that everyone is doing the same job,
but that each discipline works together to make the system function
properly. The metaphor that is presented to the children is that of a jazz
band, in which each player uses her instrument in collaboration with the
others to make beautiful music.

When the hierarchy within a system is leveled, the gatekeepers are di-
versified. Multiple perspectives are essential to the healthy functioning
of a system, and therefore the children receiving services may be given
more options. When individuals of traditionally lower-level positions
have a voice within the system, everyone benefits from the extended
and diverse experience base. The leveling of hierarchy requires a process of shared decision-making. This assumption is a core concept for
applying an antiracist framework. Here is a case example:

> John is a 15-year-old in a Sanctuary® unit at the RTC. He engages
> with his social worker in individual therapy, but remains some-
> what withdrawn in the milieu. When encouraged by his primary
> milieu counselor to participate in a group unit activity, John be-
> comes angry, is verbally aggressive with the counselor, and goes
> "out of place" (leaves the supervised area without permission).
> During a treatment conference, the team, consisting of milieu
> counselors, the unit director, social worker, and social work super-
> visor, is discussing John's progress in the program. The social
> worker is pleased with his progress and feels that John should be
> allowed to go home for the weekend. The primary milieu coun-
> selor disagrees, stating that John's action of going out-of-place au-

tomatically dismisses the possibility of a home visit for that weekend. Applying the leveling of hierarchy assumption, the team acknowledges and respects the milieu counselor's suggestion. These alternate perspectives are both honored in a team with leveled hierarchy, leading to a process of consensus building to reach a decision regarding the home visit.

This example is very common; differences of opinion in treatment planning are bound to occur, but a level hierarchy allows open, honest communication and a healthy working environment. When shared decision-making takes place, people of color have a voice in the traditionally White-dominated system. This concept is also applied to the residents. During daily community meetings, children have the opportunity to discuss community issues and to make shared decisions about key elements of their daily living. Sometimes the decisions may revolve around seemingly simple topics, such as group trips and snacks, and sometimes more complex topics, such as cottage rules and privileges. The basic process of consensus building is empowering to the group and to each member.

Shared decision-making through the leveling of hierarchy is inherently antiracist because the power is in the hands of the community members. Pinderhughes (1989) refers to this process as "power sharing." She explains that when individuals or groups share power, the power is experienced differently. "Power will be experienced not as a consequence of dominance, but as freedom from it. There is freedom from the entrapment embedded in the dominant position, from the sense of conflict, the fear and the stress, the rigidity, and need for sameness" (p. 142). When power is shared, the wealth of perspectives is an asset. In *Cultural Competence in Serving Children and Adolescents with Mental Health Problems*, SAMHSA (1996) suggests allowing the community to determine direction and goals of treatment in culturally competent practice. Although they are not referring to a community, such as a group of children and staff in a residential treatment setting, the recommendation is nevertheless important.

#4: The Team Is the Treatment

In a Sanctuary® unit, every person has something to contribute and every person's opinion counts. In a therapeutic community, the whole community provides the treatment, not just one individual who has a private office or a particular educational degree. Traditionally, the treatment was expected to take place in the therapist's office for 45 minutes a week. The child would attend therapy and then return to a chaotic and unsafe environment. Sanctuary® shifts the concept of where treatment takes place: it happens primarily in the milieu. The children, milieu counselors, clinicians, and administrators are all therapeutic agents. When a child has a problem in the milieu, she is encouraged to discuss it with her primary milieu counselor. When there is a community issue, there will be a group discussion and processing to resolve it. Children and staff have the option of "calling" an impromptu group meeting to address any community issues that are pressing. SAMHSA recommends that to achieve culturally competent work, the community should determine direction and goals. Sanctuary® does exactly this.

Community Meetings are a central component to the actualization of Sanctuary®. At the RTC, all members of the community, or "cottage," meet twice a day. One resident functions as the leader for the meeting. The children and staff are asked the following questions by the leader: "How are you feeling?" "What is your goal for today?" and "Who will you ask for help?" At the end of the day, the morning goal is followed up, and there is a time to discuss and process community issues. These questions are based in trauma theory and create a therapeutic community. "How are you feeling?" develops the ability to label affect, a common difficulty for people who have been traumatized. "What is your goal?" helps individuals to see how their actions now can impact the near or far future. "Who will you ask for help?" helps to rebuild healthy attachments or create them for the first time.

All staff members participate in the Community Meeting. Everyone sits in the same circle, and the hierarchy is leveled. Every individual in the meeting is held to the same standard. All staff members are active agents for treatment in Community Meetings and in the general therapeutic milieu. They are able to encourage children with goals, offer their help, and model affect management. When the children see the collaboration between different disciplines, they realize the power paradigm can change from what is known on the outside.

Using the whole team as the treatment is inherently antiracist in nature because it honors the multiple perspectives that different individuals may bring to the work. Having the team as the treatment requires that the individual members of a team work collaboratively so that it is not confusing for the child. When this assumption is actualized and all members are providing treatment, but not in collaboration, it can be very disruptive to the child. However, when individuals do collaborate, healing can occur. This is the same concept as "It takes a village to raise a child." When a resident knows that the milieu counselors, who are likely of the same race and ethnicity as she is, are respected and honored as essential members of the system, it provides a stronger sense of self in relation to the child's own race and ethnicity.

#5: Everyone Can Get Better, Even if Only a Little Bit

Without hope, a dream cannot be actualized. For many of these children, there is little or no internal or external hope. Sanctuary® provides a hope that all people can recover, if only a little bit, from the experiences of chronic trauma. This assumption is also based on the concept of resiliency. For example, a child comes from an impoverished neighborhood, experienced chronic physical and emotional abuse, lost a parent to incarceration, survived 11 foster care placements, and still is able to wake up each morning and go to school–*that* is resiliency.

S.E.L.F.-Based Recovery

The Sanctuary® Model is organized around a recovery framework called S.E.L.F. (Safety, Emotional Management, Loss, and Future). The residents are responsible for their own recovery by working on these areas with the treatment team and the community. All staff members are trained in the concepts of S.E.L.F., and the framework is worked into every aspect of treatment. Here are a few examples of how S.E.L.F. is integrated into treatment:

Safety is addressed through creation of Safety Plans. Staff members frequently set daily community meeting goals related to safety, such as "My goal is to keep the community safe this evening." *Emotional Management* is self-monitored through use of Safety Plans. Education around emotional management is ongoing, such as in daily Community Meetings when children answer the question, "How are you feeling?" *Loss* is addressed through Loss and Bereavement groups for children who have suffered the death of a primary caregiver. Milieu counselors also discuss issues of loss, such as children leaving home, losing friends, etc., with the children individually and in groups. A form of loss is recognized as a natural result of trauma. *Future* is a constant topic during daily Community Meeting goal-setting, independent living groups, and the motivational speaker series.

S.E.L.F. also applies to the staff and the system and provides a means to recognize and work against racism. Staff members talk with each other regularly to promote safety among themselves. If the RTC perpetuates racism, children and staff cannot feel safe alone or in relation to one another. If there is not enough safety to address racially-based inequality, a milieu counselor cannot feel that her opinion really matters. Emotional management is sometimes referred to as "managing your stuff" with the residents. The organization also has to "manage its stuff," meaning that when issues of racism and other forms of oppression arise, they have to be acknowledged and dealt with. Milieu counselors and social workers teach the children to talk about things that bother them, thereby creating an environment in which unsettling feelings can be aired. This process must be applied to the staff as well. Loss is keenly felt in social service and mental health-care settings, as funding is frequently cut and there is regular turnover of staff. Issues of loss, whether personal or institutional, create a stressful environment. Processing on a micro or macro level is an essential part of recovery. In order to stay hopeful in a stressed system, there has to be a shared vision for the future. The organization, and the people within it, need to discuss with each other what the shared vision is, so that members of the system can support and reinforce each other.

Through its application to the individual and to the organization, S.E.L.F. provides a self-monitoring and therefore antiracist framework for recovery. The power for change is within each individual and the system, and not determined by an outside force.

A LONG WAY TO GO

The RTC described in this article is at the beginning stages of a culture change initiated by the Sanctuary® Model and facilitated by a commitment to antiracist practice. The RTC continues to diversify its staff, as is demonstrated by the administrative position demographics of 56% people of color and 44% White individuals. All clinical and milieu staff are required to complete training on issues of race, ethnicity, class, and cultural competence. The RTC proudly incorporates a motivational speaker program that honors people of color as role models for the residents. Residents will soon be starting a social justice organizing group so that they can make change in the systems that have oppressed them.

Culture change is continuous and has no tangible ending or product. Some beginning tangible changes have occurred through the implementation of model, such as Safety Plans, Community Meetings, and psychoeducational modules. Application of Sanctuary® shared assumptions provides an opportunity to self-monitor the ways that racism and other forms of oppression play a role in our system. Many of the treatment teams, consisting of clinical and milieu staff, successfully work together in a non-hierarchical and team approach. The benefits are incredible for the team members, and most importantly, for the residents. Sanctuary® provides us with a framework for openly and honestly discussing racism, White privilege, and other forms of oppression, but we must be vigilant. We can easily fall into the trap of saying we honor Sanctuary® values, while not *practicing* in a Sanctuary® way. The work is hard, especially as it requires each of us to look at the ways that racism and/or White privilege have played a role in our lives, and continue to impact our work relationships and the treatment of the children inside a larger racist system and society. We must consciously turn around on the conveyor belt that Tatum (1997) describes and head in the opposite direction.

REFERENCES

Abramovitz, R., & Bloom, S. (2003). Creating sanctuary in residential treatment for youth: From the "well-ordered asylum" to a "living-learning environment." *Psychiatric Quarterly, 74,* 119-135.

Blitz, L. V., & Illidge, L. C. (2006). Not so black and white: Shades of gray and brown in antiracist multicultural team building in a domestic violence shelter. *Journal of Emotional Abuse, 6*(2/3), 113-134.

Bloom, S. (1997). *Creating sanctuary.* New York: Routledge.

Bloom, S., & Reichart, M. (1998). *Bearing witness.* Binghamton, NY: The Haworth Press, Inc.

Boyd-Franklin, N. (2003). *Black families in therapy* (2nd ed.). New York: The Guildford Press.

Chestang, L. W. (1972). Character development in a hostile environment. *Readings in Human Growth and Development,* 40-50.

Chisom, R., & Washington, M. (1997). *Undoing racism: A philosophy of international social change.* New Orleans: The People's Institute Press.

Franklin, A. J. (2004). *From brotherhood to manhood.* Hoboken, NJ: John Wiley & Sons.

Franklin, A. J., Boyd-Franklin, N., & Kelly, S. (2006). Racism and invisibility: Race-related stress, emotional abuse and psychological trauma for people of color. *Journal of Emotional Abuse, 6*(2/3), 9-30.

Gibbs, J., & Huang, L. (2003). *Children of color.* San Francisco: Jossey-Bass.

McIntosh, P. (1988). *White privilege and male privilege: A personal account of coming to see the correspondences through work in women's studies.* Wellesley, MA: Center for Research on Women.

National Association for the Advancement of Colored People (2005). *Prison project: A historical overview.* Available from, http://www.naacp.org/programs/prison/prison_index.html

National Mental Health Association (2003). *Cultural competency in mental health systems.* Retrieved December 15, 2004 from, http://www.nmha.org/position/ps38.cfm

National Mental Health Association (2004a). *Mental health treatment in the juvenile justice system: A compendium of promising practices*, p. 1, 11-12.

National Mental Health Association. (2004b). *Prevalence of mental disorders among children in the juvenile justice system.* Retrieved December 15, 2004 from, http://www. nmha.org/children/justjub/prevalence.cfm

Petit, M. R., & Curtis, A. A. (1997). *Child abuse and neglect: A look at the States.* Washington, DC: CWLA Press.

Pinderhughes, E. (1989). *Understanding race, ethnicity and power.* New York: The Free Press.

SAMHSA (1996). *Cultural competence in serving children and adolescents with mental health problems* (CA-0015). Retrieved December 15, 2004, from http://www.mental health.org/publications/allpubs/CA-0015/default.asp

Snyder, H., & Sickmund, M. (1999). *Juvenile offenders and victims: 1999 national report.* Washington, DC: Office of Juvenile Justice and Delinquency Prevention.

Tatum B. D. (1997). *Why are all the Black kids sitting together in the cafeteria?* New York: Basic Books.

doi:10.1300/J135v06n02_09

SECTION IV
RACIAL IDENTITY IN TREATMENT

Coming Together and Falling Apart:
Looking at Relationship

Libbe H. Madsen

SUMMARY. Race was an essential element in how this couple both came together and fell apart, and offers a useful lens to understand the partners and their connection. Their relationship began with pride in their shared African ancestry, and hit bottom with the threat of violence in the presence of their four-year-old daughter. Their racial identity was a source of strength for each of them, yet the effects of racism stressed them and their relationship and contributed to their undoing as a couple. The case is written by the woman's therapist, who draws upon relevant clinical and cultural literature and incorporates her increasing sensitivity

Address correspondence to: Libbe Madsen, JBFCS, 120 West 57th Street, New York, NY 10019 (E-mail: libbem@gmail.com).

The author would like to acknowledge Helaria for providing an invaluable opportunity for professional and personal growth.

[Haworth co-indexing entry note]: "Coming Together and Falling Apart: Looking at Relationship." Madsen, Libbe H. Co-published simultaneously in *Journal of Emotional Abuse* (The Haworth Maltreatment & Trauma Press, an imprint of The Haworth Press, Inc.) Vol. 6, No. 2/3, 2006, pp. 155-172; and: *Racism and Racial Identity: Reflections on Urban Practice in Mental Health and Social Services* (ed: Lisa V. Blitz, and Mary Pender Greene) The Haworth Maltreatment & Trauma Press, an imprint of The Haworth Press, Inc., 2006, pp. 155-172. Single or multiple copies of this article are available for a fee from The Haworth Document Delivery Service [1-800-HAWORTH, 9:00 a.m. - 5:00 p.m. (EST). E-mail address: docdelivery@haworthpress.com].

to how racial issues affect relationships between women and men, and between client and therapist. doi:10.1300/J135v06n02_10 *[Article copies available for a fee from The Haworth Document Delivery Service: 1-800-HAWORTH. E-mail address: <docdelivery@haworthpress.com> Website: <http:// www.HaworthPress.com> © 2006 by The Haworth Press, Inc. All rights reserved.]*

KEYWORDS. Racism, racial identity, partner abuse, race in psychotherapy

Many factors shape people's lives and many frames can be used to understand individuals and couples. This article uses the lens of race to examine a couple's relationship because race was an essential element in how these two people came together and fell apart. Helaria and Malik[1] met while studying their African heritage, and pride in being black was an essential source of attraction between them. Appreciating their history as black people helped them understand some of the prejudices and insults they experienced. As the challenges of becoming a family accumulated and were compounded by their ongoing exposure to racism, each was stressed in ways that caused injury and disappointment within the relationship. When their conflicts escalated to emotional abuse and near-violence in the presence of their four-year-old daughter and the relationship fell apart, the separation process was also affected by issues of race and racism.

This article looks at their relationship from the perspective of the therapist who was treating the woman in individual therapy before, during, and after the couple's time together. My increasing understanding of racial issues over the course of the treatment is included to show how this growing awareness affected the work. (For similar discussions, see Chapman, this volume; Kohl, this volume; and McGann, this volume.) From the beginning, I was prepared to look for the sources of strength and vulnerability in Helaria's and Malik's individual histories, to explore their early development and their family relationships. As I became more sensitized to issues of race and racism, it became increasingly clear that being black has always presented additional variables for them. Their lives have been shaped by their own experiences of racism and also by the history of black people in America. The impact of that history continues, through the intergenerational transmission of unhealed injuries and unmourned losses that are the emotional legacy of their ancestors' forced passage from Africa (Richardson & Wade, 1999).

THE PEOPLE

Helaria is an attractive dark-skinned woman, tall and muscular, with hair in locks held gracefully from her face. Her appearance supports her statement that she is proud to be black. She is introspective and thoughtful, speaks softly and concisely, and conveys a quiet strength. In addition to meditation, prayer, and yoga, she has been a long-distance runner. She works as a nanny for an upper-middle-class white Jewish family with two daughters. They sponsored her immigration process, helped her achieve some financial security, and include her warmly in holiday celebrations.

I have never met Malik. By Helaria's description, corroborated by a photograph, he also is attractive, tall, and dark, with very long and striking dreadlocks. As a young adult, he changed his first and last names to reflect his African heritage. He appears serious and intense, relates to the world more politically than spiritually, and is very alert to expressions of racism. When they met, Malik said he was working on a master's degree and had a job in a lab on campus.

I am a middle-aged, middle-class, white Jewish woman. I am a social worker who has worked in public agencies and private practice in New York City for almost 30 years. I am small, not athletic, and comfortably verbal. Like Helaria, I am emotionally reserved, and this similarity was an essential element in our early positive connection.

THE THERAPEUTIC FRAME

Presenting Problem

Helaria's employer referred her to me because she was depressed following an exploitive relationship. She engaged readily, saying she was "confused about the whole thing with men." She felt nervous meeting new people, in fact had limited practice talking to people at all because in her grandmother's home children did not speak to adults. Helaria was very reserved, careful, inclined to deal with conflict by withdrawing. She was aware others saw her as cool, aloof, and judgmental, while she felt self-conscious and unable to assert herself.

Trauma Recovery, Feminist Attunement, and Multiculturalism

From our first session, I offered support to Helaria in response to her presentation of depression and injury. As I was attuned to issues of feminism in psychotherapy, I sought to use our relationship to help Helaria develop her sense of self, do her own thinking, and find her own voice (Miller & Stiver, 1998). My stance was to offer observations for her consideration as part of an interactional dialogue, explicitly stating that "here is one way of looking at . . ." and "how would it be to think of it this way?" As stories emerged of physical and sexual abuse by family members, this stance was even more essential, as a central focus of treatment of abuse survivors is to honor the personal agency of the client (Herman, 1992). Each of these perspectives was congruent with my professional education, which included learning culturally-competent practice and also some background about diverse racial and ethnic groups. Beyond this training, the personal values that led me to social work were grounded in respecting and honoring differences.

Antiracist Framework

As I began to learn more about white racial identity and white privilege (Tatum, 1997), the work shifted. An antiracist perspective increased my awareness of the potential effects of racism on Helaria and Malik and on my relationship with Helaria. We had discussed her home, her interest in her African ancestry, her experience as a black person in New York, but we had not spoken of how it was for her to talk with me, a white Jewish therapist. My decision not to address this issue was supported by my sense that there was mutual respect and comfort within our relationship, and our later discussions have confirmed that this was so. Nevertheless, I came to view my stance as an expression of privilege, an assumption that my racial and cultural identity was simply "normal" or expected, and need not be addressed. For example, I had not considered how the fact that my role as therapist and Helaria's role as client might echo many other situations in which the white person is the leader and the black person is expected to be the responder. I gradually recognized the importance of naming this dynamic in our work together.

Relational Approach

While the antiracist perspective came to inform my questions, the relational approach in psychotherapy (Mitchell, 1988) provided the theoretical frame. The relational approach underscores the value of the therapist's acknowledging herself as a participant in the therapeutic relationship, which includes addressing racial and cultural differences.

When I did speak directly of these issues, our communication became more open. For example, when Helaria told me of her father's family's anger at white people, I sensed her caution with me as a white therapist. As I conveyed my receptivity to her feelings and experience, Helaria expressed them more. In addition, she spoke more openly about the emotional abuse in her relationship with Malik, as if letting down her guard in protecting me from her family's feelings about white people also created a freedom to talk openly about a negative aspect of her relationship with a black man.

BACKGROUND OF EACH PARTNER

Helaria

Helaria was born in Grenada, which she described with great affection. Although she occasionally referred to specific facts about its history and politics, I learned much more when I specifically asked. As Dyche and Zayas (1995) note, the therapist's attitude of naiveté helps her to limit assumptions and develop real curiosity about the client's life. Hargrove (this volume) and Hine-St. Hilaire (this volume) similarly discuss the importance of knowing about the client's culture and the history of her country of origin. I wanted to know what Helaria thought was important and why, and learned that she focused on instances of independence and strength. She was especially interested in the nearly bloodless coup in 1979 that made Maurice Bishop prime minister. Helaria was very impressed with Bishop, whom she met when she was 12, because he valued self-sufficiency and became personally involved in helping communities work together to improve their living conditions. When we later revisited this story, Helaria recalled that my interest in her praise of Bishop was an important step in our growing therapeutic alliance.

The population of Grenada, including people in positions of power and authority, is almost entirely black, which Helaria believes explains why she did not consider racism a central issue for her. A sociopolitical analysis of racism, however, includes the understanding that people of color can internalize racism and enact its dynamic within a society or within a family. Helaria stated that despite a mostly black population in her country, lighter skin is often valued over darker. Internalized racial oppression (Boyd-Franklin & Franklin, 1998), in which attitudes of white culture regarding skin color intrude into black society in subtle

and potentially destructive ways, can linger long after the obvious dominance of the white culture has ceased. An awareness of this was important to our therapeutic work. Similar to my use of a feminist perspective
to help Helaria find her voice, an antiracist frame led me to consider her
racial identity and help her transform the effects of internalized racism
into a well-integrated pride.

Helaria grew up with her maternal grandparents and their large extended family because both her parents left for New York to seek economic opportunity when she was very young. Helaria's grandfather was
gentle and playful with the children. He was the one man Helaria always
admired, although when drinking he was angry and critical of his wife.
Her grandmother relied on a rigid interpretation of the Bible to "keep everyone in place," according to Helaria. Grandmother's family, however,
had practiced the African spiritual tradition of Obiya, which many people
mistrusted and called "bad," but which fascinated Helaria. Grandmother's righteousness left Helaria vulnerable to guilt and shame, and
ill-prepared for relationships.

Helaria's father's family was less religious, less frightening, more
politically aware and interested. She once accompanied them to Carni-
val, where black people dressed in scary costumes, played music, and
made noise. Maternal grandmother punished her harshly for participating in this "devil activity," while her father's family viewed it as a symbolic re-enactment of the end of slavery that showed white people as
bad and celebrated black people's power to throw off white rulers.

Helaria now says of her adolescence, "my strength was buried." At
twenty-one, to escape maternal grandmother's strict limits, Helaria left
Grenada for New York. She began her current job and established friendly
contact with her family here. She ran and practiced yoga, earned a GED
and took courses at the local community college. She had some close girlfriends and dated a little, mostly proper Christian men like those she had
known at home. Although she missed having a religious practice, she was
wary of her grandmother's strict fundamentalism and sought something
more personal and spiritual.

Malik

I have never spoken with Malik and know him only through Helaria.
He was born in the Virgin Islands and loved it there, told Helaria of
swimming from one island to another and eating mangoes off the trees.
His parents lived together during his early childhood but his father was
also involved with many other women and had many other children.

When his mother, like Helaria's parents, moved to New York, his maternal grandmother raised him and his siblings. Malik was very attached to this grandmother, who was warm and gentle and taught him a lot, including about his African heritage.

He felt his life changed dramatically for the worse when, as a young teenager, his mother brought the children to New York to live with her and her new husband and their new children. Mother catered to this man, allowing him to control choices in music and television and, more importantly, refusing to address his sexual behavior with Malik's sister. His mother's indulgence of her husband, his stepfather's exploitation of this sister, and his father's involvement with other women must have been important unspoken messages to Malik about relationships between men and women, and also between parents and children. His mother is a traditional and religious person who sent him to Catholic schools in the Virgin Islands and resented his changing his names from those she had given him to African ones. Malik told Helaria he felt unseen and unimportant in his family.

FINDING EACH OTHER

Helaria was 33 and Malik was 45 when they met. They were among a group of people who came together to learn about their African heritage and to celebrate traditions that honored their ancestors. As her knowledge of history increased, Helaria began to think of people in her family who had emotional disturbances as coping with unhealed effects of the trauma of slavery. She began to develop a sense of self that was placed in historical context, formed in the juxtaposition of slavery and triumph, racism and racial pride.

Malik had been active in a movement that provided support to people in Africa, and was knowledgeable about the journey of black people in America. Helaria was attracted to his pride at being African, his hair in dreadlocks, his clothing often of African fabrics. She was excited to learn more about her heritage as a black woman, and to learn it from him. His perspective echoed that of her father's family, which certainly reinforced his appeal. Besides her being a warm and attractive woman, Helaria's enthusiasm for her African identity was part of her appeal for Malik. She was very attentive and interested in him, as he was exposing her to a world she wanted to know. They dated intensely, and Helaria felt excited and free. From the beginning, she also expressed some reservations about how honest Malik was about his life and about how much togetherness and privacy they each wanted and needed. Despite these concerns, she saw Malik as a strong person who also appreciated her strengths.

Helaria fits the picture Romero (2000) refers to as a Strong Black Woman who looks invulnerable and in control, strong and resilient even in the face of the multiple stresses of loss, trauma, racism, and sexism. Loss of control is seen as failure and a source of shame. Presenting herself in this way felt natural to Helaria; she had been raised to fit this picture and was in fact quite competent and liked to look and feel "together." This personal style was likely also in part an effect of the traumatic experiences in her life, as numbing and avoidance are typical long-term consequences of abuse (Herman, 1992).

In addition to emotional containment, the primary responsibility of the Strong Black Woman is as caregiver who nurtures and preserves the family (Romero, 2000). This task can cause her to overlook a man who is kind and attentive to her emotional needs, and instead respond to a man who needs her nurturing. Helaria exemplified this pattern, having been raised to keep house rather than attend school, to hide her feelings, and to keep to herself. She had learned little about relationships with men, about what might be more and less desirable qualities in a partner. She was smart but very naïve, and care giving was a reliable way of relating.

Although Malik gave Helaria an initial impression of strength, he had vulnerabilities of his own. He was drawn to her competence as a good caretaker and good problem-solver, perhaps to compensate for being ignored and disregarded by his mother when he came to New York. The "invisibility syndrome" (Franklin & Boyd-Franklin, 2000) experienced by many black men in America is probably another factor in Malik's feeling of being overlooked. Many black men, especially if they appear powerful, find that white people feel uncomfortable in their presence. In an effort to manage this discomfort, white people treat black men as if they are invisible in order to avoid having to deal with them. Black men experience this as "micro-aggressions" (Pierce, 1988), such as being ignored, disregarded, or assumed to be of lower status, which results in injury, disappointment, and anger. Having felt unseen in his family, Malik was particularly sensitive to invisibility and responded by asserting his visibility, in appearance through his hair and clothing, and in attitude through his pride and assertiveness, a stance that was attractive to Helaria.

BECOMING A FAMILY

Before either of them was ready, before they even lived together, Helaria became pregnant. She was acutely aware that she and Malik did not know each other well, and had not found ways of dealing with their differences. She also felt morally opposed to abortion, and was eager for a child. Malik was supportive, accompanied her to doctor visits, and looked forward to the baby, a girl they named Ladi. At the same time, the transition was difficult. Becoming parents is demanding for most couples, who often struggle with issues of power and power imbalance in relation to roles, money, time, privacy, and sexual satisfaction (Carter, 1999). While many cope by relying on traditional gender roles, this is difficult when the wife's income is higher or steadier. Black women are typically more readily received in the work world than black men (Boyd-Franklin & Franklin, 1998), especially in the traditional role of care giver, which does not challenge existing power arrangements. The discrepancy in their earnings can lead to tension and arguments between partners. This pattern clearly affected Helaria's and Malik's access to employment and led to the expected conflicts. Helaria assumed the role of primary breadwinner. Although she liked her job and her employers accommodated her new needs for flexibility, she resented having to return to work soon after the baby was born.

Malik's job-seeking was complicated by the fact that the appearance of strength and confidence in black men can evoke avoidance rather than acceptance (Franklin & Boyd-Franklin, 2000; also Franklin, Boyd-Franklin, & Kelly, this volume), an aspect of invisibility. As Pager (2003) suggests, employers' assessment of applicants of color may be distorted by unconscious biases. When a black man is seen as successful and smart, his race is often ignored and unseen; recognition of his competence comes at the expense of his ethnicity (Franklin, 1999). Securing and keeping a job requires that black men use interpersonal skills related to accommodating and not appearing too aggressive. Malik does not accommodate. While some black men save their anger from the workplace and express it at home (Almeida, Woods, Messineo, Font, & Heer, 1994), Malik expressed his immediately when and where he felt insulted. He has enough knowledge and experience to enter work situations that offer status, good income, and success, but his stance had complicated his previous job, which led him to charge bias and expend considerable time and energy on legal action. Asserting his visibility now made it hard for him to get past an initial interview.

Helaria understood the racial factors that complicated Malik's job search, and empathized with his frustration and anger at how the status quo affects black men. But over time, her feelings became more complicated. As Hines (1999) notes, because they recognize the special oppression of black men, black women are reluctant to add to their burden.

Rather than making their own demands, black women often find themselves carrying a heavier load in the family. Helaria was doing most of
the work, earning most of the money. Her fatigue grew as Malik spent
time and money suing his former employer rather than pursuing a new
job. His failure to contribute financially to his family and his continuing
dependence on Helaria probably degraded his self-esteem, and he
vented his frustration at home by blaming and demeaning Helaria.

For Helaria, the explanation of racism was no longer enough. From
her West Indian perspective, Malik's willingness to depend on her
rather than to compromise and get a job of any kind showed a stiff-
necked kind of pride she found shameful and unmasculine. She wondered how much he was standing on principle, how much he was ex-
ploiting her, and how much he was psychologically incapable of
flexibility. She was disappointed and angry, and her respect for him de-
clined. The assaults of racism and the partners' efforts to manage their
effects were contaminating their relationship.

DEALING WITH CONFLICT

At the beginning of their relationship, Helaria felt safe to express her
anger and sadness about the injuries racism had caused her family, and
understood and validated Malik's similar pain. Like many new couples,
however, their lack of skills for dealing with differences left them hurt
and frustrated. As the pressures of baby and job increased, Helaria was
inclined to suffer in silence. Malik found her emotionally distant and
felt the aloofness she had initially described to me. Their intimacy de-
clined. When she attended to the baby Ladi, he felt ignored, as he had by
his mother. He accused Helaria of being more devoted to the white children she was caring for than to himself and his daughter, and criticized
her disloyalty to their family and their race. He went from complaint to
attack, calling Helaria a typical black woman who emasculates her
black man, blaming her for his difficulties making a living. When she
permitted herself to acknowledge it, this felt painful and emotionally
abusive.

Because black men experience greater threats to their physical safety
outside the home, they are socialized differently from black women
(Boyd-Franklin, 2003). As the Franklins note, black parents today pay
particular attention to preparing their sons to live in a racist society
(Boyd-Franklin, Franklin, with Touissant, 2001). This fits with the view
within black culture that black families raise their daughters and love

their sons (Boyd-Franklin, 2003). The additional concern shown to sons may lay the foundation for later inequality in relationships between black men and women, as men expect more care while women expect more responsibility.

Helaria struggled to balance her sympathy for Malik's position with her own desire to be treated fairly and with respect. A black woman who feels the outside world is mistreating her man may have difficulty holding on to her own right to feel upset and angry at him for mistreating her (Mahmoud, 1998). This is part of the additional burden for women of color in abusive relationships (Geller, Miller, & Churchill, this volume). And yet, recognizing the impact of racism does not excuse abusive behavior within a relationship (Almeida & Durkin, 1999). Both racism and sexism must be addressed and challenged, and men of color must be accountable for how they treat their partners (Boyd-Franklin, 2003). Over time, Helaria came to feel that Malik used his political sophistication, blaming the racism of others to exploit her.

Jenkins (2000) notes that when the black woman's life changes in ways that distance her from her black family, she may keep those changes private. While Helaria was making an effort to speak up to Malik about their conflicts, her relationship with me may have contributed to distance and disconnection from Malik. He was somewhat taunting about the little he knew of me, saying obviously Helaria was the crazy one since she saw a therapist. His mistrust of the therapy had some validity, as I was supporting the voice that challenged him, bolstering her confidence with empathy for her pain.

Malik also kept much of himself private. Now more skeptical of him, Helaria discovered various inaccuracies: he was older than he said, he was not a graduate student, and he was active in his estrangement from his first daughter. When she viewed his lies and distortions as efforts to seduce and control her, she identified them as the beginning of his emotionally abusive behavior.

From the perspective of individual psychology, Malik's misrepresentations seem to be self-protective responses to threats to his self-esteem that convey a somewhat paranoid vigilance. From an antiracist perspective, however, his statements may be seen as efforts to resist the perceptions and assumptions about a black man in a racist society as he confronts the challenges of invisibility. Newhill (1990) suggests that because of the pervasiveness of racism in the United States, especially for young black males, behaviors that might be considered symptoms of paranoia are more accurately seen as adaptive coping. For example, the suspiciousness and lack of trust that characterize paranoia might be appropriate wariness about how information could be used by people in authority. The paranoid fear of loss of autonomy might be an accurate response to the experience of powerlessness. Under conditions of racism, caution about self-disclosure and vigilance about being controlled may well be signs of good reality testing.

While Helaria tried to understand Malik, however, she could not find a way to talk with him about her own struggles. As Romero suggests (2000), the Strong Black Woman is cautious about showing feelings. Meanwhile, Malik avoided communicating his needs or acknowledging when he had hurt Helaria. To survive in the world, black men are socialized to present themselves as tough and invulnerable, while expressing feelings is seen as weakness (Boyd-Franklin, 2003). Both partners felt isolated and lonely. Instead of joining, they fought both silently and verbally. Their life as a family was burdened by disappointment, distance, and competition with white people. The injuries each experienced in a racist society, initially a source of connection and refuge, compounded their frustrations with one another.

FALLING APART

Malik's behavior became increasingly controlling and furtive. He went through Helaria's pockets looking for money and for information about other men he believed she was seeing. He explained that since they were still in a relationship he had the right to go to any lengths to know what she was doing. Meanwhile he was staying out late and apparently seeing other women, who occasionally called him at home. As she realized he was lying to her, stealing from her, and sneaking out with other women, Helaria began to disengage emotionally and look for a way to separate. When another apartment became available, she seized the opportunity.

Once she had moved, Helaria saw how she had displaced herself in the service of the relationship. To help her regain her grounding, she and I looked for ways to draw on the spiritual presence of African ancestors as an aid to survival (West, 1999) in addition to her yoga and meditation practice. We spoke of family members who would wish her success and be proud of her efforts. She began to attend church, feeling freer to appreciate and draw on grandmother's religious faith and steadfastness as a model.

Malik came to the new apartment regularly to visit Helaria and Ladi, and gradually began to stay until he was again living with them. Helaria tried to set limits but was inconsistent, a common pattern in emotionally abusive relationships (Geller, 1992). Frustrated, she tried to think of other people Malik might listen to and found she knew very little of the people in his life. We considered an intervention based on the Cultural Context Model (Almeida & Durkin, 1999), which addresses the intersecting of a range of factors, so that the impact of race, class, and other issues are explicitly acknowledged along with holding the person accountable for his abusive behavior. We discussed a referral to a black male colleague committed to working with black men. She did not act on these steps, however, wary of Malik's reactions.

Four years after they met, three years after their daughter was born, after at least two years of mostly unhappy relating, Helaria had had enough. She found Malik's presence oppressive; she wanted to move on with her life and insisted that he move out. As often happens, when Malik felt threatened with separation he became more controlling. He spent more time in the apartment, kept track of Helaria's whereabouts, and secretly taped her phone calls. When she discovered this she was outraged, and considered legal action but felt constrained by two factors. First, she wanted to protect her daughter's connection with her father. Second, she did not want to bring public systems into her private life because she could not trust how they would intervene and how Malik might react. In particular, she worried that in response to exposure and humiliation he might become physically assaultive to the police or other authorities.

As discussed by Geller et al. (this volume), public exposure of intimate violence has been shown to be empowering for white women and a deterrent to repeat offenses for white men. A study of mandatory arrest (Paternoster, Brame, Bachman, & Sherman, 1997) found significantly fewer repeat offenses among suspects who felt they had been treated fairly. But black abusers, who often feel unfairly treated because of class and race bias in the criminal justice system, are more susceptible to perpetrating further violence against their partners (Mills, 2003). These findings support Helaria's intuitive concern.

One night as they were arguing in the kitchen, Malik took a knife from the drawer and threatened Helaria with it. She called 911, he hung up the phone, and Ladi saw everything. Realizing what he had done, he backed away. The injury he had experienced in the outside world, compounded by his failure at home, had overwhelmed him. As bell hooks (1981) states, in American culture overpowering another is considered a way to assert strength and masculinity. Malik asserted the power of male over female, losing sight of the solidarity he had felt with his black partner. Yet feeling so out of control, perhaps seeing himself being abusive like his stepfather, sounded an alarm. It was at this point that he finally made a real plan and moved out.

Helaria was furious that he would subject her, and especially their daughter, to such danger. She decided to go to the police, to report the incident, and get an order of protection. She went to the station three times, but could not make herself enter. No longer concerned about the impact on Malik, she was afraid that Ladi would be removed from her custody. Helaria had no confidence the police and child protective services would accept her story and act on her behalf. In her view, relying on public systems was too risky; she needed to deal with the situation in private in order to retain more control. Her concern was not unreasonable, as children have been removed from mothers who are deemed neglectful for continuing to live with their children in abusive situations. While the practice of removing children who witness domestic abuse has been blocked in New York (*Nicholson v. Williams*, 2002), the perception in the community, and particularly among women of color, is that the danger remains.

REFLECTIONS ON THE THERAPY

When she met Malik, Helaria was less depressed than she had been at the beginning of treatment and we were meeting irregularly. She resumed steadier contact when their conflicts became more difficult, as she needed support and felt safe in her connection with me. Still, it was some time before I learned about the nature and extent of her distress in the relationship. In retrospect, Helaria had a number of explanations for this. She said she avoided giving me an accurate picture of how Malik was harsh and critical in order to protect him. I wonder if she worried that as a white woman I might privilege sexism over racism, might encourage her to speak up to Malik about how he was treating her without sufficiently honoring the stresses on him as a black man. While I was active in stating my awareness of his challenges, this might not have been sufficient.

Helaria also explained she was protecting me and did not want me to worry about her. We considered that she might also have been protecting herself, avoiding seeing how bad things had become. In what Jenkins (2000) refers to as the "central relational paradox" (p. 76) for African American women, surviving in both the black and white worlds requires isolating aspects of the self, including isolating experiences in the black world from a white therapist. The black woman client may not be fully authentic with her white therapist, expecting that the white therapist will not fully understand contextual aspects of her life such as racism, classism, and other cultural factors. While Helaria felt generally accepted and respected in her connection with me, not directly addressing these issues left them unspoken and laid the ground for other issues to also remain unspoken.

In retrospect, I realize that while I was quite attentive to the possibility that Malik might mistrust me, I did not address how Helaria felt about this. As noted, an antiracist perspective led to my asking directly about the effects of our racial difference in our relationship. This directness ultimately led her to be more open with me about her relationship with Malik. This raised a difficult issue for me. If I had attended to and addressed the differences between us earlier in our work, might Helaria have more readily told me things that were hard for her to say? Might she then have been able to deal more directly with Malik?

Helaria's decisions about what to tell and not tell me had a racial component. Her stance with me was similar to her stance in relation to outside systems such as child protection and police. She was careful to avoid involving them even if they might be helpful, out of concern for developments beyond her control, and she was reticent with me to protect my picture of her. While I might hope for access to more of her experience, honoring her choices has been central to our work. She makes decisions about what to tell me and what to keep private. Choosing silence is itself an exercise of her voice.

The increasing openness between us led Helaria to speak more directly with the woman she works for as well. She is more assertive about work issues, such as prioritizing tasks, and also about their racial, religious, and other differences. They are both pleased with how their connection has deepened as a result. Helaria is also more confident about expressing her opinions and needs to her friends. She looks forward to a new relationship with a man and feels able to engage in a more balanced and satisfying way.

When we met, Helaria was eager to celebrate the African American history she knew, and to learn more. She was hurt and angry at the racism she felt and observed. She was also depressed, insecure, looking for meaningful connections, and vulnerable to exploitive relationships. She used our sessions to ground herself, to get support, and to clarify her thinking. Now, she is deeply disappointed and sad about the loss of her relationship with Malik and about her daughter not living with her father, but she is not depressed and she is eager for new and sustaining relationships.

Helaria's experience with me in therapy has helped her to find her voice. Directly addressing both her racial experiences and our racial differences has made room for her to articulate other differences as well, disagreeing with my interpretations and asserting her own views. Helaria considers her race one essential aspect of who she is as a person. In her view, hers is primarily "the story of a person" learning to speak up on behalf of herself and her child. In this statement I see a parallel with the quality of Maurice Bishop she so admired, that of working with people to support their self-sufficiency. We are pleased with what we have accomplished together.

NOTE

[1] Names and other identifying information have been changed to protect the privacy of the individuals.

REFERENCES

Almeida, R., & Durkin, T. (1999). The cultural context model: Therapy for couples with domestic violence. *Journal of Marital and Family Therapy, 25*, 313-324.

Almeida, R., Woods, R., Messineo, T., Font, R. J., & Heer, C. (1994). Violence in the lives of the racially and sexually different: A public and private dilemma. In R. Almeida (Ed.), *Expansions of feminist family theory through diversity* (pp. 99-126). New York: The Haworth Press, Inc.

Boyd-Franklin, N. (2003). *Black families in therapy*. New York: Guilford Press.

Boyd-Franklin, N., & Franklin, A. J. (1998). African American couples in therapy. In M. McGoldrick (Ed.), *Revisioning family therapy: Race, culture, and gender in clinical practice* (pp. 268-281). New York: Guilford Press.

Boyd-Franklin, N., & Franklin, A. J. with Touissant, P. A. (2001). *Boys into men: Raising our African-American teenage sons*. New York: Plume.

Carter, B. (1999). Becoming parents: The family with young children. In B. Carter & M. McGoldrick (Eds.), *The expanded life cycle: Individual, family and social perspectives* (3rd ed., pp. 249-273). Needham Heights, MA: Allyn & Bacon.

Chapman, R. T. (2006). Internalized racism of the clinician and the treatment dynamic. *Journal of Emotional Abuse, 6*(2/3), 219-228.

Dyche, L., & Zayas, L. H. (1995). The value of curiosity and naiveté for the cross-cultural psychotherapist. *Family Process, 34*, 389-399.

Franklin, A. J. (1999). Therapeutic support groups for African American men. In L. E. Davis. (Ed.), *Working with African American males: A guide to practice* (pp. 5-14). Thousand Oaks: Sage.

Franklin, A. J., & Boyd-Franklin, N. (2000). Invisibility syndrome: A clinical model of the effects of racism on African-American males. *American Journal of Orthopsychiatry, 70*, 33-41.

Franklin, A. J., Boyd-Franklin, N., & Kelly, S. (2006). Racism and invisibility: Race-related stress, emotional abuse and psychological trauma for people of color. *Journal of Emotional Abuse, 6*(2/3), 9-30.

Geller, J. A. (1992). *Breaking destructive patterns: Multiple strategies for treating partner abuse.* New York: The Free Press.

Geller, J., Miller, J., & Churchill, P. (2006). Triple trouble: Battered women of color– "Being black, being battered and being female . . . I ask myself, where do I begin?" *Journal of Emotional Abuse, 6*(2/3), 77-96.

Hargrove, P. (2006). Social work practice with Mexican clients: Service provision with illegal entrants to the United States. *Journal of Emotional Abuse, 6*(2/3), 47-60.

Herman, J. L. (1992). *Trauma and recovery: The aftermath of violence–From domestic abuse to political terror.* New York: Basic Books.

Hine-St. Hilaire, D. (2006). Immigrant West Indian families and their struggles with racism in America. *Journal of Emotional Abuse, 6*(2/3), 173-196.

Hines, P. M. (1999). The family life cycle of African American families living in poverty. In B. Carter & M. McGoldrick (Eds.), *The expanded life cycle: Individual, family and social perspectives* (3rd ed., pp. 327-345). Needham Heights, MA: Allyn & Bacon.

hooks, b. (1981). *Ain't I a woman: Black women and feminism.* Boston: South End Press.

Jenkins, Y. (2000). The Stone Center theoretical approach revisited: Applications for African American women. In L. C. Jackson & B. Greene (Eds.), *Psychotherapy with African American women: Innovations in psychodynamic perspectives and practice* (pp. 62-81). New York: The Guilford Press.

Kohl, B. G., Jr. (2006). Can you feel me now? Worldview, empathy and racial identity in a therapy dyad. *Journal of Emotional Abuse, 6*(2/3), 173-196.

Mahmoud, V. (1998). The double bind dynamics of racism. In M. McGoldrick (Ed.), *Revisioning family therapy: Race, culture and gender in clinical practice* (pp. 255-267). New York: The Guilford Press.

McGann, E. P. (2006). Color me beautiful: Racism, identity formation, and art therapy. *Journal of Emotional Abuse, 6*(2/3), 197-217.

Miller, J. B., & Stiver, L. (1998). *The healing connection.* Boston: Beacon Press.

Mills, L. (2003). *Insult to injury: Rethinking our responses to intimate abuse.* Princeton, NJ: Princeton University Press.

Mitchell, S. A. (1988). *Relational concepts in psychoanalysis: An integration.* Cambridge: Harvard University Press.

Newhill, C. E. (1990). The role of culture in the development of paranoid symptomatology. *American Journal of Orthopsychiatry, 60*(2), 176-185.

Nicholson v. Williams, 203 F.Supp. 2d153 (EDNY 2002).

Pager, D. (2003, November 20). Newsfeed on the Observer Online, news for the Northwestern University community. Retrieved June 16, 2004 from, http://www.northwestern.edu/observer/issues/2003-11-20/newsfeed.html

Paternoster, R., Brame, R., Bachman, R., & Sherman, L. W. (1997). Do fair procedures matter? The effect of procedural justice on spouse assault. *Law and Society Review 31*, 163.

Pierce, C. M. (1988). Stress in the workplace. In A. F. Conner-Edwards & J. Spurlock (Eds.), *Black families in crisis* (pp. 27-33). New York: Brunner/Mazel.

Richardson, B. L., & Wade, B. (1999). *What Mama couldn't tell us about love: Healing the emotional legacy of racism by celebrating our light.* New York: Harper Collins.

Romero, R. (2000). The icon of the strong black woman: The paradox of strength. In L. C. Jackson & B. Greene (Eds.), *Psychotherapy with African American women: Innovations in psychodynamic perspectives and practice* (pp. 225-238). New York: The Guilford Press.

Tatum, B. D. (1997). *Why are all the Black kids sitting together in the cafeteria? And other conversations about race.* New York: Basic Books.

West, T. C. (1999). *Wounds of the spirit: Black women, violence, and resistance ethics.* New York: New York University Press.

doi:10.1300/J135v06n02_10

Can You Feel Me Now?
Worldview, Empathy, and Racial Identity
in a Therapy Dyad

Benjamin G. Kohl, Jr.

SUMMARY. Mental health professionals have long recognized the importance of empathy in individual therapy. Practitioners and researchers continue to identify the complex role race and other aspects of social identity group membership have on client assessment, engagement, and service utilization. Recent applications of racial identity theory and the worldview construct have contributed to an understanding of the dynamics of therapeutic intervention and clinical supervision. This article describes the work of a Black, Haitian, female client and a White, Anglo-Saxon, male therapist at a community-based family service program. The roles of empathy, racial identity, and worldview on the dynamics of the therapeutic alliance are discussed. doi:10.1300/J135v06n02_11 *[Article copies available for a fee from The Haworth Document Delivery Service: 1-800-HAWORTH. E-mail address: <docdelivery@haworthpress.com> Website: <http://www.HaworthPress.com> © 2006 by The Haworth Press, Inc. All rights reserved.]*

KEYWORDS. Worldview, empathy, racial identity, social identity

Address correspondence to: Benjamin G. Kohl, 38 Wyckoff Street, Brooklyn, NY 11201 (E-mail: bkohl@jbfcs.org).

[Haworth co-indexing entry note]: "Can You Feel Me Now? Worldview, Empathy, and Racial Identity in a Therapy Dyad." Kohl, Benjamin G., Jr. Co-published simultaneously in *Journal of Emotional Abuse* (The Haworth Maltreatment & Trauma Press, an imprint of The Haworth Press, Inc.) Vol. 6, No. 2/3, 2006, pp. 173-196; and: *Racism and Racial Identity: Reflections on Urban Practice in Mental Health and Social Services* (ed: Lisa V. Blitz, and Mary Pender Greene) The Haworth Maltreatment & Trauma Press, an imprint of The Haworth Press, Inc., 2006, pp. 173-196. Single or multiple copies of this article are available for a fee from The Haworth Document Delivery Service [1-800-HAWORTH, 9:00 a.m. - 5:00 p.m. (EST). E-mail address: docdelivery@haworthpress.com].

Available online at http://jea.haworthpress.com
© 2006 by The Haworth Press, Inc. All rights reserved.
doi:10.1300/J135v06n02_11

The accelerating diversification of the United States population has cemented the mandate that mental health practice be culturally competent. The need for professionals to develop clinical skills that will integrate dimensions of social identity, such as race, gender, ethnicity, class, faith tradition, and sexual orientation, into therapy practice has been well-prescribed (Adams, 2000; Carter, 1995; Sue, 2003). The importance of including social identity group membership awareness in service provision is buoyed by an accumulation of research that documents differential mental health treatment of racially and ethnically diverse clients in areas such as assessment bias and diagnostic error (Ibrahim, Roysircar, & Ohnishi, 2001). The resulting underutilization of mental health services by people of color has been linked to a lack of non-white service providers (Diller, 1999), a dearth of bilingual practitioners (Lu, 1996), and manifestations of structural racism in the mental health professions (D'Andrea et al., 2001).

During the past decade, an understanding of this crisis has been deepened by a growing recognition of the theoretical biases upon which many of our practice principles have been predicated (Sue, Ivey, & Pedersen, 1996). Social work educators have argued that dominant theories in clinical curricula are limited in their application to diverse clients (Perez Foster, 1996). Dismantling what has been called the *universal approach*, or the application of majority White cultural standards and theories to ethnic/racial minorities, has become an important goal of many scholars and practitioners (Robinson & Morris, 2000). Similarly, there has been a challenge to the cultural myopia of psychoanalysis (Altman, 1995; Perez Foster, 1996), and a number of thinkers have sought to expand the application of psychodynamic principles to the treatment of an increasingly diverse population (see Mishne, 2002). In short, many mental health researchers, educators, and practitioners have been diligent in their response to the pervasiveness of inadequate mental health care and inequitable social service provision for people of color.

Despite the gathering momentum of the multicultural movement (Robinson & Morris, 2000) and a growing awareness of structural racism and White privilege (see Goodman, 2001; Hitchcock, 2002), mental health providers are often frustrated by a lack of specific practice skills that facilitate discussion about social identity and foster healing around social inequity. To be sure, cross-cultural dynamics in psychotherapy are complex (Pedersen, 2000). Research has shown that even when training has increased practitioners' multicultural awareness, knowledge, and skills, the efficacy of their interventions can still be limited

(Helms & Richardson, 1997). Thus, even when therapists accept the importance of being aware of their own social identities and challenging their own culturally influenced biases, they can be at a loss about how to monitor this process in treatment and supervision. When therapists are sensitive to clients' experiences of oppression (or unearned advantage), they can remain uncertain about how to manage these experiences in the context of presenting problems and treatment contracts. In short, social identity awareness and social justice consciousness are necessary, but not sufficient, conditions for successful clinical intervention.

THEORETICAL BRIDGES FOR MULTICULTURAL PRACTICE

Given the complexity of providing mental health services across social identity differences, it is important to question which conceptual frameworks best inform clinical strategies for culturally competent practice. Are there ideas that can help connect, for example, a practitioner's growing awareness of unearned White privilege (see McIntosh, 1996) with a Black client's struggle to give voice to the daily micro-aggressions or feelings of invisibility that are a product of living in a racially structured society (see Franklin, 2004)? One clue as to how to bridge a gap between social justice consciousness and clinical acumen is to consider the values upon which psychodynamic practice principles have been established. For example, Sodowsky, Kuo-Jackson, and Loya (1997) draw a useful parallel in which they characterize social consciousness and political awareness as a foundation of multicultural counseling "just as psychodynamic and humanistic principles set the origins of mainstream forms of counseling" (p. 16). Helms and Richardson (1997) extend this analogy by arguing that multicultural training should prioritize the development of therapists' philosophical orientation over their acquiring a unique set of clinical interventions. This recommendation highlights the perhaps obvious idea that therapists' values have an interdependent relationship with how they understand their own (and their clients') social identity. Understanding the feedback loop between the saliency of a therapist's social identity group membership and her ability to address and integrate with clients the effects of oppression and advantage has been increasingly identified as vital to successful mental health treatment (Pedersen, 2000; Sue, 2003). Many authors stress the need for more precise theoretical models that will lead to a practitioner's increased flexibility in the integration of relevant sociopolitical dynamics (Helms & Richardson, 1997). This need

is particularly acute with White practitioners who are often unaware of
their social privilege and its expression during the treatment process
(see Goodman, 2001; Hitchcock, 2002).

Three theoretical frameworks that have been empirically correlated
with practitioners' development of multicultural awareness, knowledge, and skills are worldview, empathy, and racial identity theory. This
article briefly reviews recent literature regarding these three conceptual
constructs. It then describes a course of treatment of individual therapy
between a Black, Haitian, female client and a White, Anglo-Saxon,
male therapist at a community-based family services program in New
York City. It continues by integrating the literature with the case example in order to illustrate how these conceptual frameworks can enhance
an understanding of interpersonal dynamics and therapeutic alliances in
cross racial-cultural practice. The article concludes by discussing ways
in which progressive empathic attunement and racial identity awareness
can increase the potential for successful treatment.

Worldview Overview

Because of its potential to capture both therapist and client cultural assumptions, and their relationship to cognitive and affective structures, the
worldview construct has become one of the most popular paradigms in
the multicultural counseling literature (Ibrahim et al., 2001). Worldview
constitutes our psychological orientation in life and determines how we
think, behave, make decisions, and define events. It includes one's group
and individual identities, beliefs, values, and language that construct a reality for perceiving life events. As used in multicultural counseling,
"worldview is a set of beliefs, values, and assumptions that undergirds a
person's behavior and emotional reactions. It provides an implicit frame
of reference for interpretation of the world and its experiences and is de-
rived from one's social and cultural world" (Ibrahim et al., 2001, p. 445).

The worldview construct offers a way of defining mental health, appropriate service provision, and acceptable methods of intervention that
integrates competing perspectives and belief systems (Sanchez, 2001).
For example, having an awareness of a client's worldview toward work,
education, family, and gender norms is essential for career counselors
working with diverse populations (Hargrove, Creagh, & Kelly, 2003).
However, it is important to recognize that the domains of worldview are
most often defined from the perspective of the majority Western culture
(Vazquez & Garcia-Vazquez, 2003). As noted previously, the theoreti-

cal constructs and standards of comparison that are used to establish psychopathology are limited in their universal application. Therefore, while the worldview construct can help clinicians reframe misunderstandings and miscommunications that lead to misdiagnosis and early termination in cross racial-cultural practice (Ibrahim & Kahn, 1987), its efficacy is limited by the clinician's willingness to apply it to her or his own experience and theoretical perspective. For example, Sodowsky et al. (1997) related multicultural competency to graduate counseling psychology students' increasingly flexible worldview and greater sense of personal adequacy. These variables are important because they introduce the relationship between practitioners' life experiences and values, and their perceived ability to relate to and help a variety of culturally different clients. Similarly, Mahalik, Worthington, and Crump (1999) found that therapists' values were stronger predictors of worldview than racial/ethnic membership. Although 73% of the therapists sampled were minorities, the values associated with this worldview tended to be White and middle-class. Their provocative findings support the idea of a therapist culture in the United States wherein practitioners are operating with a professional value set that partially eclipses their culturally specific beliefs. This and similar research has prompted a call for the further specification of a counseling worldview that may be operating to shape how we observe, assess, define, and approach client problems (Sanchez, 2001). Ultimately, the importance of research that correlates worldview with cultural competency may be to match clients and therapists on value dimensions rather than solely on demographic variables.

Empathy: Implications for Cultural Competence

Empathy has been identified as a construct critical to the development of multicultural clinical competency (Constantine, 2000; Mishne, 2002; Ridley & Lingle, 1996; Shonfeld-Ringel, 2001). In their summary of empathy's relationship to cross-cultural social work practice, Dyche and Zayas (2001) argue that both cognitive and affective elements are present in empathy. Similar to effective utilization of the worldview construct, the authors conceive of empathy as tapping therapists' ability "to balance competency of craft with openness and receptivity to the client's point of view" (p. 256). Mishne (2002) has further emphasized the cognitive and affective aspects of empathy in her discussion of the essential relevance of self-psychology and intersubjectivity theory to cross-cultural practice. She argues that because these theories emphasize mutuality as inherent to the therapeutic process, they are naturally inclusive of differences in social identity.

Despite the theoretical succor offered by these authors, there is less understanding of how empathy is activated, operationalized, and sustained in cross racial-cultural therapy. One promising area of investigation is in the relationship between practitioners' perception of their cultural competency and understanding of themselves as victims of discrimination (Ponterotto, Fuertes, & Chen, 1996). These authors found that measures of multicultural awareness, knowledge, and skills predicted self-reported levels of discrimination. The implications are that if a therapist believes she shares experiences of oppression with a client, she may be more likely to understand herself as culturally competent. In one of the only studies to empirically investigate this relationship, Constantine (2000) found that both gender and empathy were significantly predictive of self-reported multicultural counseling knowledge and awareness. Constantine hypothesizes that women's feelings of self-efficacy about working with culturally diverse clients may be heightened because of the salience of sexism in their own lives. Clearly, there is not a necessary relationship between a therapist's experience of oppression and his or her development of empathy with clients. As will become clear in the discussion of racial identity development, an individual's affective reaction to social group membership and the cognitive mechanisms used to process information about race and racism might preclude or encourage empathic attunement. Although future research would need to investigate the empirical connection between racial identity status, empathy, and experiences of oppression, the notion of an association between affective empathy and dimensions of self-perceived cultural competency is a compelling theoretical construct. It offers a logic model wherein subjective experiences of oppression, understood by the therapist as shared with the client, function to increase the practitioner's perception of multicultural clinical efficacy.

Despite the recent emphasis in the practice literature on empathy's importance for working across social identity differences, its actualization in the therapeutic process can remain difficult. For example, studies of the development of a commitment to antiracism in White people have noted subjects' reported difficulty sustaining empathy in their relationships with people of color (O'Brien, 2003). This research suggests that, despite Whites' good intentions, they may establish a false empathy in which their enthusiasm to correct social injustice becomes paternalistic and their associations with people of color are under-examined, especially for the role of White privilege. It is important to consider how this phenomenon is informed by racial identity theory and to illustrate how it can impact cross cultural-racial therapeutic relationships.

Racial Identity Theory: Recent Applications

A number of theoretical frameworks explore the relationship between racial group membership and identity. For anything beyond this cursory summary of these ideas, and for overviews of the history of their development or recent research applications, the reader is referred elsewhere (see Fischer & Moradi, 2001; Helms, 2001; Thompson & Carter, 1997 especially). Although William Cross (1971) was the first to present a theory of Black racial identity, Janet Helms' expansion of his work has had the most realized potential for clinical application. As Helms and her collaborators refined White, Black, and People of Color racial identity concepts and scales (see Helms, 1990, 1992; Helms & Carter, 1990; Helms & Cook, 1999), their work came to be characterized as a mature subset of behavioral science (Ponterotto, Fuertes, & Chen, 2000). Helms (1984, 1990) initially argued for two phases (abandonment of racism and defining a nonracist identity) and six stages (Contact, Disintegration, Reintegration, Pseudoindependence, Immersion/emersion, and Autonomy) of White racial identity development. In her refinement of the model, she reconceptualized the stages as ego statuses and linked them to specific information-processing strategies (IPS; Helms, 1994, 1995; also Blitz, this volume). Although still conceived as epigenetic, the statuses now better capture the fluidity of racial identity development and afford the mitigation of situational variables. This is a welcome improvement, for as Carter (1997) notes it "is important to emphasize that each level of White racial identity, excepting perhaps the last (Autonomy), are intimately intertwined with individual, institutional, and cultural racism" (p. 200). In order to understand how racism is embedded in the policies and practices of institutional structures, it is especially necessary to focus on how racial identity is often invisible to White people. It has been emphasized that practitioners whose identities are privileged by the dominant culture need to ferret out their conscious and unconscious convictions related to racial inequalities (McIntosh, 1996). Recent research has built on Helms' ideas to consider how Whites develop an antiracist identity and the implications of this process for multicultural education strategies (Clark, 2004).

While human service educators have emphasized the need to help White people address and deepen their awareness of the impact of White privilege on clinical practice (Goodman, 2001; Tatum, 1994), considerable research of racial identity development theory involves therapists and clients of color (see Cross, Parham, & Helms, 1991; Helms, 1995). Although Black racial identity, or psychological Nigrescence, was the first to be fully elaborated, Helms has since argued that there is enough shared experience between non-White American racial-cultural groups to expand the theory to include all people of color. Similar to White people, the development of a racial identity for people of color generally proceeds through a number of statuses within which various information process strategies are used. The five sequential statuses for People of Color Identity Theory are: Conformity, Dissonance, Immersion-Emersion, Internalization, and Integrative Awareness. Helms (1995) clarifies that racial identity development is not necessarily a linear process, and it is likely that several statuses will exist simultaneously with a different one dominating. Although the space allotted here does not allow for full delineation of each status, as an example, note that the individual moving from conformity to dissonance initially believes that poverty and other oppressed social conditions (e.g., disproportionate incarceration) of people of color are of their own making. When a person progresses to the dissonance stage, it is often motivated by a jarring personal or social event that results in the recognition that most Whites will actively or passively see him or her as inferior. As we shall see in the case presented below, this healthy movement to a more fully realized racial self can be misunderstood as treatment resistance.

Germane to this discussion is the idea that cross-race dyadic interactions are affected by the primary racial identity status from which the therapist and client are each operating. Helms (1984, 1990) has proposed three basic topographies in which the interaction between therapist and client can either be regressive, progressive, or parallel. An example of a regressive relationship would be a White therapist with a less-developed racial identity working with a Black client who has a worldview that recognizes White privilege as unearned. By contrast, in the progressive relationship the person in the position that has implicit authority, in this case the clinician, is functioning at a more advanced status level than the client. And in the parallel relationship, each individual in a therapy dyad has a similar dominant racial identity status. Chapman (this volume) and Blitz (this volume) offer further exploration of the impact of racial identity on the treatment.

It is important to note that Helms has mapped out the utility of the interaction model for both cross-racial relationships and between persons of similar social identity group memberships. This model has been applied to cross racial-cultural supervisory relationships by researchers who investigated the relationship between racial identity attitudes and operationalized multicultural competencies (Ottavi, Pope-Davis, & Dings, 1994). It has been found that supervisee competency increased when the supervisor held a higher racial identity status regardless of the supervisee's scores (Ladany, Brittan-Powell, & Pannu, 1997). Interestingly, racial identity scores accounted for more variability in students' multicultural competency scores than the racial configuration of the supervisory dyad. In other words, when it came to helping trainees become more culturally competent, supervisors' awareness of their race was more important than their actual race. This research might be replicated with therapy dyads to empirically investigate how racial identity development mitigates therapy outcomes.

THE CASE OF CAROL

Carol, a 30-year-old Haitian American Black woman, was referred to a community-based family service program by a public hospital when her 14-year-old step-daughter developed acute catatonic symptoms immediately after witnessing her paternal grandmother being struck by a car in front of their New York City home. Grandmother suffered minor injuries and recovered quickly. Carol and her husband Claude believed that the girl's symptoms were related to the fact that her mother, Claude's first wife, was killed in a car accident when the child was five years old. After several weeks of individual and family therapy, the girl's symptoms dissipated; at the family's request, she was referred to our after-school program and Carol asked to be seen individually.

Carol is an attractive, slightly overweight, deeply dark-skinned woman who was born in Haiti and brought to New York City as an infant by immigrant parents of modest wealth. She had a Bachelor's degree, had worked as a secretary for several Wall Street firms, and dressed in a conservative corporate style. The presenting problem was difficulty "keeping my house," by which she meant managing her and Claude's five-year-old daughter, setting limits with her step-daughter, and pleasing her ailing mother-in-law, who also lived in the home. She reported feeling emotionally abandoned by and angry with her husband, who she suspected of infidelity. Finally, she complained of "letting people walk all over me." We contracted for weekly individual therapy; the material presented below is culled from a two-year course of treatment.

Early in our work together, Carol described herself as feeling torn between "the American value system" and her Haitian culture. She located the meaning of this bifurcation in her role as a parent and feeling "too soft" in disciplining her five-year-old daughter and 16-year-old step-daughter. She recounted her own history of childhood physical abuse during which she was frequently beaten by her mother, often with extension cords and other objects, from as young as she can remember until she left home at age 21. She noted that her two older sisters and younger brother were seldom, if ever, abused. Her father never hit her, nor did he intervene or comfort her afterwards. She stated, "I guess he was around. I don't think he cared much about what was going on. In Haitian families discipline is not the man's job anyway." In the several months during which she disclosed her abuse history, she presented with escalating feelings of despondency and dissociation. She noted some relief from discussing her childhood abuse; however, she reported an inability to thwart her growing sadness. During one particularly poignant session, she stated, "I often feel like crying, but I can't." When asked what might happen if she cried during therapy, she remembered that her mother would admonish her not to cry during beatings, and if she whimpered she was hit harder. At this point, she wept uncontrollably and afterwards gave voice to rage towards her mother.

In the following months, Carol explored the relationship between her childhood physical abuse and her frustrations disciplining her daughter and step-daughter. She discovered that her daughter, who she described as "joyful, but willful and stubborn," was now the same age as Carol's earliest memories of her own abuse. Carol recounted moments when she felt overwhelmed with anger at her daughter's behavior and feared she would lose her temper and become violent. Using positive reinforcement as well as giving her daughter time-outs seemed to help control the child's behavior; nevertheless, Carol reported a growing dread that she was "turning into my mother and will come to hate my child." This concern was compounded by Carol's increasing exasperation at her husband's lack of involvement in parenting and lack of communication in their relationship. She discussed the waning of sexual intimacy during their seven years of marriage. During one session, she disclosed with great hesitancy that she suspected Claude of more than just infidelity, and was nearly certain that he had a second family that he secretly supported in Florida. After observing my relatively neutral response, she expressed great relief that I did not think she "was an idiot for staying with him." She stated that as a White American male, I might not understand that this was not uncommon for Haitian men. And although his polygamy disturbed her, she was somewhat comforted by his ability to "take care of his business" and by the fact that he spent almost all of his time with her and his daughters in New York City.

Carol and I did not avoid or minimize our differences. Throughout the work, we explored how our gender, cultural, and racial differences might be affecting our ability to understand each other. When I early on asked how she felt about working with a White male therapist, Carol remarked that she thought I would be more open-minded about her personal history than another Black person or especially another Haitian woman. Carol initially stated that my ignorance of Haitian familial mores made her feel more comfortable and less judged. I emphasized our need to share the responsibility for understanding each other and invited her to offer whatever cultural information she felt would be helpful in my understanding her better. For example, she explained to me that it is the custom of widowed Haitian mothers to live with an adult daughter rather than a son. Claude had three adult sisters in New York City, any of whom could have cared for their mother. Carol understood this breach in tradition as another example of how she let herself be "stepped on." She linked this situation with her being scapegoated by her mother while her siblings escaped childhood beatings.

During the first year, Carol was hardworking and increasingly self-directed in our weekly sessions. Yet, despite our working alliance being solidified I had the consistent feeling that Carol and I were not connecting. During a session in which I had initiated "re-contracting around treatment goals," I asked her to comment on her experience of the therapy and how I might better help her. She quickly lauded my skills as a therapist and said that for the first time in her life she felt fully understood. Despite my gratified narcissism, I managed to express surprise that our identity differences were so easily bridged. She stated, "I can tell that you really care about me so all that other stuff doesn't matter." At the time, it was easy for me to believe that she was right.

About a year into our work together, she announced with great determination that she wanted to share with me a period of her life about which she was confused. Over the next several sessions, she related the story of her courtship with her husband. Her mother did not approve of Claude because he was much older and she forbade Carol, who was 21 at the time, from seeing him. After only a few months, they eloped and Carol cut off all communication with her mother. Immediately following her moving in with him, she developed hammertoes in both feet and required surgery. During her recovery, alone each day while Claude worked, she began to suffer from acute olfactory, auditory, and visual hallucinations. These were accompanied by near catatonic symptoms of immobility and time distortion. These phenomena persisted for about six months during which time she was visited by her older sister, who urged her to make reparation with her mother. Her sister consulted a Haitian spiritualist and learned that the visions Carol was experiencing were particular to a Voodoo sect to which, the sister suggested, Claude belonged. For example, she heard the hooting of owls, smelled rope burning, and saw patterns of light emerging from her body; and her sister provided Carol with written material "proving" she was being possessed. Carol was advised to leave Claude by a certain date or risk permanent loss of her will. On the evening before that date, her mother and two sisters rescued her and spirited her away first to Florida and then to Haiti. Over the next six months, she "got medicine" from a variety of spiritualists and then returned to New York City. She returned to her mother's home for a short time and described eventually reuniting with her husband as "just sort of happening."

As Carol told this part of her story, she pressed me to tell her what had happened to her. Although I was wildly fascinated by her narrative, I managed to agree that she had survived a very difficult experience and to gently give her question back to her. One session she remarked, "I know you're not going to tell me whether I went crazy or was possessed. It's something I have to decide on my own." Nevertheless, there were occasions when Carol still sought my advice. She worked full-time as an executive assistant at a Wall Street firm and I was often asked to judge the fairness of a given situation at work, such as her feeling under appreciated by her White male boss. I might observe, "It seems important that I tell you whether you are being mistreated." Initially, she doubted the benefit of any introspective efforts on her part, but gradually became more tolerant of my refusal to tell her what to do, and sometimes celebrated situations where she stood up for herself at work. During this time, I occasionally heeded the suggestion of my supervisor–a psycho-dynamically oriented White male–that I "bring it more into the transference." For example, when Carol playfully admonished me for not advising her about an unfair situation at her office I might ask, "I wonder if there are ways here in therapy that I am treating you unfairly?" These types of comments invariably were met with puzzlement or simple reassurances that I was "doing great."

I never directly answered Carol's question concerning my beliefs about the ontological reality of her possession experience. She now seldom asked me what to do, and rarely required prompting to explore her associated affect. Nor did I prompt deeper discussions of our racial or gender difference outside of parallels between our relationship and her hoped-for resolutions with other White men in her life. We did at times broaden our conversation to include topics like affirmative action, prejudice between West Indian immigrants and African Americans, and other current events in New York City. During her second year of therapy, Carol made several significant changes in her life. She quit her Wall Street job and founded a successful real estate company in the New York Haitian community. She was also able to set a strong enough limit with her husband for him to negotiate that his mother go live with one of his sisters. Perhaps most significantly, she initiated several contacts with her own mother so that she could get to know her granddaughter.

I counted this as one of my most successful and interesting cases and was trying to come to terms with my supervisor's reminders that it was time to initiate a discussion about termination. One week that summer, as I was planning to bring up our ending treatment, Abner Louima, a Black Haitian immigrant, was brutally beaten and tortured by White police officers in the community where Carol lived and my family services program is located. She immediately brought it into treatment and reported that she could not stop thinking about it. She described the event as making her feel unsafe and noted she had even joined in some of the protest demonstrations outside the precinct. At the same time, we agreed that after two years in therapy Carol had finished a piece of work and we should begin to say good-bye.

During the last months of our work together, Carol no-showed two sessions and came late to others. When I tried to process this with her, she was gently dismissive and offered vague excuses. When I eventually asked whether she felt safe in therapy, she noted that her sister and several friends involved in the community protests at the precinct had questioned her continuing to come to see a White man. She reported that their questions had surprised her and that she felt guilty about not standing up for herself and the hard work she had done in therapy.

As our ending approached, Carol seemed distant and I was increasingly dissatisfied. I rationalized that the strain in our relationship was due to a normal cooling of intimacy during termination. However, I felt that I had failed to protect our alliance from the impact of the Louima incident. I was angry and hurt, and blamed the White cops who had tortured Louima for reminding Carol and me of our differences. I also blamed myself for being unable to sustain further discussion about our differences or about the Louima incident. Nevertheless, we ambled

through the final sessions, and our review of our work was characterized by shared sadness, celebration, and relief.

DISCUSSION

This case can be understood through a number of theoretical frameworks. For example, Carol is an adult survivor of childhood abuse, and
her dissociative process and other cognitive coping strategies are certainly informed by trauma theory. At the time, I was guided by considerations of how our transference and countertransference processes
reflected known paradigms in work with sexual abuse victims (see for
example, Davies & Frawley, 1994). However, as the years went by, and
I slowly became more aware of my identity as a straight, White, middle-class, American male, I came to wonder whether my understanding
of the work with Carol was complete or even accurate. Several years
ago, I wrote about this case as a doctoral candidate because I was proud
that our social identity differences had been explored and successfully
bridged. However, as I began to question my relatively color-blind orientation to service provision and to become increasingly aware of myself as White, I was less sure how I had helped Carol. In this context, I
hope to use the three theoretical frameworks discussed previously to
reframe how our social identity group memberships impacted the work.
I am interested in illustrating how modest efforts to capture the dynamics of difference can change what is understood as healthy behavior and
successful clinical intervention.

Worldview and Countertransference

In my work with Carol, I felt it was important to improve my understanding of Haitian culture and family systems. I balanced reading literature and research with encouraging Carol to share what she understood
and valued as culturally specific, similar to the process discussed by
others in this volume (Hargrove, this volume; Hine-St. Hilaire, this volume, Madsen, this volume). Carol educated me about parenting and
gender norms of Haitian households, expectations for social relations in
the extended family, the prevalence of polygamy, and the role of
religion. Even before sharing her story of Voodoo possession, her willingness to clarify how cultural values related to her self-concept and self-
esteem grounded our work. Understanding Carol's worldview was largely
a process of probing for, rather than ascribing, the meaning that Carol as-

signed to the problems she chose to work on in therapy. Because Carol was actively questioning her worldview, she readily shared her understanding of how her cultural beliefs related to her current thoughts and feelings. Clarifying her cultural values then afforded me the flexibility to suspend my own beliefs about wellness and mental health.

The openness of my beliefs about healing systems notwithstanding, our attempt to develop a shared worldview was not without consequences. One of the most common countertransference reactions in cross-cultural therapy is to romanticize or become excessively curious about the client's culture (Dyche & Zayas, 2001). I was fascinated by Carol's story, by her Voodoo victimization, and by her questions, "What happened to me? Do you think I went crazy?" My curiosity was not mollified by our clinic's psychiatrist, who emphasized the extreme suggestibility of patients suffering a psychotic break. She hypothesized that Carol's psychosis was initiated by the sudden separation from her abusive mother. The Voodoo particulars were interjects suggested by the sister and brought to life by Carol's punitive superego and fear of retribution by an internalized object. Indeed, Carol herself eventually formulated something close to this. Even so, the most useful consultation was with a Haitian colleague, a psychologist and immigrant, who offered a Creole phrase as, "You have to work with both hands." He noted that to continue to work effectively with Carol, I needed to remain flexible in my own belief system, neither overemphasizing a Western understanding of her experience nor de-emphasizing the ontological reality of her possession.

This prescription relates to an important unresolved theoretical issue in the worldview literature: whether empathy can help create a shared worldview that then becomes the base for reaching the client's subjective reality (Ibrahim et al., 2001). In this case, I believe we shared enough of our beliefs and feelings that it created a shared worldview. However, this had a lot to do with how we understood the purpose of our work together. For example, from the beginning Carol was actively exploring her ambivalence about acculturation. She consistently used therapy to discuss being torn between middle-class values and Haitian beliefs regarding parenting, the world of work, and the actual conceptualizing of her "pathology." Our consulting psychiatrist's medical training and belief in the primacy of Western scientific method prohibited her from conceptualizing Carol's possession as anything other than a psychotic break within the context of an indigenous faith tradition. By contrast, my general fascination with voodoo and willingness to suspend a definitive explanation about Carol's experience created a mutual cognitive empathy where numerous interpretations for her experience were possible. What remained under-examined was how my counter-transference related to my beliefs about race and racism. For example, to what extent did Carol's expressed opinion that voodoo was primitive and unsophisticated validate my own thoughts about the inherent supe-riority of a White middle-class worldview? How did Carol's request for a diagnosis and psychodynamic explanation of her experience play into my confidence that I could help her at all? It is important to explore how our group memberships related to our ability to understand each other.

Empathy and Social Identity Group Membership Differences

While it is not unusual for me when beginning with a new client to adopt a reserved tone, there was something about Carol's initial presen-tation that elicited in me an almost laconic response. A formal style is congruent with my upbringing as a White Anglo-Saxon Protestant (WASP), where a reserved emotional disposition is often preferred. This formal style has been reinforced by my socialization as a straight White American male. That is, I have internalized the unearned privi-lege and social power of being a White male and have come to antici-pate being responded to as an authority (see Goodman, 2001). Like many Caribbean and Latino clients, Carol immediately treated me as an expert who could both understand and help her. It is possible that my initially limited empathic reaction to her story may have reflected a healthy emerging recognition of White male hubris. That is, despite de-cades of service in communities of color while working with Carol, I was beginning to question whether I could or should work with clients from other backgrounds. My early formal response to Carol may have been a response to our extreme differences and an acted-out concern to whether she would feel understood and whether I would be able to un-derstand her. On the other hand, a truncated affective reaction in cross-racial dyads has been linked to the covert racist belief that people of color are unsuitable for analysis (Perez Foster, 1996). It may have been that my nascent awareness of my unearned White privilege clued me to unexplored racist beliefs that I held.

Nevertheless, I was reassured by my early supervisions where I ex-plored how my increased formality and persistent feelings of being dis-connected might be examples of complementary identification (Racker, 1968). For example, I was enacting Carol's internalization of her indif-ferent father, who did not rescue her from her mother's beatings, and as

I listened to her story with measured professional interest I had been reflexively accepting the role that Carol was offering in the transference. With this formulation in tow, I began to find Carol an exciting and curable client. Indeed, few practitioners would have questioned Carol's ability to benefit from treatment. I considered her a hard-working client whose intelligence buoyed a solid neurotic defensive structure. In a short time I felt we had successfully transcended our social identity differences and were working with material, whether related to trauma and/or early object relations, that was universal to the human condition. My timid explorations of whether and how Carol felt cared for by me were motivated by an attempt to offer her a corrective emotional experience, and at the time my interventions were almost completely blanched of reference to our racial and gender differences. I cared about her as a human being and sustained an empathic responsiveness to her in therapy. Carol reacted with an almost hyper-cooperative disposition in which we both genuinely believed she could be helped.

After the Louima incident, I maintained a cognitive understanding of what Carol might be feeling as a Haitian woman living in a precinct area where White police officers torture Black citizens; however, my ability to affectively empathize with her was limited. I lacked awareness of how her feelings about my being White could change after Louima was brutalized. This blind spot reflected my inability to see our work and myself in the context of a racially structured society. That is, I was unable to appreciate how I shared, and could potentially abuse, power resulting from unearned White privilege, just like the police officers that had committed the crime. I saw myself primarily as a social worker, not as a White male. It is important to understand how this failure to recognize myself as White, and Carol's resultant emotional distancing, were products of our respective racial identity statuses.

Analysis of Racial Identity Dynamics

When this case is viewed through the lens of racial identity theory, several perspectives can be illustrated. Like many mental health practitioners, my ideas about the role of race in treatment were dominated by my commitment to service. Despite 20 years of practice with poor people of color, I did not think about what it meant to be White, with the consistent exception of considering how clients of color might react to me as a member of the dominant culture. As a therapist, I was convinced of the importance of initiating discussions of racial and gender difference and I saw these differences as something to work through. I operated with the belief that even if a client of color did not take me up on the offer, I had at least signaled that the topic was discussable (and that I was not a racist). With Carol, I was proud that we had worked to move beyond our differences and that they had not become an impediment to treatment. I lacked the perspective to see how the Louima incident had helped Carol move towards a status of racial identity where she became actively aware of racism. In Helms' model, I was firmly in the pseudo-independent status of White racial identity development that is characterized by an intellectual commitment to the White racial group and stated tolerance of other groups (Helms, 1990, 1995). Most of my professional efforts were focused on helping change people of color and Blacks so that they could better assimilate in the world of Whites. While I appreciated the importance of discussing racial differences, I seldom considered the importance of discussing racism and its impact on clients (or friends) of color. Although I was quite aware of the disparities of access to resources between myself and clients of color, I seldom considered what it meant to be White beyond a feeling that I did not have to suffer discrimination. If anyone had suggested that I was taking the beginning steps towards constructing a positive White identity, I would have been baffled to consider what further progress would look like. I saw little positive in being White, but rather it seemed something to often ignore and sometimes justify.

In this way, Carol and I were at first a strong match. Through most of our work, she primarily operated from the conformity status of Helms' People of Color identity model. While she admitted racism, she also believed in American meritocracy and often espoused prejudiced views towards African Americans, whom she saw as entitled. For example, the presence of a single Black vice president at the firm where she worked was evidence that organizational racism could be overcome. Her lamentations about unfair treatment in the workplace were not about her as a victim of racism, but about her not being recognized for the hard work and effort she made.

Carol and I were clearly ascribing to White standards of success and failure, and initially had a parallel interaction relationship. Despite our differences, we shared many middle-class values and this cemented our complicity with cultural racism. For example, even when Carol became a landlord in her Haitian neighborhood–a decision that might have indicated a move towards immersing herself in her community–she did so with the idea that it was a good business decision. At the time, I had nothing but encouragement and support for her entrepreneurial efforts. She soon began to complain that her African American tenants–many of whom were single mothers–did not take care of their apartments, were lazy, and could not be trusted. At the time, I addressed these beliefs as I would with a White client by gently suggesting that there were social factors, like poverty, that eclipsed her tenants' individual shortcomings. Other than this intellectual interpretation, I did little to challenge Carol's opinions and had no awareness of how I might interpret them to help her modify her self-concept. My unconscious assumption that Carol's failures and successes were solely due to her individual efforts reflected my denial of White privilege and prohibited me from understanding how Carol was idealizing White cultural norms.

I believe that Abner Louima's torture and the subsequent mobilization of the Haitian community propelled Carol from a conformity into a dissonance status of racial identity. This is characterized by an increased recognition of racial inequity and discrimination and a subsequent reconsideration of American meritocracy. Theorists note that this progression is often triggered by a shocking social or personal event (Helms, 1990). Information processing strategies that previously had helped Carol maintain a denial of racism were now overwhelmed. Her feelings of a lack of safety, confusion about our relationship, and withdrawal from therapy all reflected her movement away from a worldview characterized by conformity. Her attending protests and development of a successful business in her community now offered her the support she needed to progress in her racial identity development.

Our racial identity interaction now changed from parallel to regressive as I was unable to consider how her identification with the Louima protests was in fact healthy. In the regressive model, "the counselor is unable to perceive how the client's racial identity development status characteristics may impede or facilitate his or her growth therapeutically" (Thompson & Carter, 1997, p. 27). I could only see Carol's withdrawal and avoidant behavior as acting out related to our termination. My narrow and defensive reaction prohibited me from exploring how Carol's behavior after Louima was a healthy step towards accepting her racial identity, modifying her worldview, and empathizing with her community. If I had been more advanced in my own racial identity development and actively examining what it meant to me to be White, I might have been more able to interpret and support Carol's development during this period in time. This is not to suggest that my blind spots and Carol's avoidant behavior were solely a product of our racial identity development; they were also clearly related to our termination. However, because I had not considered her behavior through the lens of racial identity development, I understood the end of this case as my failure, when in fact it was Carol's success.

CONCLUSION

This article has described the evolution of a cross racial-cultural therapy dyad and suggested the importance of considering worldview, empathy, and racial identity theory in individual treatment. While I hope this article has provided some clarity regarding multicultural practice, I am sure it has raised numerous questions and issues for further research. For example, what are the best models of training for clinicians, and how should they differ for White therapists and therapists of color? How can human service providers best integrate a social justice perspective into practice? What is the role of supervision in furthering an understanding of the dynamics of oppression and advantage in clinical work? What is the human service providers' obligation to incorporate current and historical events that relate to oppression in treatment and program administration? The inclusion of social identity group membership differences in treatment works to restore the self through the promotion of healthy racial identity functioning. As we communicate our understanding of the other's experience of oppression and advantage, we create the possibility of change. As we recognize the mutuality of change, we perpetuate the possibility for justice and hope.

REFERENCES

Adams, J. M. (2000). Individual and group psychotherapy with African American women: Understanding the identity and context of the therapist and patient. In L. C. Jackson & B. Greene (Eds.), *Psychotherapy with African American women* (pp. 33-61). New York: Guilford Press.

Altman, N. (1995). *The analyst in the inner city.* Hillsdale, NJ: The Analytic Press.

Blitz, L. V. (2006). Owning whiteness: The reinvention of self and practice. *Journal of Emotional Abuse, 6*(2/3), 241-263.

Carter, R. T. (1995). *The influence of race and racial identity in psychotherapy: Towards a racially inclusive model.* New York: John Wiley & Sons.

Carter, R. T. (1997). Is White a race? Expressions of White racial identity. In M. Fine, L. Weis, L. Powell, & L. Wong (Eds.), *Off White: Readings on race, power and society* (pp. 198-209). New York: Routledge.

Chapman, R. T. (2006). Internalized racism of the clinician and the treatment dynamic. *Journal of Emotional Abuse, 6*(2/3), 219-228.

Clark, C. (2004). White antiracist identity development: Implications for multicultural education. In R. L. Hampton & T. P. Gullotta (Eds.), *Promoting racial, ethnic, and religious understanding and reconciliation* (pp. 49-86). Washington, DC: CWLA Press.

Constantine, M. G. (2000). Social desirability attitudes, sex, and affective and cognitive empathy as predictors of self-reported multicultural counseling competence [Electronic version]. *Counseling Psychologist, 28,* 857-872.

Cross, W. E., Jr. (1971). The Negro-to-Black conversion experience: Toward a psychology of Black liberation. *Black World, 20,* 13-27.

Cross, W. E., Jr., Parham, T. A., & Helms, J. E. (1991). The stages of Black identity development: Nigrescence models. In R. L. Jones (Ed.), *Black psychology* (pp. 319-338). Berkeley, CA: Cobb & Henry.

D'Andrea, M., Daniels, J., Arrendondo, P., Ivey, M. B., Ivey, A. E., Locke, D. C., et al. (2001). Fostering organizational changes to realize the revolutionary potential of the multicultural movement: An updated case study. In J. G. Ponterotto, J. M. Casas, L. A. Suzuki, & C.M. Alexander, (Eds.), *Handbook of multicultural counseling* (2nd ed., pp. 222-254). Thousand Oaks, CA: Sage Publications.

D'Andrea, M., Daniels, J., & Heck, R. (1991). Evaluating the impact of multicultural counseling training. *Journal of Counseling and Development, 70,* 143-150.

Diller, J. V. (1999). *Cultural diversity: A primer for the human services.* New York: Brooks/Cole.

Dyche, L., & Zayas, L. H. (2001). Cross-cultural empathy and training the contemporary psychotherapist [Electronic version]. *Clinical Social Work Journal, 29,* 245-258.

Fischer, A. R., & Moradi, B. (2001). Racial and ethnic identity development: Recent developments and future directions. In J. G. Ponterotto, J. M. Casas, L. A. Suzuki, & C. M. Alexander (Eds.), *Handbook of multicultural counseling* (2nd ed., pp. 341-370). Thousand Oaks, CA: Sage.

Franklin, A. J. (2004). *From brotherhood to manhood: How black men rescue their relationships and dreams from the Invisibility Syndrome.* Hoboken, NJ: Wiley.

Goodman, D. J. (2001). *Promoting diversity and social justice: Educating people from privileged groups.* Thousand Oaks, CA: Sage Publications.

Hargrove, B. K., Creagh, M. G., & Kelly, D. B. (2003). Multicultural competencies in career counseling. In D. P. Pope-Davis, H. L. K. Coleman, W. M. Liu, & R. L. Toporek (Eds.), *Handbook of multicultural competencies in counseling and psychology* (pp. 392-405). Thousand Oaks, CA: Sage Publications.

Hargrove, P. (2006). Social work practice with Mexican clients: Service provision with illegal entrants to the United States. *Journal of Emotional Abuse, 6*(2/3), 61-76.

Helms, J. E. (1984). Towards a theoretical explanation of the effects of race on counseling: A black and white model. *Counseling Psychologist, 12,* 153-165.

Helms, J. E. (Ed.) (1990). *Black and white racial identity: Theory, research and practice.* Westport, CT: Greenwood.

Helms, J. E. (1992). *Race is a nice thing to have.* Topeka, KS: Content Communications.

Helms, J. E. (1994). Racial identity and other "racial" constructs. In E. J. Trickett, R. J. Watts, & D. Birman (Eds.), *Human diversity* (pp. 285-311). San Francisco: Jossey-Bass.

Helms, J. E. (1995). An update on Helms' White and People of Color racial identity model. In J. G. Ponterotto, J. M. Casas, L. A. Suzuki, & C. M. Alexander (Eds.), *Handbook of multicultural counseling* (2nd ed., pp. 143-192). Thousand Oaks, CA: Sage Publications.

Helms, J. E. (2001). Life questions. In J. G. Ponterotto, J. M. Casas, L. A. Suzuki, & C. M. Alexander (Eds.), *Handbook of multicultural counseling* (2nd ed., pp. 22-29). Thousand Oaks, CA: Sage Publications.

Helms, J. E., & Carter, R. T. (1990). Development of the White Racial Identity Inventory. In J. E. Helms (Ed.), *Black and White racial identity: Theory, research and practice* (pp. 67-80). Westport, CT: Greenwood Press.

Helms, J. E., & Cook, D. A. (1999). *Using race and culture in counseling and psychotherapy: Theory and process.* Boston: Allyn and Bacon.

Helms, J. E., & Richardson, T. Q. (1997). How "multiculturalism" obscures race and culture as differential aspects of counseling competency. In D. B. Pope-Davis & H. L. K. Coleman (Eds.), *Multicultural counseling competencies: Assessment, education and training, and supervision* (pp. 61-79). Thousand Oaks, CA: Sage Publications.

Hine-St. Hilaire, D. (2006). Immigrant West Indian families and their struggles with racism in America. *Journal of Emotional Abuse, 6*(2/3), 47-60.

Hitchcock, J. (2002). *Lifting the white veil: An exploration of white American culture in a multiracial context.* Roselle, NJ: Crandall, Dostie, & Douglass Books, Inc.

Ibrahim, F. A., & Kahn, H. (1987). Assessment of worldviews. *Psychological Reports, 60*, 163-176.

Ibrahim, F. A., Roysircar, G., & Ohnishi, H. (2001). Worldview: Recent developments and needed directions. In J. G. Ponterotto, J. M. Casas, L. A. Suzuki, & C. M. Alexander (Eds.), *Handbook of multicultural counseling* (2nd ed., pp. 425-456). Thousand Oaks, CA: Sage Publications.

Ladany, N., Brittan-Powell, C. S., & Pannu, R. K. (1997). The influence of supervisory racial identity interaction and racial matching on the supervisory working alliance and supervisee multicultural competence. *Counselor Education and Supervision, 36*, 380-388.

Lu, Y. E. (1996). Underutilization of mental health services by Asian American clients: The impact of language and culture in clinical assessment and intervention. *Psychotherapy in Private Practice, 13*, 45-69.

Madsen, L. H. (2006). Coming together and falling apart: Looking at relationship. *Journal of Emotional Abuse, 6*(2/3), 155-172.

Mahalik, J. R., Worthington, R. L., & Crump, S. (1999). Influence of racial/ethnic membership and "therapist culture" on therapists' worldview. *Journal of Multicultural Counseling and Development, 27*, 2-17.

McIntosh, P. (1996). White privilege and male privilege: A personal account of coming to see correspondences through work in women studies. In Paula Rothenberg (Ed.), *Race, class and gender in the United States* (6th ed., pp. 188-192). Belmont, CA: Wadsworth Publishing.

Mishne, J. (2002). *Multiculturalism and the therapeutic process.* New York: The Guilford Press.

O'Brien, E. (2003). The political is personal: The influence of white supremacy on white antiracists' personal relationships. In A. W. Doane & E. Bonilla-Silva (Eds.), *White out: The continuing significance of racism* (pp. 253-270). New York: Routledge.

Ottavi, T. M., Pope-Davis, D. B., & Dings, J. G. (1994). Relationship between white racial identity attitudes and self-reported multicultural counseling competencies. *Journal of Counseling Psychology, 41,* 149-154.

Pedersen, P. (2000). *A handbook for developing multicultural awareness* (3rd ed.). Alexandria, VA: American Counseling Association.

Perez Foster, R. M. (1996). What is a multicultural perspective for psychoanalysis? In R. M. Perez Foster, M. Moskowitz, & R. A. Javier (Eds.), *Reaching across boundaries of culture and class: Widening the scope of psychotherapy* (pp. 3-20). Northvale, NJ: Jason Aronson, Inc.

Ponterotto, J. G., Fuertes, J. N., & Chen, E. C. (2000). Models of multicultural counseling. In S. D. Brown & R. W. Lent (Eds.), *Handbook of counseling psychology* (3rd ed., pp. 639-669). New York: John Wiley & Sons.

Ponterotto, J. G., Rieger, B. P., Barrett, A., Harris, G., Sparks, R., Sanchez, C. M., et al. (1996). Development and initial validation of the Multicultural Counseling Awareness Scale. In G. R. Sodowsky & J. C. Impara (Eds.), *Multicultural assessment in counseling and clinical psychology* (pp. 247-282). Lincoln, NE: Buros Institute of Mental Measurements.

Racker, H. (1968). *Transference and counter-transference.* New York: International Universities Press.

Ridley, C. R., & Lingle, D. (1996). Cultural empathy in multicultural counseling: A multidimensional process model. In P. B. Pedersen, J. G. Dragons, W. J. Loner, & J. E. Trimble (Eds.), *Counseling across cultures* (pp. 21-46). Thousand Oaks, CA: Sage.

Robinson, D. T., & Morris, J. R. (2000). Multicultural counseling: Historical context and current training considerations [Electronic version]. *Western Journal of Black Studies, 24,* 239-253.

Sanchez, A. R. (2001). Multicultural family counseling: Toward cultural sensibility. In J. G. Ponterotto, J. M. Casas, L. A. Suzuki, & C. M. Alexander (Eds.), *Handbook of multicultural counseling* (2nd ed., pp. 672-700). London: Sage Publications.

Shonfeld-Ringel, S. (2001). A re-conceptualization of the working alliance in cross-cultural practice with non-western clients: Integrating relational perspectives and multicultural theories. *Clinical Social Work Journal, 29,* 53-63.

Sodowsky, G. R., Kuo-Jackson, P. Y., & Loya, G. J. (1997). Outcome of training in the philosophy of assessment: Multicultural counseling competencies. In D. B. Pope-Davis & H. L. K. Coleman (Eds.), *Multicultural counseling competencies: Assessment, education and training, and supervision* (pp. 3-42). Thousand Oaks, CA: Sage Publications.

Sue, D. W. (2003). *Overcoming our racism: The journey to liberation.* San Francisco: Jossey-Bass.

Sue, D. W., Ivey, A. E., & Pedersen, P. D. (Eds.) (1996). *A theory of multicultural counseling and therapy.* Pacific Grove, CA: Brooks/Cole.

Tatum, B. D. (1994). Teaching white students about racism: The search for white allies and the restoration of hope. *Teachers College Record, 95,* 462-475.

Thompson, C. E., & Carter, R. T. (Eds.) (1997). *Racial identity theory: Applications to individual, group, and organizational interventions.* Mahwah, NJ: Lawrence Erlbaum Associates.

Vazquez, L. A., & Garcia-Vazquez, E. (2003). Teaching multicultural competence in the counseling curriculum. In D. P. Pope-Davis, H. L. K. Coleman, W. M. Liu, & R. L. Toporek (Eds.), *Handbook of multicultural competencies in counseling and psychology* (pp. 546-561). Thousand Oaks, CA: Sage Publications.

doi:10.1300/J135v06n02_11

Color Me Beautiful:
Racism, Identity Formation,
and Art Therapy

Eileen P. McGann

SUMMARY. A primary task of adolescence is the consolidation of one's identity. To successfully achieve this, the adolescent must experience and internalize validation from her immediate community and the culture at large. For young women of color, the effects of intra-family prejudice and societal racism can severely compromise their ability to embrace their ethnic identity. In art therapy, this can manifest as self-rejection in the desire to portray themselves with physical characteristics that are unlike their own. The impact of racism on identity formation for young women of color and the effects of art therapy as a forum treatment will be examined in this article. doi:10.1300/J135v06n02_12 *[Article copies available for a fee from The Haworth Document Delivery Service: 1-800-HAWORTH. E-mail address: <docdelivery@haworthpress.com> Website: <http://www.HaworthPress.com> © 2006 by The Haworth Press, Inc. All rights reserved.]*

Address correspondence to: Eileen P. McGann, Montague Day Treatment, 57 Willoughby Street, Brooklyn, NY 11201 (E-mail: emcgann@jbfcs.org).

[Haworth co-indexing entry note]: "Color Me Beautiful: Racism, Identity Formation, and Art Therapy." McGann, Eileen P. Co-published simultaneously in *Journal of Emotional Abuse* (The Haworth Maltreatment & Trauma Press, an imprint of The Haworth Press, Inc.) Vol. 6, No. 2/3, 2006, pp. 197-217; and: *Racism and Racial Identity: Reflections on Urban Practice in Mental Health and Social Services* (ed: Lisa V. Blitz, and Mary Pender Greene) The Haworth Maltreatment & Trauma Press, an imprint of The Haworth Press, Inc., 2006, pp. 197-217. Single or multiple copies of this article are available for a fee from The Haworth Document Delivery Service [1-800-HAWORTH, 9:00 a.m. - 5:00 p.m. (EST). E-mail address: docdelivery@ haworthpress.com].

Available online at http://jea.haworthpress.com
doi:10.1300/J135v06n02_12

KEYWORDS. Racism, adolescents, art therapy, ethnic identity, identity formation, racism, relational aggression, self-portrait

The impact of racism on identity formation is an interest born of my many years working as an art therapist with adolescent girls. Young women I have seen in treatment struggle with life experiences that leave the hidden scars of emotional abuse. In these young women of color, I have repeatedly observed self-rejection in their professed desire and active attempt to portray themselves with fair skin, blonde hair, and blue eyes. I refer to this as the "blue eye phenomenon." As a female therapist with fair skin and blue eyes, I struggle to form a therapeutic alliance with these young women that is not based on physical identification. To accept or collude with a young woman of color representing herself with blue eyes would promote a deeper self-rejection. I challenge their perceptions through the metaphor of the art-making. This article examines the impact of racism and intra-family color prejudice as a form of internalized racial oppression for young women of color as they negotiate the passage of identity formation in adolescence. Other authors in this volume (Blitz & Illidge, this volume; Chapman, this volume; Samuel-Young, this volume) offer discussions on internalized racial oppression. Art therapy as a treatment modality is presented along with case examples.

IDENTITY FORMATION IN ADOLESCENCE

Adolescence, the developmental period that bridges childhood and adulthood, is a time of change, hope, promise, and, for some, great confusion. Leaving childhood offers great promise, of what is to come, but entering adulthood may also bring fear and confusion about identity, life choices, and commitments. In his seminal work, Erik Erikson (1975a) describes the process of identity formation during adolescence. "The term identity expresses such a mutual relation in that it connotes both a persistent sameness within oneself (self-sameness) and a persistent sharing of some kind of essential character with others" (p. 179). Within this, the adolescent must achieve a sense of himself or herself that remains constant, one that is not subject to fluctuations of character. The "maintenance of an inner solidarity with a group's ideals and identity" (p. 179) is essential in the process of identity formation.

Standards of value, beauty, and acceptance are outlined for adolescents in the messages sent forth from the culture. As adolescents begin to make purposeful choices about how they will model themselves, they naturally turn to their families and society to evaluate and develop opinions and beliefs about the world and their place within it. In beginning to find and develop an authentic sense of self, adolescents rely on affirmation and feedback from those around them. The community at large needs to accept and recognize the young person for who he or she is. This goes beyond recognition for any particular achievement; rather, it is a reciprocal process in which the adolescent values the community and society and is in return recognized and accepted (Erikson, 1975b).

Young women have a particularly difficult time in developing an authentic sense of self. In their studies of adolescent girls, Pipher (1994) and Gilligan (1993) note that young women experience demands from society to develop and conform to ways of being that are often in opposition to their true feelings and beliefs. Adolescent girls are subject to pressures from society to model themselves after notions of preferred submissive behavior and ideals of beauty. Pipher (1994) states, "Girls experience a pressure to split into true and false selves . . . the pressure comes not from parents but from the culture" (p. 22). The community in which they live impacts the ethnic identity of all adolescents (Canino & Spurlock, 1994); young women of color additionally experience the effects of racism, which further complicates their process of identity formation.

The Impact of Racism

Young people of color struggle when they become aware that society is judging them based upon their skin color and ethnic origins and not their individual capabilities. In such instances, the young person is likely to feel invalidated. Negative messages from the dominant culture about their inherent value and worth compromise the process of positive identification for adolescents who have minority status. As a result, these young people of color often become ambivalent about their appearance and ethnicity (Klein, 1980; Schwartz, 1998).

Ambivalence about ethnic identity will severely impact if, and how, an adolescent forms a stable sense of self. Problems arise for the adolescent when they experience a strong conflict between good and bad self-images. Adolescents are not able to integrate the conflicting good and bad self-images if they feel powerless, helpless, or overwhelmed by negative messages about their existence. When this identity integration

of opposing self-images does not occur, adolescents will dissociate
from the negative self-image (Klein, 1980) and it becomes a split-off,
hated part of themselves.

Dissociation from negative self-images can also be seen in family relationships. When families subscribe to the dominant White culture's
standards of beauty and worth, darker-skinned members are rejected
and resentment of the lighter-skinned family members can occur. This
dynamic of racial hierarchy and inter-family color prejudice among
families in the Black community has its roots in slavery. Light-skinned
children with White physical features, born to African American slave
women who had been impregnated (often raped) by White plantation
owners, received privileged treatment. Darkskinned children were not
granted any special treatment. A class system based upon color and
physical characteristics developed (Tatum, 1977). This system promoted inclusion of those who appeared to be part of the White dominant
group while simultaneously excluding those from the Black community.

The Effects of Exclusion

In studies on aggression among children, Crick (2002) reveals significant differences in the way boys and girls express their aggression. For
boys, the aggression is more often physical, while for girls it is predominantly relational. Girls experience relational aggression more frequently than do boys and are more severely affected. Difficulties in
social adjustment, peer relationships, and self-concept are some of the
problems that develop for young girls who have been victimized by
relational aggression.

Relational aggression is not expressed directly; it is duplicitous and
confusing. "Relationally aggressive acts are those in which damage to
relationships (or the threat of damage) serves as the means of harm (e.g.,
using social exclusion as a form of retaliation)" (Crick, 2000, p. 1).
Overtly there may be no attack, yet this pattern of exclusion sends a
clear message of not being wanted, valued, or needed (Simmons, 2002).
To be included or excluded sends a strong message about whether
someone or something is of value. For young women, their developing
identity is greatly determined within the context of their relationships
(Gilligan, 1993). Exclusion by their peers can have devastating effects
on a young woman's sense of self. The experience of betrayal and frac-
ture in their emotional ties leads to significant problems in social functioning and self-concept (Crick, 2002). When internalized, this message

rips away at the adolescent's emergent and often fragile sense of themselves.

On a societal level, the dynamics of exclusion and social aggression become part of the way racism is expressed and experienced. Racism promotes inclusion and acceptance of the dominant group along with insidiously excluding and rejecting others. Simmons' (2002) interviews with adolescent girls illustrate the deleterious effects of exclusion and racism. When adolescent girls were polled about what constitutes a desirable, beautiful, "good girl," they responded by saying they thought a beautiful girl was one who is fair-skinned with blonde hair and blue eyes. These girls indicated that an undesirable physical appearance, someone who would not be beautiful, would be a dark-skinned girl.

Tatum (1997) looks at the role of omission in defining racism. She notes that what we believe about others and the ideas and perceptions we form are often based on what we have not been taught or what we are not exposed to. In regard to racism and concepts of feminine beauty she states,

> Consider this conversation between two White students following a discussion about the cultural transmission of racism:
> "Yeah, I just found out that Cleopatra was actually a Black woman."
> "What?"
> The first student went on to explain her newly learned information. The second student exclaimed in disbelief, "That can't be true. Cleopatra was beautiful!" (p. 5)

The implications are profound. Members of the White culture often have not deemed darker-skinned women beautiful. So, too, members of the African American community have not always deemed darker-skinned women beautiful. Celious and Oyserman (2001) look at the impact of skin tone within a wider consideration of the effects of race on life experiences. Citing research by Neal and Wilson (1989), Harvey (1995), Wade (1996), Bond and Cash (1992), Hall (1992, 1995), Keenan (1996), Drake and Cayton (1945), and Okazawa-Rey, Robinson, and Ward (1987), Celious and Oyserman indicate that skin tone has been ascribed as a marker of beauty and that there are different consequences for men and women of color. These studies showed that among African Americans, women perceive darker skin tone as being connected with a negative sense of self. Conversely, African American men perceive darker skin tone as being attractive and desirable. Skin tones that are either very light or dark tend to be extremely stigmatized. A very light skin tone has associations of a lack of racial purity, as well as associations of beauty and status. Consequently, the authors indicate that among African Americans skin tone that is medium, neither too light nor dark, is the preferred.

Color is just one physical trait that lends itself to racial prejudice. Indeed, physical characteristics such as body size, facial features of nose, eyes, hair, and lips, as well as other characteristics, have all been used to evaluate the worth and value of a person. In order to conform to the dominant culture's standards, many young women (of any race) will alter their appearance. Mild and temporary forms of alteration can be noted in cosmetic products, while more extreme and permanent alterations are seen in skin bleaching creams and plastic surgery (Tatum, 1997). For young women of color, extreme efforts to change their appearance inherently encompass a rejection of their ethnicity.

IMPLICATIONS FOR ART THERAPY

Art therapy combines practices from the fields of psychology and fine arts; thus, the theoretical and practical approaches used in art therapy draw from these disciplines. My work as an art therapist encompasses psychodynamic perspectives, object relations theory, child and adolescent development, and art education. Within this framework, an integrative understanding is applied in assessment and interventions as they relate to each individual client. A therapeutic alliance with the client is formed through the process of artistic exploration.

Program Description

The setting in which the art therapy occurred is a day treatment program for adolescent girls with emotional disturbances ranging in age from 12 to 18. The comprehensive services offered at this day treatment program include individual, group, and family psychotherapy, milieu treatment, special education classes, and art therapy. The psychotherapeutic treatment is generally long-term, and it is not uncommon for a girl to be in the program for several years. The adolescent girls are referred to this day treatment program in a number of ways, such as from school settings, hospitals, outpatient clinics, or by self-referral. All of these adolescent girls have life histories of abuse and neglect and most come from families who experience economic hardship. Some live with a biological relative and others are in foster care. The make-up of the program's clients and staff encompasses a range in ethnic origins, including African American, Caribbean, Puerto Rican, other Latin countries, European immigrants, and White Americans. The effects of racism and struggles with their ethnic identity are not the primary reasons these young women seek treatment, yet they share the impact of societal racism. For young people of color, the destructive effects of racism can cause extreme impediments to their emotional, social, and psychological functioning (Zayas, 2001).

Art as Therapy

My practice of art therapy is rooted in the pioneer work of Edith Kramer (1971). In this approach of *art as therapy*, the art-making is utilized as the primary vehicle of expression and communication. The art therapist and client form what is known as a "therapeutic art alliance," whereby the interpersonal connection is established and supported through the art-making processes. Specific art directives are not given so that the client can feel free to decide upon choice of media and subject matter. While verbal exchange can and does occur, the emphasis is not necessarily upon fostering verbal interactions with the therapist or interpreting unconscious meaning from the images. As stated by Kramer,

> Instead, art therapy is conceived of primarily as a means of supporting the ego, fostering the development of a sense of identity, and promoting maturation in general. Its main function is seen in the power of the art to contribute to the development of psychic organization that is able to function under pressure without breakdown or the need to resort to stultifying defensive. So conceived, art therapy becomes both an essential component of the therapeutic milieu and a form of therapy which complements or supports psychotherapy but does not replace it. (p. xiii)

The art therapist's continuous assessment and interventions, without interpreting to the young person, guide the therapeutic art process. Functioning as the "third hand" (Kramer, 1986), the art therapist sets up an environment that invites and supports genuine investment and value in the art-making processes. This includes having an adequate work area and an ample supply of durable art materials. Functioning as "the third hand" also involves non-intrusive interventions in the art-making that support the artistic process such as offering the proper tools or changing media in keeping with an individual's need in the moment. At times, an art therapist may model use of media, offer instruction about the technical aspects of the work, or create art side-by-side with an individual. "The Third Hand must be capable of conducting pictorial dialogues that complement or replace verbal exchange" (p. 71). A pictorial dialogue involves communicating through the art-making processes and in the images. Here, verbal dialogue is generally not emphasized. Rather, it is the visual creation by the art therapist that sends a message and can influence the work of the individual in treatment. This could include the art therapist mixing paints to create colors such as peach, amber, caramel, toffee, and chestnut brown, to counter a client using black or white paints for skin tones. The client is then presented visually with options and an example of how to achieve subtle, or not so subtle, change in their work.

During the art-making processes, the art media often sustains repeated efforts and struggles. At times, the young women may paint over and over an image, or cut the clay and to reform sculpture. Engaging with art materials is a stimulating sensory experience that often leads to a release of emotions. In art therapy, helping an individual facilitate expression that can lead to a catharsis may be a first step in treatment. For some, a strong release of emotion or connecting with unconscious processes that are involved in any art-making experience may become over-stimulating.

Externalizing emotions and experiences in the art allows these young women to place their feelings and life events at a distance to be examined. It is possible, then, for them to consider alternate possibilities and develop alternate perceptions while working with the art materials. It is the role of the art therapist to recognize when an individual is either comfortable or experiencing undue anxiety as a result of the art-making processes and intervene accordingly.

In the art therapy arena, reference materials such as books or magazines and artwork illustrating people of different cultures and race provide a model of acceptance and celebration of diversity. When a young person enters a treatment arena where there are paintings, drawings, and sculptures that reveal cultural differences, a strong message is given that can be experienced viscerally. The impact of these images speaks to and can promote an atmosphere of safety, tolerance, and worth. "It is useful for the success of therapy to be able to use a tangible art product as a reference point. While the process reveals the meaning of the product, it is helpful to use the artwork as a focal point from which the dialogue emerges" (Riley, 1999, p. 200).

When young women of color create self-portraits with fair skin, blonde hair, or blue eyes, it suggests that they have created "defensive, unattainable ego ideals that can bring no comfort" (Kramer, 1986, p. 77). Therefore, I challenge their work by asking questions such as "How does this look like you? Is this what you want?" and in response to their questioning me "Isn't she pretty?" I would reply, "I don't know. . . . Pretty is different for everyone. What do you think is pretty?" Further questioning would include asking about the women they know who are strong, attractive, or stand as role models and why. These types of questions generally reveal what perceptions these young women of color have internalized from a racist society. Through words, we explore the ambivalent and/or negative messages about their origins, who they are, and who they would like to become.

Additionally, the naturally narcissistic gratification that can occur in the art-making, if the art is seen as a mirror of the artist, further supports the young person. Their efforts can leave a tangible product that has traversed emotional, psychic and physical realms. These processes parallel the range of emotional and psychic struggles for the adolescent who is attempting to achieve a sense of inner constancy. The ability to make purposeful choices and revisions in the art stands as a metaphor to the decisions of inclusion and exclusion that an adolescent has in terms of identity consolidation.

Considerations for the Therapist

As with all therapists, art therapists need to understand the cultural background of the people they see in treatment. It is common for people to embrace and accept their own cultural background as the norm. People innately subscribe special meaning to their own backgrounds (Dosamantes-Beaudry, 1977). In order to avoid the pitfalls of the color-blind therapist (Acton, 2001; Blitz & Illidge, this volume), it is necessary to acknowledge and discuss the differences in race and culture that may exist between therapist and client. Being a color-blind therapist means that one would enter into the treatment relationship with the belief that all people should be treated in a similar manner "without acknowledgement of race or culture" (Acton, 2001, p. 109). For a therapist to operate under such a premise, it would follow that their position could not include a genuine understanding of the clients with whom they work. It is equally

important to recognize, understand, and be sensitive to what impact the
cultural background of the therapist has upon the therapeutic relationship (Coseo, 1997). Therapists must be attuned to any inclination toward identification with clients of similar cultural background, and
distancing toward clients from dissimilar cultural backgrounds. The
cultural similarities or differences between client and therapist will influence unconscious identifications and defense mechanisms (Bradshaw, 1978). "Self-knowledge can control such maneuvers and enable
the therapist to be more sensitive toward people of different cultures
and races" (Pinderhughes, 1989, as cited in Canino & Spurlock, 1994,
p. 130).

As a White therapist working with young women of color, it is essential to explore and clarify the differences and similarities that arise in
treatment. So much of what can occur in the art-making process is emotionally laden and beyond the borders of conscious awareness. Art therapists need to identify and recognize how their own biases and prejudices
might present in the visual realm. It is irresponsible and unethical for an
art therapist to attempt to guide their clients through processes that they
have not explored or resolved themselves (American Art Therapy Association, 2003).

As such, art therapists often create their own art to explore the issues
that arise within any treatment relationship. Figure 1, a mixed media
painting titled *Issues in Identity*, explores my role as a White art therapist working with young women of color. Within this work are three
faces, overlapping and layered. The central figure, whose eye color has
yet to be determined, stands between what I envisioned as the ancestor
on the left and me on the right. Initially placed with equal clarity, my
self-portrait was ultimately layered over, leaving only a shadow of my
presence. It was important for me to clarify the impact of my role and to
balance my presence and influence in the dynamics of identity formation with young women of color. The following case vignettes are examples of some of the exchanges that have occurred in the art therapy
arena.

CASE EXAMPLES:
THE BLUE EYE PHENOMENON IN ART THERAPY

When I first began to read Toni Morrison's (1970) Pulitzer Prize win-
ning work, *The Bluest Eye,* I was working with Lakendra, a young African American girl who was horribly abused for most of her 13 years.

FIGURE 1. Issues in Identity

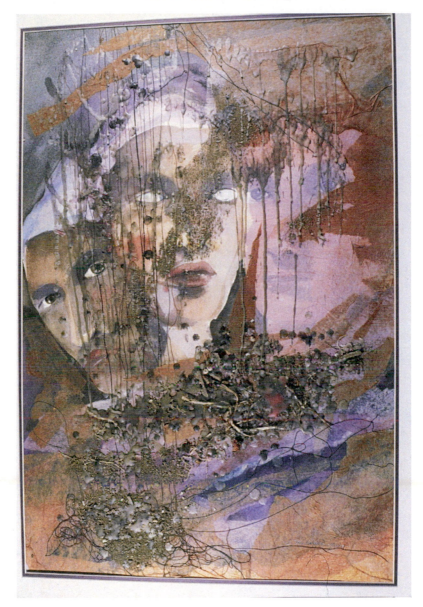

Reprinted with permission.

Lakendra was steadfast in her desire to have blue eyes instead of the brown eyes that she was born with. The parallels between Morrison's Pecolla Breedlove and Lakendra's experiences of abuse and desire for a physical appearance so unlike her own were profound. Lakendra, working in a silent and focused manner, painted an image of herself with blue eyes (see Figure 2). Absorbed in her artwork and internal processes, Lakendra was non-responsive to external stimuli. She did not react affectively or reply when spoken to. Efforts to have her share the meaning of her work or enter into any verbal or art-making dialogue went unfulfilled. In the milieu, she escalated in psychotic thought processes and was beset by emotions that she could not contain. Lakendra was not able to make use of the multitude of services, including art therapy, at the day treatment program. She continued to deteriorate psychically and was hospitalized for a higher level of care.

A year later, when the English teacher at the day treatment program assigned *The Bluest Eye,* students were asked to write a response paper. The only student to write that she would keep her own brown eyes was a White girl. Without any expressed ambivalence, these young women of color were subscribing to the dominant culture's standards of beauty and acceptance based on skin tone.

FIGURE 2. Girl with Blue Eyes

Kayla

Kayla, a 14-year-old African American girl, and her mother participated in weekly art therapy sessions for over two years. During the first year of treatment, Kayla was completing work on a sculpture of a female figure that had taken the better part of the year to construct. Clearly, her persistent work on this clay figure demonstrated tremendous care and investment in what appeared to be a self-portrait. It is notable that while all parts of Kayla's female figure were approached with great care and detail, the face remained untouched for many months (see Figure 3). Leaving the figure without a face suggested ambivalence and uncertainty in her sense of personal identity. Modeling work on a separate piece of clay, I invited Kayla to evaluate and make choices as a means of practicing before attending to her own sculpture. When it came time to paint the figure, I assisted by mixing a range of colors to choose from, in addition to the flat brown, black, or white available in the paint containers. Art therapists must be able to mix a range of skin tones using art materials such as paints, chalks, or colored pencils. It requires certainty and determination to spend time mixing paints to the exact color desired. For individuals who may be ambivalent, the process of mixing colors may be too demanding and they will often use media simply because it is right in front of them.

Kayla began to mix a dark shade of brown similar to her own skin color. Her mother looked up from her own work, a colored pencil drawing of a platter of food, wrinkled her nose in disgust and said, "Eww . . . yuck! It looks like dog shit." Kayla's face was crestfallen. She sat down and abandoned her painting. The mother's overt rejection and comparison of her daughter with feces was shocking. Rage toward a child was not a new phenomenon to me; however, the rejection of a child based on color was. Both mother and daughter appeared to have similar skin tones. During a clinical meeting, other staff indicated that within this family there was a hierarchy among family members according to skin tone. Greater status was granted to family members with lighter skin tone, and Kayla was the darkest-skinned member of her family.

In response to the mother's disgust, I intervened by talking about many things that were the color brown. A comparison was made between the various paint tones to skin colors, the earth, elements of nature, and even some of the food in the drawing the mother was working on. The intention here was to neutralize the rage, make it possible for work to continue, and present a possibility of acceptance of many shades of brown. By working in the metaphor, this intervention was

FIGURE 3. Kayla, Self-Portrait Unpainted/No Facial Details

Reprinted with permission.

successful: Kayla ultimately opted to continue with the dark brown skin tone and complete her work (see Figure 4).

Rejection of ethnic identity by adolescent girls is demonstrated frequently in their approach to self-portraits. Cries of "the lips are too big, the nose is too flat or wide" have been the words of many young women of color. While self-rejection is not uncommon for traumatized adolescents, self-rejection based upon race is something that I have witnessed

FIGURE 4. Kayla, Self-Portrait, Clay and Paint

almost exclusively by girls who identify themselves with the Black community.

Tanya

Tanya, a 15-year-old girl, participated in individual art therapy for over a year. Her father was from Trinidad and her mother from Guyana. Tanya's mother was a drug runner and was physically abusive of Tanya. During individual art therapy sessions, Tanya was initially unsure how to respond to the individual attention. She presented herself in a seductive manner, attempting to undress to her bra or undershirt, saying it was hot in the room. Tanya would continuously bump into me and ask to have her clothes adjusted or an itch on her body scratched. Physical boundaries were adhered to, a smock was worn by both of us at all times, and work area was established. The clinical staff suspected that Tanya had been sexually abused. Tanya seemed to understand her worth and value were based upon seductive physical contact.

In the beginning stages of treatment, Tanya's work in clay encompassed fragmented body parts and snakes that transformed into penises. Interventions were geared toward integrating these fragmented forms to humanize her creations and lead her away from perceiving people as objects. To reduce the potential for Tanya embracing the role of abuser or perpetrator, it was important that she begin to perceive people as whole beings. Additionally, before Tanya could begin to explore her own identity, she had to be able to understand herself as fully present and not dissociate from her physical experiences or presence. This work spanned the better part of her first year in art therapy.

In her final work of the second year, Tanya began a clay sculpture of a head, which she claimed to be a self-portrait (see Figure 5). In sculpting the features, Tanya cut and slashed at the nose and lips of the figure. Her manner was aggressive and bordered on lethal. While working in clay, she spontaneously stated that her family had her nose broken when she was a baby to prevent it from getting too big. Her ambivalence in crafting life-like features was marked. She would tear, cut, and rip away the clay, only to apply it again and again.

Clay is forgiving. It is a medium that can withstand tremendous shifts, changes, cuts, and aggressive energy. It has the potential for reintegration, sustained energy, and construction. Over several weeks, I modeled work on a separate sculpture. Tanya observed my process of forming the head and reshaping the facial features. Most often this exchange occurred in silence. Tanya would watch, return to her own work, and at times implement

FIGURE 5. Tanya, Self-Portrait, Clay/Unpainted

Reprinted with permission.

some of the techniques I had used. Ultimately, Tanya was able to reintegrate the assaulted features. She sustained work on her sculpture revealing a solid, well-formed, life-like self-portrait. Her approach in completing this work was tender. The smoothing of the form suggested a dramatic shift from self-mutilation to self-care. Additionally, the clay, like skin, covers a multitude of inner scars and wounds that had been exposed in her art-making processes. These hidden wounds were now being tended to and incorporated into her work, her sense of self.

My role with Tanya was to bear witness, support her struggle, and continuously offer options and materials. Tanya was able to accept the interventions. By the end of the construction of this clay head, there was a notable shift in her energy and demeanor in session. Tanya approached painting of the head in a calm and focused manner. An exploration of various skin tones occurred through mixing paints. Colors ranging from light peach to dark brown were created and then tested on paper. These color samples were also held up near Tanya's face for comparison with her own skin coloring. At one point, Tanya painted her arm with several bands of brown, waited for the paint to dry, as she wanted to be sure "to get it right." I questioned her about choosing a color to match her hair and eyes. She selected and used colors on her sculpture that were clearly akin to her own coloring. Tanya abandoned her initial desire for blue eyes in favor of dark brown eyes, similar to her own eye color. Concluding work on this piece was the painting of the headdress. Tanya was specific in color choice. She used colors from the flags of Trinidad and Guyana, the homeland of her parents (see Figure 6).

Tanya's final work in art therapy was sculpting with clay a seated female figure that she identified as an image of her mother. Tanya was able to bring the figure to completion within a few sessions. She was clear in her choices and steadfast in the clay process. Her approach during this work was gentle. Tanya gave particular attention to the flowing, long braided hair and smoothing the surface in a tender manner that appeared to be caressing the skin. Tanya stated in one of her last art therapy sessions that she felt she had "done all I need to do here."

DISCUSSION

In the cases presented, the effects of racism and intra-family color prejudice were evidenced in the words and initial images of these young women of color. Internalizing negative messages from family members and the culture at large, these young women embraced ideals that were unattainable. In art therapy, aiding a fantasy by supporting images and ideals that lead to emptiness and self-rejection can destroy a young person's self-concept. Acknowledging cultural differences, providing modeling, and encouraging exploration will support young women of color in acceptance and celebration of their ethnic identity. For the art therapist, one manner of responding to cultural diversity lies in the very tools we use. Mixing paints, comparing colors and media to achieve visual representations is the metaphoric language of identity as seen in the art. Communication and exchange in art therapy occurs through both pictorial and verbal dialogue.

In any clinical work, the art therapist will strive to provide a progressive and integrative experience for the individual. For some individuals, as seen in the work of Lakendra, the art making processes may indicate psychic and emotional disintegration. For Tanya and Kayla, who were able to embrace therapeutic interventions, their work in art therapy led to experiences of competency with the media and a sense of empowerment through the art making. Kayla's and Tanya's life-like, naturalistic self portraits suggest that they were able to begin to work through negative identifications based upon intra-family prejudice and societal racism, and move toward accepting and embracing their ethnic identity.

FIGURE 6. Tanya, Self-Portrait, Clay and Paint

Reprinted with permission.

REFERENCES

Acton, A. (2001). The colorblind therapist. *Art Therapy, 18,* 109-112.

American Art Therapy Association (2003). *Ethical principles for art therapists.* Available from http://www.arttherapy.org/aboutarttherapy/ethicsfinal2003.pdf

Blitz, L. V., & Illidge, L. C. (2006). Not so black and white: Shades of gray and brown in antiracist multicultural team building in a domestic violence shelter. *Journal of Emotional Abuse, 6*(2/3), 113-134.

Bond, S., & Cash, T. (1992). Black beauty–Skin color and body images among African American college women. *Journal of Applied Social Psychology, 22,* 874-888.

Bradshaw, W. H. (1978). Training psychiatrists for working with Blacks in basic residency programs. *American Journal of Psychiatry, 135*(12), 1520-1524.

Canino, I., & Spurlock, J. (1994). *Culturally diverse children and adolescents.* New York: The Guilford Press.

Celious, A., & Oyserman, D. (2001). Race from the inside: An emerging heterogenous race model. *Journal of Social Issues, 57*(1), 149-165.

Chapman, R. T. (2006). Internalized racism of the clinician and the treatment dynamic. *Journal of Emotional Abuse, 6*(2/3), 219-228.

Coseo, A. (1997). Developing cultural awareness for creative arts therapists. *The Arts in Psychotherapy, 24*(2), 145-157.

Crick, N. (2002). Relational and physical victimization within friendships: Nobody told me there'd be days like these. *Journal of Abnormal Child Psychology, 30*(6), 599-607.

Dosamantes-Beaudry, I. (1997). Embodying a cultural identity. *The Arts in Psychotherapy, 24*(2), 129-135.

Drake, S., & Cayton, H. (1945). *Black metropolis.* New York: Harcourt Brace.

Erikson, E. (1975a). The concept of ego identity. In A. Esman (Ed.), *The psychology of adolescence* (pp. 178-195). Guilford, CT: International University Press.

Erikson, E. (1975b). The problem with ego identity. In A. Esman (Ed.), *The psychology of adolescence* (pp. 318-346). Guilford, CT: International University Press.

Gilligan, C. (1993). *In a different voice.* Cambridge, MA: Harvard University Press.

Hall, R. (1992). Bias among African-Americans regarding skin color: Implications for social work practice. *Research on Social Work Practice, 2,* 479-486.

Hall, R. (1995). The bleaching syndrome: African Americans' response to cultural domination vis-à-vis skin color. *Journal of Black Studies, 26,* 172-184.

Harvey, A. (1995). The issue of skin color in psychotherapy with African Americans. *Families in Society: The Journal of Contemporary Human Services, 76,* 3-10.

Keenan, K. (1996). Skin tones and physical features of Blacks in magazine advertisements. *Journalism of Mass Communication Quarterly, 73,* 905-912.

Klein, J. W. (1980). *Jewish identity and self-esteem: Healing wounds through ethnotherapy.* New York: Institute on Pluralism and Group Identity.

Kramer, E. (1971). *Art as therapy with children.* New York: Shocken Books.

Kramer, E. (1986). The art therapist's third hand: Reflections on art, art therapy, and society at large. *American Journal of Art Therapy, 24,* 71-86.

Morrison, T. (1970). *The bluest eye.* NewYork: Plume Books.

Neal, A., & Wilson, M. (1989). The role of skin color and features in the Black community: Implications for Black women and therapy. *Clinical Psychology Review, 9,* 945-965.

Okazawa-Rey, M., Robinson, T., & Ward, J. (1987). Black women and the politics of skin color and hair. *Women in Therapy, 6,* 89-102.

Pinderhughes, E. (1989). *Understanding race, ethnicity and power: The key to efficacy in clinical practice.* New York: Free Press.

Pipher, M. (1994). *Reviving Ophelia.* New York: Ballantine Books.

Riley, S. (1999). *Contemporary art therapy with adolescents.* London: Jessica Kingsley.

Samuel-Young, L. (2006). Staying whole in a fragmented world: One Afro-Caribbean social worker's journey through wholeness—A psycho-spiritual perspective. *Journal of Emotional Abuse, 6*(2/3), 229-239.

Schwartz, W. (1998). The identity development of multicultural youth, *CUE Digest,* Number 137, Clearinghouse on Urban Education, NY.

Simmons, R. (2002). *Odd girl out: The hidden culture of aggression in girls.* San Diego: Harcourt Books.

Tatum, B. D. (1997). *Why are all the Black kids sitting together in the cafeteria?* New York: Basic Books.

Wade, T. J. (1996). The relationship between skin color and self-perceived global, physical, and sexual attractiveness, and self-esteem for African Americans. *Journal of Black Psychology, 22,* 358-373.

Zayas, L. (2001). Incorporating struggles with racism and ethnic identity in therapy with adolescents. *Clinical Social Work Journal, 29*(4), 361-373.

doi:10.1300/J135v06n02_12

SECTION V
RACIAL IDENTITY DEVELOPMENT
OF THE THERAPIST

Internalized Racism of the Clinician
and the Treatment Dynamic

Rene T. Chapman

SUMMARY. This article examines the transference and countertransference found in an interethnic treatment dyad where the therapist is a heterosexual Black woman and the patient is a homosexual White man. The core issues examined are racial and sexual identity, power and privilege, internalized racism, and shame. Clinical examples, including dream material, are presented in an effort to explore the unconscious aspects of identity and internalized introjects. doi:10.1300/J135v06n02_13 *[Article copies available for a fee from The Haworth Document Delivery Service: 1-800-HAWORTH. E-mail address: <docdelivery@haworthpress.com> Website: <http://www.HaworthPress.com> © 2006 by The Haworth Press, Inc. All rights reserved.]*

Address correspondence to: Rene T. Chapman, LCSW, 26 Court Street, Suite 610, Brooklyn, NY 11242 (E-mail: RTChapman@nyc.rr.com).

[Haworth co-indexing entry note]: "Internalized Racism of the Clinician and the Treatment Dynamic." Chapman, Rene T. Co-published simultaneously in *Journal of Emotional Abuse* (The Haworth Maltreatment & Trauma Press, an imprint of The Haworth Press, Inc.) Vol. 6, No. 2/3, 2006, pp. 219-228; and: *Racism and Racial Identity: Reflections on Urban Practice in Mental Health and Social Services* (ed: Lisa V. Blitz, and Mary Pender Greene) The Haworth Maltreatment & Trauma Press, an imprint of The Haworth Press, Inc., 2006, pp. 219-228. Single or multiple copies of this article are available for a fee from The Haworth Document Delivery Service [1-800-HAWORTH, 9:00 a.m. - 5:00 p.m. (EST). E-mail address: docdelivery@haworthpress.com].

KEYWORDS. Racism, racial identity, internalized racism, transference, countertransference, shame

"Haven't you ever felt shame?" This was one of the first questions asked of me by a supervisor with reference to my beginning work with a White, homosexual, male patient who was to become key to my own development as a clinician. I did not know it at the time, but this patient was to teach me everything that would become the bedrock of my understanding and skill in challenging my internalized racism. I also learned to identify and work with the transference-countertransference dynamic as the main tool in the treatment process.

I was in psychoanalytic training at the time, and so naïve. I was intimidated by the status of the very thing I was trying to become. I was so intimidated that I did not even admit to myself that I wanted to become an analyst. I told myself that as long as I was getting something out of the training that would lead to deeper work with clients that I would continue. I gave myself permission to drop out, to not complete, and to take it slowly. What I did not understand at the time was that I was allowing my feelings of internalized racism to protect me from the harsh reality and my fears of not being good enough to become an analyst due to being a Black woman. I had given myself permission to fail in order to protect myself from the feeling that Black women are not "supposed to" become analysts. A Black analyst is contrary to the world order.

My maternal grandmother was a civil rights activist and I had been a pawn in the movement from the time I was a child. *Brown vs. the Board of Education* was decided in 1954, and I began school in 1955, first in my neighborhood, and then a few years later in a White neighborhood. I had been trained to fight the world order simply by living. I lived in a Black neighborhood, was "carpooled"–not bussed–to White schools, and had to be "the only" and isolated in the classroom. Forget a social life; I was ostracized. The isolation that results from being ostracized and fighting the social order did not suit my social nature, but fit "the cause" and as a child I had no choice in the matter. I knew I was smart, actually smarter than most people were, but in White environments, I felt small, inadequate, and downright stupid sometimes. Most days were hard because I struggled to maintain an authentic self-view while considering the views of the Whites around me. I found myself beginning to wear a shame that did not quite fit. I was afraid of disappointing my parents, who tried to provide a learning environment meant to be challenging but was, in truth, oppressive. I overcame, mastered the "learning to learn" process with some difficulty, and went on to become a social worker.

As my professional life progressed, I would hit treatment impasses with some of my clients. I could go no deeper, and knew that the key to breaking down the walls of these impasses lay in my learning a new skill. While managing symptoms and problematic behaviors was still my goal, I began to realize that an inability to identify and address the underlying issues that resulted in those problematic behaviors led to new symptom formation or stalemated work. I realized that I needed psychoanalytic training to better serve my clients. I had no idea of the impact it would have on me personally.

SHAME AND INTERNALIZED IDENTITY ISSUES IN TREATMENT

Race carries weight in our society, and the treatment situation is no different. I have chosen to discuss my treatment of a White homosexual man because of the poignancy of the difference in our races and how that difference affected the treatment. In this therapeutic dyad, a Black woman therapist treating a White homosexual man was fraught with reversals. Being Black is a primary part of who I am as a person. I was ashamed of being Black, while simultaneously voicing pride at being Black. I had committed no crime and had nothing of which to be ashamed. My race simply was, as my client's homosexuality simply was.

A word about shame and racism: both are interpersonal in nature, shame relating to an operation in a dyad while racism relates to an operation in society. The effects are the same. Shame has been described in depth by Broucek (1991) in *Shame and the Self*. Shame refers to an "I am-ness." In guilt, the operating factor is that one has done something wrong; in shame the operating factor is, "I am something wrong." This is the parallel to racism. Part of the power of racism that becomes internalized lies in the acceptance of the "I am something wrong" identity, often unconsciously. The psychic problem with the internalization of shame is that it is often in conflict with who you are as a person. The effects, however, are seen in the behavior and attitudes in the world and in the emotional life of the individual. The mantra antiracists have been challenging is "White is right" by saying that White people have been given unearned privilege. Using race to determine privilege and status must come to an end. Blacks have been fighting for equality and respect since slavery, and that battle continues even in the treatment room. Samuel-Young (this volume) also discusses this struggle with internalized racism and the importance of faith and resiliency to overcome it.

This same process of instilling shame in individuals is true for other objects of societal oppression, such as homosexuals. In homophobia, society identifies the homosexual as "being wrong," and some homosexuals internalize this status and the attendant shame. Both external and internal evidence of this may be seen in the defense mechanisms used. My work with this homosexual White man became a dance between his internalized homophobia and my internalized racism.

So when my White male supervisor asked me, "Haven't you ever felt shame?" I did not know how to answer. I became immobilized. He had used his privilege. He assumed that I had felt shame. He did not know me. How could he know about a feeling that I was only dimly aware of myself? I did not yet have the language to tease out the threads of what I had been feeling in the treatment room with my White, male patient who was a homosexual,[1] and therefore a member of a hidden minority. My patient was also suffering from emotional whiplash. As a White man he is privileged by our society; yet every time he "comes out" (i.e., identifies himself as homosexual), he loses some of that privilege. He could not tolerate the mobilization of a homophobic society against his being. And he was being treated by a Black woman. The power differential established by society was at play in the treatment room in every session. My patient often thought, "Can she help me?" I knew I could help him. Our minority status occasioned an area of identification that could be used in the service of the treatment. I was not prepared, however, for the overwhelming reaction I would have to that identification.

KNOWING THE PATIENT THROUGH TRANSFERENCE AND COUNTERTRANSFERENCE

Treatment uses the powerful tool of the exploration of transference and countertransference in the treatment process to effect change. Transference and countertransference not only apply to elements found in the family drama, but in our experiences in society as well. I will review several examples from different points in the treatment to demonstrate how the exploration of transference and countertransference affected the treatment of this patient. The examples progress from the earliest part of the treatment, into the middle phase when the treatment alliance was secure, and the final example comes from the termination phase of the treatment. All of the transference and countertransference examples have the issue of race as a major component.

It is through transference that we learn the most about the unconscious processes of our patients and their needs. They enter the treatment room, a special and private space, and fill it with their lives. The family and social dramas emerge in that room, that space. But the therapist is there as well, providing a screen for the viewing of this live production. One aspect of this screening is the content of the material itself; the other is the nature of the screen and the ability to show what is projected. Ideally, the screen displays without distortion. Unlike the screening room, however, there is a dynamic between the production and screen that bears on the treatment. Being human, both the producer of the material and the screen have distortions. The working-through process of these distortions is what leads to the change. The distortions in content we call transference, and in the screen the countertransference.

Comas-Diaz and Jacobsen (1991) speak of the unique dynamics of interethnic transference. Some indicators that these factors are operational include overcompliance and friendliness, denial of ethnicity and culture, ambivalence, clinical anthropology, guilt, pity, and aggression in either process. (Clinical anthropology refers to the therapist's overly curious activity about the patient's ethno-cultural background at the expense of the treatment; p. 396.) The power differential must be taken into account as well. In this therapeutic dyad, the therapist is a member of a minority racial group while the patient is a member of the majority racial group. In some instances, my patient's transference reaction was used defensively to mask deeper emotional reactions, similar in emotional content to his struggles with being a member of a hidden minority.

My patient's core issue was one of identity. He had entered his first session speaking of how he was "shamed" and my unconscious responded to this feeling and became trapped in its power. Shame makes you hide. I would often comment on how he presented with a "smoke and mirrors" routine. "From the first session, though he spoke for most of the session, afterwards I realized that he had shared nothing concrete about the specifics of his life, where he worked, lived or friends" (Chapman, 1997, pp. 4-5). It was as if he had brought a smoke screen into the room with his words.

In the next session, I explored the "smoke and mirrors" behavior with my patient and observed the difference in our races. He had assigned me special powers. He said that he felt comfortable enough with me to just begin. I am Black and therefore empathic, comfortable in and with my body and with my sexuality, and able to be a compassionate nurturer, the perfect parent. This was recognized as a positive transference and I took it at face value. I used denial and avoided exploring the possible negative reactions he may have had at that time to my being Black.

Racism and Stereotypes in the Transference

The positive transference deepened as the treatment progressed when he associated me with a Black maid in the civil rights-torn South portrayed in a TV series. For me, in the countertransference images of "mammy" came to mind, and though I could see the positive maternal transference, the "good mother," I experienced feelings of rejection based on color and felt discounted as a person in my own right. My instincts were not wrong. The shame of his association to my being a Black maid in his mind emerged: "It was as if I called you a nigger." I certainly felt as if he had. I also knew that my handling of this material would be critical in our ability to continue to work together. I acknowledged the fact, despite the rage welling up inside of me. My feeling of being victimized by his unconscious racism was on target. By the time this material emerged, I was able to really hear his comment, could identify my own countertransference, reaction to the "mammy" position, and stay with the material to permit him the experience of exploring the pejorative feelings he had been harboring. I also began to wonder about the ways in which he might devalue his own mother.

If the positive transference was difficult for me to handle, the negative was almost impossible at times. His rage and aggression became unmanageable. In many ways, he devalued me. He devalued me by testing the boundaries, coming late, withholding payment, and questioning my judgement, all the while acknowledging that there was an improvement in his functioning. When he was enraged, he attacked on the race axis. He devalued himself as well. I had missed the sense of castration and shame he experienced as a homosexual man. I was unaware of how my own helplessness as a member of a feared and hated minority would negatively affect the work.

His feelings toward me started appearing in the dream material. In an early dream, he told of seeing two minority men. He thought that they were Black. He was frightened of them and thought they would hurt him. As we explored the material, it was clear that the transference implication was to me, but he had difficulty acknowledging this. Nonetheless, I listened to the material and realized how violent he saw Blacks as being. I had become a real threat to his existence, and I was his therapist. Communicating this realization seemed to help him. This dream also gave me a clue to the closeness he was beginning to feel in the therapeutic relationship and the fears that were beginning to emerge. What I missed, however, was the warded-off part of himself and his anger that was also implied in that Black men might hurt him, in the dream and in reality.

Identity Issues in the Countertransference

I thought: how could I possibly help? He cannot trust me. My reaction was to pull away to protect myself, and indeed this was a stance that I maintained for some time. My defensive and protective withdrawal was interpreted as aggression, the very thing that he feared. I also missed the fact that the Black men also represented his fears of his own rage connected to his minority status, going out of control.

In many ways I felt sorry for him, so that pity was one of my reactions. Here, it was from the standpoint of my position as a member of the heterosexual majority, enriched with my understanding of the dynamics of the minority status in this society. White society had not prepared him for the reality of being homosexual within a heterosexual world. As a Black woman, I grew up in a family that taught me a variety of ways of coping with my minority status. Threats were something that came from outside of the home. There was strength in affiliation. For him, however, he was a stranger within his own home and rejected by his family. They did not understand how he came to be a part of them, and given his difference, he was shunned. There were almost no models of difference for him to emulate. I felt unequal to the task of becoming a role model for him. He responded to me as he responded to his own family. He hated me.

Both of us had to struggle with the isolation he was feeling in his life and in the treatment. He was aware that he had pushed me away, but unlike his family I tried to stay close, to understand why he felt he needed to be alone. What we discovered was that he had not had the experience of feeling that he belonged anywhere. Again, my memories of elementary school flooded me . . . alone, isolated, not by choice, but by circumstance. My empathic responses to his material produced mending in the therapeutic relationship. I had understood his longing to belong. His parents apparently never understood this. He began to explore the difference between his longed-for parents and his real parents, accepting their limitations. He started to value the work again. I got paid. He discussed his treatment with friends, but they questioned our accomplishments. "Can she really help you?" they would ask. He shared that race was a factor in their concern. The conflicts appeared in the dream material again.

Division, Defense, and a Sense of Danger

The dream revolves around a "murderous Black apartment superintendent" who kills two people, a couple, by cutting their throats, and a neighbor acts as if everything is perfectly fine. The superintendent is also seen as being in his childhood room and taking a TV from him, maybe borrowing it. Next, the superintendent is in bed and over him, big, powerful, and intimidating. There were a specific number of old photos involving some espionage. There are rambling building scenes, an elevator, and this superintendent that he wants to like more than he does says, "don't worry, no one will hurt you here." In his telling of the dream, he sensed an unknown danger. He went on and finally said, "I don't feel OK to say it. You're Black and I'm not. There is an obvious difference. I have this fear of not being understood under the guise of helping me."

My thoughts were of controlling my own rage. I knew that the dream conveyed a feeling in the transference of my incompetence, and his being unsure of my efficacy, all hanging on my being Black. It hit too close to home. Despite the gains he had made, I was not secure in my role in those gains. I said nothing meaningful, and simply encouraged him to talk. I did not want to treat him. I was tired. I wanted to withdraw and was relieved when the session ended. It gave me a chance to work on my responses to this material and prepare for the next day's session.

I remarked how the murdered couple resembled his parents. For some time now, he was talking of the difference between his real parents and the parents in his head, and in his memory. I, "the Black superintendent," had killed the parents of his fantasy life and he now had to live with the knowledge of his real parents. We had produced together a positive therapeutic outcome. He was not so much afraid of my being inadequate as he was of experiencing me as being effective.

A new conflict arose. His friends wanted him to stop treatment with me. Where would his allegiances fall? He felt really uncomfortable behaving how others wanted him to behave. He was not sure if he wanted to please his friends, and stop treatment with me, or if he wanted to continue to please me. He was not yet sure of what he wanted to do for himself. He referred to the fact that dreams carry precious information. He said that he would have ended with me if he had felt uncomfortable with me, but he was also aware of how resistant he was to treatment. "In a way there is a way in which I trust you and I don't . . . You know, though, you are in training and I wonder if maybe I should leave treatment . . . like sometimes I feel that you just don't get it . . ." But I did "get it," very much so. And he did as well.

After these sessions, I realized that he wanted to stop treatment, to leave before he was left, to protect against his expectation of my retaliatory rage, and also to block the feeling that he had with reference to me perhaps using him for my own purposes and not being truly there for him. I identified this and the floodgates opened. He was relieved that I was willing to explore this "murderous" feeling. He had put out on the table what he had been feeling and talking with his friends about for a long time: can a Black woman help him? I would ask myself how much abuse I was willing to accept in the name of helping someone who hated me.

HEALING AND WHOLENESS

Being able to identify the gains that one is making in treatment and reducing the unconscious defensive reactions signal the beginning of the end of the work. Although it took some time, the work between us became more genuine. I was less defensive, and the work became less painful as I was able to acknowledge that what was brought in the treatment room was his emotional pain, and his own healing. I could sit with his feelings and empathize without tearing myself apart in the process.

My hope is that this paper is helpful to those who are struggling with their own reactions to clients and patients who raise the countertransferential material. What issues are raised? Are they from the family drama, or from broader society? Are they issues that have lain dormant or conflicted? Are they unidentified issues? Is it race? As therapists we have to start asking about the impact of race on the life of the patient on a regular basis, irrespective of the perceived racial identity of that patient. As a part of American society, we all have internalized aspects of institutional racism into our sense of self. Being mindful of race helps us to include it in our psychoanalytic thinking and our treatment of patients.

Being a clinician on any level requires courage in managing the emotional land-mines that can develop when there is a parallel between internalized views, which are so intricately intertwined. As we unravel the tapestry of our patient's lives, we must simultaneously unravel the tapestries of our own, mending as we go along to assure that our clients are best served by whole people, willing to be real in the process, and willing to take the risk to walk with them through their experiences.

NOTE

1. Some identifying facts and specifics of the treatment have been changed to protect the identity of the patient.

REFERENCES

Broucek, F. J. (1991). *Shame and the self.* New York: The Guilford Press.
Brown v. Board of Education, 347 U.S. 483 (1954).
Chapman, R. (1997). *A case of narcissism in a homosexual man.* Unpublished case study.
Comas-Diaz, L., & Jacobsen, F (1991). Ethnocultural transference and counter transference in the therapeutic dyad. *American Journal of Orthopsychiatry, 61,* 392-402.
Samuel-Young, L. (2006). Staying whole in a fragmented world: One Afro-Caribbean social worker's journey through wholeness–A psycho-spiritual perspective. *Journal of Emotional Abuse, 6*(2/3), 229-239.

doi:10.1300/J135v06n02_13

Staying Whole in a Fragmented World: One Afro-Caribbean Social Worker's Journey Through Wholeness– A Psycho-Spiritual Perspective

Lesley Samuel-Young

SUMMARY. Racism is an unnecessary evil and is a complex, man-made construct that continues to destroy many bright futures of people of color. Racism is intricately layered and interwoven in the fabric of life and is a disease of the spirit that has its origin in a lack of brotherly love and could also be described as a lack of reverence for God. This is a personal story of staying whole in a fragmented world through spiritual transformation found in Christianity. It begins in the Caribbean and discusses some aspects of nurturing and upbringing that fostered a sense of positive self-worth, which helped in grooming for social work practice and preparation for dealing with the effects of racism in America. doi:10.1300/J135v06n02_14 *[Article copies available for a fee from The Haworth Document Delivery Service: 1-800-HAWORTH. E-mail address: <docdelivery@haworthpress.com> Website: <http://www.HaworthPress.com> © 2006 by The Haworth Press, Inc. All rights reserved.]*

KEYWORDS. Racism, Christianity, social work practice, racial identity

Address correspondence to: Lesley Samuel-Young, P.O. Box 629, Far Rockaway, NY 11691 (E-mail: lyoung@jbfcs.org).

[Haworth co-indexing entry note]: "Staying Whole in a Fragmented World: One Afro-Caribbean Social Worker's Journey Through Wholeness–A Psycho-Spiritual Perspective." Samuel-Young, Lesley. Co-published simultaneously in *Journal of Emotional Abuse* (The Haworth Maltreatment & Trauma Press, an imprint of The Haworth Press, Inc.) Vol. 6, No. 2/3, 2006, pp. 229-239; and: *Racism and Racial Identity: Reflections on Urban Practice in Mental Health and Social Services* (ed: Lisa V. Blitz, and Mary Pender Greene) The Haworth Maltreatment & Trauma Press, an imprint of The Haworth Press, Inc., 2006, pp. 229-239. Single or multiple copies of this article are available for a fee from The Haworth Document Delivery Service [1-800-HAWORTH, 9:00 a.m. - 5:00 p.m. (EST). E-mail address: docdelivery@haworthpress.com].

Envy thou not the oppressor and choose none of his ways.

–Proverbs 3:31

There are different views of what constitutes racism. Although there is variation within groups, Whites often conceive of racism as individual acts of prejudice or egregious and blatant attacks or denial of rights. People of color often view racism as a pervasive part of our social fabric, woven into culture, institutions, social structure, relationships, and both the collective and individual psyches of our nation (Miller & Donner, 2000). Franklin, Boyd-Franklin, and Kelly (this volume) offer a detailed overview of the impact of racism and the many ways it is enacted in society and in relationships.

While this paper supports these definitions of racism, it also holds the view that racism is an unnecessary evil and is a complex, man-made construct that continues to destroy many bright futures of people of color. Intricately layered and interwoven in the fabric of life, racism is a disease of the spirit that has its origin in a lack of brotherly love that could also be described as a lack of reverence for God. Racism is a canker of our humanity and is a sad commentary on the otherwise brilliant accomplishments of our human race.

Racism affects every human being in some way or another. Whites benefit from being members of the dominant group, which brings power and a significantly greater portion of wealth. With people of color, the internalization of racist ideas from society is oppressive and can affect the individual's feelings of self-worth. At the extreme, the institutionalization of racism and its perpetuation in our culture sets up a system that allows the kind of discriminatory practices that deny people of color basic rights, sometimes including their right to life. People of color often have to struggle to attain many of the basic amenities afforded free citizens, and have limited access to well-paying jobs, promotions, good education, and housing.

Racism is so deeply embedded in society that oppressed people seem to ascribe to well-defined roles that have been thrust upon them by the dominant class. Pinderhughes (1989) quoted Erikson as saying that "The sad truth is that in any system based on suppression, exclusion and exploitation, the suppressed, excluded and exploited unconsciously accept the evil image they are made to represent by those who are dominant" (p. 9). In essence, oppressed people have believed the lie and bought into the stereotypes. While many people of color have done so, many others like myself have chosen a different way of living in the world.

When oppression is based on race, it begins with the assumption of the superiority of the White race, and a system is institutionalized that rarely acknowledges, appreciates, or rewards difference in people. Instead, the system seeks to steal from, kill, and destroy those who are not of the ruling class. Whites who uphold racism rarely promote any interest other than their own or their own group. Too often, however, even when Whites appear to advocate for diversity, their efforts result in deceiving the public about the subtle cruelty of institutionalized racism (see Blitz, this volume; McGlade & Ackerman, this volume). Yet people of color continue to exist and have made significant contributions to the societies they live in anyway. As a result of the reality of racism, however, people of color are especially made to call upon the resources of their resilient spirits, and their faith is often a major part of their strength.

This is a personal story of staying whole in a fragmented world; a journey about discovering self not defined by the yardstick of racism, but through spiritual transformation found in Christianity. This spiritual transformation and sense of wholeness is evidenced by a strong faith in God and adhering to the principles in the Bible, which for Christians is the will of God for our lives. The story begins in the Caribbean, considered part of the developing world, and discusses some aspects of nurturing and upbringing that fostered a sense of positive self-worth. I can dare say that my grooming for social work practice and preparation for dealing with the effects of racism in America began there as well. Values, culture, and beliefs shape early identity formation, and this paper examines the impact of Caribbean culture and incorporates the striking resemblance between social work values and Christian beliefs. My essay is meant to provoke thought in oppressor and oppressed alike to reconsider their positions as they relate to themselves, each other, and a belief in an Almighty God, and offers a differential perspective for dealing with or thinking about racism.

THE EARLY YEARS:
CULTURE, ETHNICITY AND IDENTITY FORMATION

> Train up a child in the way that he should go and when he is old he will not depart from it.
>
> *—Proverbs 22:6*

I grew up in Trinidad and Tobago during the 1970s, at a time when life was still relatively simple. The age of technology had not fully exploded in our island and we were protected from many of the effects of globalization. As part of my family's values, I was expected to go to school and do well. I was taught to be respectful to all adults, especially elderly adults. I was taught to defer to authority. I was not to be seen with rowdy, boisterous children. Sometimes I had to temper my laughter if it got too loud. I was taught that young ladies did not laugh too loudly or sit with their legs uncrossed. (I laughed loudly but crossed my legs anyway.)

I do not recall specific discussions in my family about class and race as a child, but at that time we still used the term "Negro." I had not known that it was the term used by Whites to dehumanize all African peoples (Chisom & Washington, 1997). I did not feel dehumanized. At that time, we used it as people used the term Indians to describe those of East Indian descent. Elements of racism and classism, however, did not elude me as an individual or us as a nation.

When I attended high school, I was enrolled at one of the local high schools known for producing students who almost always attended a university as a natural progression of their diligence. As an elementary school student, if you did well on the national entrance exam for high-school admission, you were selected to attend this school or one of several others with similar reputations. In high school, I was exposed to an initial understanding of class and interracial discrimination among people of color. Since it was an all-girls' school, daughters of doctors and lawyers certainly received preferential treatment over others, as did children of "fair" complexion. If you were neither but diligently applied yourself to your schoolwork, you also gained tremendous respect. Education was highly valued in our society. When I was at least 13 years old, I remember being told that the literacy rate in our tiny nation was 98%. At some point in my high-school education, I began to apply myself and received good grades. I now think that it was there, perhaps, that I received some sense of power or mastery, although I was not conscious of this and did not think about it. Having power and using it effectively is an important component in dealing with adversity, as noted by Edwards (this volume) in her discussion about the role of resiliency in resisting racism.

My family valued respect for people of all races. I remember thinking as I eulogized my grandmother that she modeled excellent social work values for me. She was, in essence, one of the first social workers I knew. She was held in high esteem in the family and in the community: she fed the poor, visited the sick, was a model housewife, and read her Bible and prayed earnestly daily. As a child, I did not understand why she did that or why my mother insisted that I go to church almost every Sunday. I do remember pondering this God who is omnipresent and omnipotent and wondered exactly how He fit into my life. At some point in my teenage years, I spent a lot of time thinking about God and would "war" within my soul as to whether I would ever be a disciple. I wondered what I would become, whether I would "make it" in this life. I am not even sure that I understood what that meant. I thought to be rich was to be free and to be without problems. I never thought about "glass ceilings" or oppression. In truth and in fact, I never understood that being "Negro," being Black or a person of African descent, would have a different–not to mention negative–connotation once I came to America. Nonetheless, I could now look back and see that I was getting ready for some important experiences of my life. These experiences would definitely shape the way I thought about racism.

COMING TO AMERICA–MELTING INTO WHOSE POT?

Wisdom is the principal thing; therefore get wisdom; and with all thy getting get understanding.

–Proverbs 4:7

It is not surprising that most newly arriving immigrants experience myriad issues pertaining to acculturation and assimilation. Acculturation, described as "the degree to which a person subscribes to mainstream culture" (Greene, 1994, p. 31), affects those coming to America from a different place that used to be extremely familiar. Assimilation, described as "the process of diverse and racial and ethnic groups coming to share a common culture" (p. 31), might not be considered a worthwhile goal as long as the effects of racism permeate American society. Similarly, this also seemed to have been the concept behind the "melting pot theory," which presumptuously suggests that people would give up their cultures altogether (p. 29). Biculturalism, or the ability to move freely between a person's ethnic community and the larger culture, offers some degree of consolation for new immigrant people of color, but the way can still be paved with frustration for people of color who have dreams of "making it" in a racist society.

I did not come to America with visions of "making it big." America is known as the land of opportunity, and it seemed obvious that based on its technological advances, its opulence, its abundance and waste of food that God has certainly blessed America. (I am not suggesting that He has not blessed other nations.) Based on family values and personal ambition, it was important for me to migrate to a place where I could stretch myself academically, and explore and refine my God-given abilities and talents. Only then, I thought, would I be equipped to contribute in some way to the larger society.

As a result of my immigration, I have made some stark observations of what it means to live in a racist society. First of all, I was not "brown" as I have been all my life; I was suddenly Black. The reality of my own internalized racism overwhelmed me. In Trinidad, the use of the word "Black" referred to the darkest skin tone, mostly despised in our culture and a reflection of our nation's acceptance of racism. How dare Americans call me Black? For a moment, I had bought into the lie and had forgotten that I am "fearfully and wonderfully made" (Psalm 139:14) by my Creator, regardless of skin color. Our faith reminds us about who we are in Christ Jesus, but I had not yet been the Christian that I am now. Now I know that Americans call all people of African descent "Black"– and "so what?" is my response.

Another of the effects of racism I observed was the internalization of people of color as not being "as good as" White people because many people of color have not amassed the wealth that Whites have acquired. Since Blacks have generally not had several generations of accumulated wealth to be passed on to their families, there remains a highly significant difference in the average wealth between races. White people value wealth and all its trappings as the most important attributes of success, as do many people of color. I am certainly not opposed to having good fortune, or of enjoying hard-earned success. When a particular ethnic group of people has systematically devised ways to amass great fortune by oppressing others, however, there is something morally decrepit about such a system. I contend that greed is also a sickness of the spirit.

On the other hand, the lie about being "less than" gets perpetuated for those who have bought into a race-based system. This is especially seen in youth of color who seemingly idolize quick money, fast cars, adopt "gangster" mentalities (kill first), and act out "gangster" roles. The social and economic impact of racism has hindered many young people of color from being able to develop healthy egos, a strong sense of community, and cultural pride. Instead, they may tend to compensate for their perceived "lesser than" status by competing with the economic advantage of the wealthy Whites they see around them. In this way, they hold the love of money in high regard above the love of people and hence defy the second great commandment, given by Jesus Christ to his disciples, "Thou shalt love thy neighbor as thyself" (St. Matthew

22:39). There is too much death and destruction in impoverished Black communities.

Parents play a vital role in the process of helping their children develop healthy egos. "Ego psychology views people as born with an innate capacity to function adaptively" (Goldstein, 1984, p. xv). Noted behavior theorist Otto Rank, in his expounding on man's will, viewed man as "Born with an innate push toward assertion and creativity . . . Man has choice and dignity. He is not bound by the past, and there are no limits to his ultimate capability. Individuals grow against asserting their wills against those of others" (Goldstein, 1984, p. 15). Certainly parents can nurture and facilitate this drive towards healthy ego functioning in their children, despite racism. Our children are apt to be equipped and better prepared to counteract the adverse effects of racism. We ought to raise our children in a way that gives them hope for the future.

Racism does not dictate that people of color must see themselves as failures. Racism is a stumbling block, but not powerful enough to deter a resilient human spirit, especially one rooted in God's principles. With belief in God first, I now know better that we are nothing without Him, whether or not we humble ourselves long enough to consider the awesomeness of His being.

As a Christian, I understand Christ's words to me. "In the world ye shall have tribulation: but be of good cheer; I have overcome the world" (John 16:33). Mine is an attitude of unwavering faith in the word of God. Those who know sacrifice understand that standing for an ideal that benefits the larger whole comes with a price. I dare say: look at the life of Jesus Christ. There is something about deep-rooted spirituality that connects us to each other and to God. My perspective is Christian because its teachings are what continue to keep me whole in a fragmented world. I doubt that God has an expectation that any of us play victims, just as He does not expect us to oppress our brothers and sisters. He says so in His Word.

SOCIAL WORK PRACTICE: JESUS CHRIST, MASTER OF SOCIAL WORK

If a man say, I love God, and hateth his brother, he is a liar; for he that loveth not his brother whom he hath seen, how can he love God whom he hath not seen?

–I John 5:20

At the heart of any spiritual teaching is the acknowledgement of God and concern for the welfare of others. This genuine positive regard for others is honored by social workers, who ought not to entertain racism as a power dynamic in the worker-client relationship. The preamble in the National Association of Social Worker's (NASW) Code of Ethics, states that "the primary mission of the social work profession is to enhance human well-being and help meet the basic human needs of all people, with particular attention to the needs and empowerment of people who are vulnerable, oppressed, and living in poverty" (Mattaini, Lowery, & Meyer, 1999, p. 327). To do this effectively, the social worker must understand the inherent power dynamics in a race-based society, and be able to respond to the client in a way that supports and empowers them.

The Bible teaches us that Christ so revolutionized the teachings of the religious right of His day that he paid dearly for it with His life. That is a gross oversimplification of His overall purpose on earth, but as a true master of social work, it speaks to the fact that He ignored class, one of the primary systems of oppression of His day. He also ignored gender and He served the people, sacrificially I might add. The concept of race had not been invented in His day, but there are many examples in scripture that he saw beyond the superficial and related to the soul and the Spirit in people without regard to their appearance or ethnicity. He was the very embodiment of the love of God, and emulating His attitude towards people gives me joy and great strength to press on in the face of adversity. Though racism exists and many oppressed people of color internalize it, as a follower of Christ, I am called upon to walk in excellence of thought, speech, and action in the face of this spiritual crisis. I am called upon to love those who perpetuate this cruel ideology of hate. Since I am created ". . . in the image and likeness of God," and God has created people of color, I must adhere to what this means and the Bible teaches me that God is both a God of love and of excellence. One can say that He is also "of color" and beyond color. My clients, regardless of race or color, are given the respect they deserve as those also created by God.

While in my earlier life I did not think that I would be a social worker, as I matured as a compassionate human being and empathized with the plight of the downtrodden and the oppressed, I found myself being drawn to social work. Again, the attraction to things of the Spirit cannot be underestimated. Social work allows you to engage in the rich and complex dynamics of the human experience. It teaches you to cherish simple things in life. When a human soul is suffering, there is no color.

WHERE THERE IS NO VISION, THE PEOPLE PERISH

Unfortunately, as a result of institutionalized racism and a culture of oppression, many people who receive social services are people of color. The stigma of people of color who live below the poverty line and are dependent on government assistance to live reverberates all too loudly. It reinforces in American society the largely held notion that people of color are lazy, that they lack ambition, that they lack character.

In July 2004, noted entertainer Bill Cosby came under attack by some groups for his remarks about our Black youth who cannot read or write, and hence have no command of the English language. He said he cannot understand what they say. He observes also that they wear sneakers that cost hundreds of dollars, and have no jobs. Many are in prison. He slammed people of color for blaming our failures on the "White man." This infuriated many people of color, although it was true. Many people of color have bought into the lie that racism requires that we fail. We have internalized and projected back unto ourselves what has been deemed typical of the imposed sense of inferiority of African Americans.

People dared call Bill Cosby elitist, while Bill Cosby himself was obviously infuriated by our constant perpetuation of internalized racism. Images in the media that glamorize fast cars, fast money, and esteem the notion that women are playthings portray Blacks as primitive. If we look at many of the music videos hosted by Black Entertainment Television (BET), we can see how the subliminal serves the purpose of reinforcing the stereotype. We seem unaware that "at the core of racism is the shaming of the African identity and culture. . . . The subjugation and oppression are built on the foundation of the purported inferiority of the African" (Watts-Jones, 2002, p. 593). I worry about what we are teaching our children. When immigrants come to America, many make extraordinary sacrifices to go to school. To repeat an earlier point, God does not expect us to play victims to our circumstances.

CONCLUSION: WHAT NOW?

But I say unto you, Love your enemies, bless them that curse you, do good to them that hate you, and pray for them which despitefully use you and persecute you.

–St. Matthew 5:18

This is my journey through wholeness. I am a work in progress, and that will continue until I take my last breath. I was never encouraged to hate. If anyone ever paid close attention to two toddlers (one Black, one White) at play, one would see that before they are taught to hate, they are clueless about issues of race.

For me, my belief in God is crucial to my survival and my work. Adhering to God-given principles of love and forgiveness makes me effective in dealing with people of all races. Despite my many experiences within a racist society, I rise. By following God's instructions in upholding excellence as a standard, in demeanor, attitude, and service, I have been granted favor in moving among the strata of human existence with success. The Bible says that "The fear of the Lord is the beginning of wisdom; but fools despise wisdom and instruction" (Proverbs 1:7). It also says that "It is appointed unto men once to die, but after this the judgment" (Hebrews 9:21). I fear God. We are not unaccountable in this life. We are not aimlessly put on this earth to oppress each other, to be corrupt in our affairs and hoard wealth to consume on our lusts. That is the oppressors' way. As extraordinarily challenging as it may be at times, I understand my purpose as serving God. In doing so, I must not fail to love, despite afflictions, despite persecutions.

I do not believe racism is going to go away in my lifetime. This is not pessimistic, but truly evident. Whites have invested too much in creating and maintaining a system that works to their advantage and excludes others who do not look like them. Therefore, it will continue to exist as long as our current system remains unchanged.

I feel an obligation to encourage my brothers and sisters of color. The Bible admonishes us to be ". . . Transformed by the renewing of our minds" (Romans 12:2). For people of color, it means first holding unto our faith in God, and obeying His Word, then a breaking off the yoke of bondage of internalized racism by putting on a spirit of excellence. The Bible says ". . . We are more than conquerors . . ." (Romans 8:37). We have faith because we know God is our source of strength. For social workers, it means that ensuring our work is not vain; by doing it truly in love, while upholding the mandates found in our Code of Ethics. For Whites, it means learning to fear God who holds all destinies in His hands.

Finally, we need to learn the secrets of love; if we did, racism and all other "-isms" that serve the purpose of dividing a wedge in our humanity would not exist.

REFERENCES

Blitz, L. V. (2006). Owning whiteness: The reinvention of self and practice. *Journal of Emotional Abuse, 6*(2/3), 241-263.

Chisom, R. & Washington, M. (1997). *Undoing racism: A philosophy of international social change.* New Orleans: The People's Institute Press.

Edwards, B. L. (2006). The impact of racism on social functioning: Is it skin deep? *Journal of Emotional Abuse, 6*(2/3), 31-46.

Franklin, A. J., Boyd-Franklin, N., & Kelly, S. (2006). Racism and invisibility: Race-related stress, emotional abuse and psychological trauma for people of color. *Journal of Emotional Abuse, 6*(2/3), 9-30.

Goldstein, E. (1984). *Ego psychology and social work practice.* New York: The Free Press.

Greene, R. R. (1994). *Human behavior theory: A diversity framework.* New York: Aldine De Gruyter.

Mattaini, M. A., Lowery, C. T., & Meyer, C. H. (Eds.) (1999). *The foundations of social work practice: A graduate text* (2nd ed.). Washington DC: NASW Press.

McGlade, K., & Ackerman, J. (2006). A hope for foster care: Agency executives in partnerships with parent leaders. *Journal of Emotional Abuse, 6*(2/3), 97-112.

Miller, J., & Donner, S. (2000). More than just talk: The use of racial dialogues to combat racism. *Social Work with Groups, 23*(1), 31-53.

Pinderhughes, E. (1989). *Understanding race, ethnicity, and power: The key to efficacy in clinical practice.* New York: The Free Press.

Watts-Jones, D. (2002). Healing internalized racism: The role of a within-group sanctuary among people of African descent. *Family Process, 41*, 591-600.

doi:10.1300/J135v06n02_14

Owning Whiteness:
The Reinvention of Self and Practice

Lisa V. Blitz

SUMMARY. White therapists must accept, confront, and understand the fabric of oppression, and have a treatment model that helps them understand their own racial identity as well as that of their clients. Disowning Whiteness, stepping away from the experience and responsibility of White racial identity, inhibits genuine acknowledgement of privilege, and leads to the unintentional perpetuation of racism. Therapists have a responsibility to go beyond cultural competency and recognize that raising consciousness about racism is as valid and important for White clients as it is for people of color. This paper uses the Helms Racial Identity Model (1995) and a socio-historical analysis of racism to present an antiracist framework for psychotherapy and counseling. doi:10.1300/J135v06n02_15 *[Article copies available for a fee from The Haworth Document Delivery Service: 1-800-HAWORTH. E-mail address: <docdelivery@ haworthpress.com> Website: <http://www.HaworthPress.com>* © 2006 by The Haworth Press, Inc. All rights reserved.]

KEYWORDS. Whiteness, racial identity, White privilege, antiracism, antiracist framework in psychotherapy

---

Address correspondence to: Lisa V. Blitz, 85 Fifth Avenue, #936, New York, NY 10003 (E-mail: lisablitz@hotmail.com).

[Haworth co-indexing entry note]: "Owning Whiteness: The Reinvention of Self and Practice." Blitz, Lisa V. Co-published simultaneously in *Journal of Emotional Abuse* (The Haworth Maltreatment & Trauma Press, an imprint of The Haworth Press, Inc.) Vol. 6, No. 2/3, 2006, pp. 241-263; and: *Racism and Racial Identity: Reflections on Urban Practice in Mental Health and Social Services* (ed: Lisa V. Blitz, and Mary Pender Greene) The Haworth Maltreatment & Trauma Press, an imprint of The Haworth Press, Inc., 2006, pp. 241-263. Single or multiple copies of this article are available for a fee from The Haworth Document Delivery Service [1-800-HAWORTH, 9:00 a.m. - 5:00 p.m. (EST). E-mail address: docdelivery@haworthpress.com].

I became White in the summer of 1977, a few months before my 16th birthday. I had been Caucasian all along, of course. My father, being Jewish, was not necessarily considered White when he was born in 1931, and he maintained a tension between his identity as a White man and a Jew throughout his life. My mother, a Christian of Scandinavian decent, was born into Whiteness, although her ancestors had been "swarthy" at best, at least according to Benjamin Franklin (Hitchcock, 2002, p. 18). By the time I came along in 1961, it was a moot point: pale skin, blue eyes, I was declared Caucasian. My identity as a White person, however, was slower to develop.

Racism seems to be something I absorbed through cultural osmosis. Notions of White superiority or the need to stay separate from black or brown-skinned people exist in my earliest memories, even though neither of my parents consciously ascribed to such ideas. At the age of four, shortly after my family moved into a new, predominately White, neighborhood, I sat speechless as my mother encouraged me to ask a young neighbor girl to play. My mother thought it was perfectly reasonable that I should play with this girl, based solely on the fact the she was also four and also new to the neighborhood. I could not believe that my mother—who certainly knew everything—did not know that I was not supposed to play with Black girls. I also knew that I could not say that to her, because she would think me a terrible person for such a declaration. I do not know where I got the notion that I was not to play with Black children; I assume I overheard adult conversations or picked up something from television. I clearly knew, however, that I could not share my feelings with my mother. My mother did not want her child to be a racist, but there I was.

HELMS RACIAL IDENTITY MODEL

The dilemma of the forced choice between pleasing my mother and conforming to some intangible social rule triggered my journey into racial identity development. To make sense of this journey, I refer to the White racial identity model developed by Janet Helms (1995; also Kohl, this volume). The Helms model proposes six distinct statuses through which the White individual's ego evolves: contact, disintegration, reintegration, pseudo-independence, immersion/emergence, and autonomy. In the contact status, the individual is aware of racial differences but is satisfied with the status quo. Disintegration refers to the process of recognizing that being White has social implications, and comes with profound feelings of guilt and confusion. As the disintegration status resolves, the person moves into reintegration, at which point they begin to idealize White culture, adopting an attitude that Whites have the best because they are the best. They deny any responsibility for racism, and may feel hostile or fearful of people of color.

White people who move beyond this status grow into pseudo-independence, which signals the first major movement toward a positive nonracist identity (Helms, 1995). The pseudo-independent White person is dependent on people of color, however, to help her define her racial identity, uncover unconscious racism, and validate her nonracist principles. In immersion/emergence, the individual engages in a sincere search to develop a White identity that feels right and moral, and brings with it powerful emotions about how other White people deal with racial issues. Those who continue in this evolution will eventually reach autonomy, where they no longer depend on people of color for validation of their identity. At this point they have internalized a realistic view of Whiteness that can be nurtured and thoughtfully examined. In autonomy, an individual realizes a stronger sense of self, a capacity to relinquish the privileges of racism, and maintains an active commitment to social justice.

Like all stage models, the development process is not linear. Individuals frequently revisit prior statuses as they progress in their growth, and do not always proceed through all six stages. Unfortunately, when it comes to issues of race, racism, and racial identity in our culture, people are vulnerable to foreclosing on an identity that is not fully actualized. In this way, they can become "stuck" in an immature status, and, intentionally or not, perpetuate racism.

A THERAPIST'S JOURNEY

Race Is Recognized: From Contact to Disintegration and Reintegration

As I sat with my mother that day, I was jolted from the contact status. My mother's attempts to persuade me to march down the cul-de-sac of our new suburban neighborhood and ask if Peggy could play shocked me into my first experience of disintegration. I was faced with a truly irresolvable moral predicament: I knew my mother was right in some moral sense I could not grasp, *and* I feared that there would be some unknowable social repercussions if I followed her advice. I was torn between my mother's humane sensibilities and loyalty to my own racial group. Tough stuff for a four-year-old, and a little part of my inner world began to crumble.

Racism was impossible to ignore as I grew up in the 1960s, but it was also impossible to understand. The families who lived in my neighborhood were almost exclusively White (Peggy and her family notwithstanding) and conservative in their social views. In spite of this, I had regular contact with people of color, constant exposure to liberal social views, and some experiences of social prejudice. My parents were divorced when I was six, and my mother was the only single mother in the neighborhood. During my childhood and pre-adolescent years, my mother had a couple of significant relationships with Black men, and her closest friend was a Black woman who was also a single mother. As a result, we often had Black people visiting our home, causing something of a scandal in the neighborhood. In addition, in order to afford the mortgage and other living expenses, my mother rented out our two extra bedrooms to students of the local university. Many of these were international students who were visible members of racial and cultural minority groups. My home was an intriguing salad bowl of diversity, and also a source of confusion. My nonconformist family became suspect and some parents in the neighborhood instructed their children not to play with me. As a consequence, I experienced painful discrimination around race issues first-hand at a young age. Nonetheless, it did not appear to me that my mother's friends and the university students were oppressed or discriminated against and I was not really able to understand the impact of racism.

Television, on the other hand, was full of news of riots, protests, civil disobedience, and assassinations. In my pre-adolescent years, I struggled to grasp the complexity of our race-based society and I vacillated between the developmental stages of disintegration and reintegration. I gaped at the incomprehensible horror of what I was seeing and hearing through the media and felt bewilderment and anxiety in the face of racial injustice (disintegration). When this became too uncomfortable, I would idealize my social and racial group, and blame other racial groups for their troubles, concluding that there must be something wrong with "those people" being depicted on TV (reintegration). Unable to reconcile the apparent dichotomies between the people I knew and the people I heard about, I began to think racial injustice was a bad thing that happened to some, perhaps deserving, people, and racism was an act that "good" people just did not "do."

Do I Have to Be White? Pseudo-Independence and Color-Blind Ideals

As a young teenager, I began to recognize broader systems of oppression. My mother enthusiastically embraced the Woman's Liberation Movement and taught me to understand that the oppression of women was not limited to individual acts of discrimination or unfairness, but was tied to a history of inequality built into our culture and governmental and social institutions. Furthermore, she taught me to recognize these dynamics from the vantage point of a member of the oppressed group, heightening my empathy for members of other oppressed groups. My eventual understanding of institutionalized and culturally reinforced racism was a natural extension of these ideas. As these ideas about racism took hold, I began to understand that all Whites were culpable in some form and that I was part of the dominant/oppressor group.

In my budding pseudo-independence, Whiteness was something I sought to overcome. Color-blindness, the concept that race does not matter (Tatum, 1997), was my ideal. Several of my friends were varying shades of brown and black, and our friendship was comfortable because we focused on our commonalities, not acknowledging any real difference between us. My struggle to make sense of racial injustice was primarily an intellectual query about "others." It was clear to me that some people were worse off than I was in this world, and I made a commitment to work for their betterment. But even in my best intentions, my vision was limited; I wanted simply to help others to have what I have and to be more like me.

Becoming White: Immersion/Emergence

White, with the full thrust of its burden, obligation, and privilege, was something that hit me for the first time at the age of 15. It happened one evening while I sat with a group of friends, laughing, playing a board game, when I suddenly looked down at myself and realized that I was the only white-skinned person in the room. My color-blind veil was lifted. I sat in startled amazement and wondered for the first time what my friends thought of me as a White person. At that moment, and forever after, being White had profound and emotional meaning. I had taken my first step into the "immersion/emergence" status (Helms, 1995).

My early experiences in the immersion/emergence are closely linked to my sexual identity development. I have eventually come to describe myself as bisexual, or "queer" when I'm feeling playful, but as an adolescent and young adult I lived and socialized as a lesbian. My lesbian identity made me the target of other people's hatred and required that I come to terms with another form of culturally embedded oppression. It also allowed me to be part of a multiracial and multicultural lesbian and gay community in Los Angeles, a community bonded together by our common experience as sexual outlaws. My new friends responded to my need to talk about Whiteness and race by confronting me on White privilege and sharing intimate details of their experiences with racism. My real education on race and racism had begun.

During this time, I became hypervigilant, attentive to racism in every form, and acutely conscious of the many social privileges of being White. Often appalled, frequently angered, I also began to see what I had not seen before: the beauty, depth, and complexity of cultures and ways of being in the world other than my own. I became curious about people and their experience in society, and started looking for answers about how American culture grew to be so deeply entrenched in racism. I needed to find my place in our society. I spent the next couple of decades grappling with my racial identity in this stage, fully immersed, emerging now and again to take a peek at autonomy. Unable to fully accomplish this, however, I was pulled again and again into immersion, and occasionally rested back on pseudo-independence.

Giving up White privilege is confounding. During difficult years in young adulthood, I got jobs not available to people of color (being Black or brown-skinned was not appropriate "front office appearance" for the investment bank that hired me as a secretary in the 1980s). In college, I was aware that I was being tracked to graduate school while talented Black and brown students were not–and I enjoyed the attention, albeit with guilt and ambivalence. I listened supportively while my actor friend, a second generation Black West Indian, raged about another lost part because he refused to do the reading one more time "a little more Black." I cringed when White friends used racist language or exposed flagrant ignorance of their privilege, but my ability to confront their racism would depend on circumstance, not an internally motivated and secure sense of self and social justice.

Throughout the years, paralleling my professional development, I have actively sought opportunities to learn more and develop my racial consciousness. I attended several conferences and workshops focusing on developing sensitivity, promoting cultural competency, or teaching about the socio-historical origins of racism. Ongoing discussions with colleagues, supervisors, and mentors, as well as my friends, have been critical in my development. My patients have often been my best teachers, as my commitment to developing empathic alliances with them has challenged me to explore nuanced facets of myself and society I might have otherwise ignored.

Owning Whiteness: Movement Toward Autonomy

As I got stronger, I believed that if I had not yet fully achieved autonomy, it was certainly within reach. I took risks, confronting racism more boldly and consistently, and got hurt because of it. I was accused of using racism, or the "appearance" of confronting it, for subversive and manipulative purposes, or personal gain. I was accused of hypocrisy and learned how to tolerate attack and mistrust. I learned that too direct an approach can make people nervous, too much exposure leads to vulnerability, and that too soft an approach may come across as insincere. I learned how to be honest–very, very honest. I also learned how to accept love in new ways, listening to and acknowledging quiet support from those who could not give it loudly. I got bolder, found more support, and continued to move forward.

Then one day I filled out a form for yet another conference on cultural competency, and gaped at how my identity got summarized: 40-year-old-White-female-social-worker. "White," highlighted as one of the six most important words to describe me, reduced my identity down to a social construct (Anderson, 2003) that still held stereotyped images I did not like. Object relations theory (Kernberg, 1976) and ego psychology (Hartman, 1964) had taught me enough about internalized objects, good/bad object splitting, and projection to understand what my reaction was representing. I was feeling the effects of the enduring remnants of internalized racial superiority, split off from my conscious self-representation as "bad," and projected onto the generalized "other" of White people. I certainly did not want to be one of "*them*"!

The conference itself began with another eye-opener. In my first group of the day, I sat with a dozen other mental health professionals, each with years of experience working in urban settings, whom I identified as White. As we went around with introductions, however, they all identified themselves as "beige," "pink," or by their ethnic, supposedly not-quite-White, heritage, thus disowning the sociopolitical power carried by their race. I stated that I was White, and began to uncover another layer of what this means to me as a social worker and therapist.

"White" is what we are because others see us that way and it has meaning in our society, not because it is the best description of our skin color. Disowning Whiteness, stepping away from the experience and responsibility of White racial identity, inhibits genuine acknowledgement of privilege and leads to the unintentional perpetuation of racism (Thompson & Neville, 1999). Hearing my colleagues renounce their racial identity helped crystallize my conviction that as therapists we have a responsibility to go beyond mere cultural competency and include an understanding of power and oppression in our work with patients and clients.

SOCIAL JUSTICE AND ANTI-RACISM IN THE THERAPY ROOM

As therapists, we are, among other things, healers. We are responsible for the souls entrusted to us, souls that have been injured by life circumstance. The impact of living in a society constructed around racial oppression cannot be factored out of that injury, regardless of the race of the individual. To heal others, we must accept, confront, understand, and undo the fabric of oppression, and start first with ourselves.

The Therapist's Racial Identity Status and Understanding Racism

To do the work of racial identity development responsibly with clients of any race, the therapist must first be clear on his/her own racial identity status (Kohl, this volume; Ottavi, Pope-Davis, & Dings, 1994; Pope-Davis, Menefee, & Ottavi, 1993). She or he also needs adequate and appropriate supports in continuing development in this area. One need not be "finished," or have achieved autonomy (Helms, 1995), to do work around racial identity issues with others. As in other complex issues, however, it is vital that we maintain an attitude of self-awareness, including knowing our blind spots and internalized biases, to allow us to talk comfortably with our clients. It is also essential to have regular access to others who will challenge us in ongoing self-reflection and encourage us as we progress.

The therapist needs two basic tools: (a) a clear model for racial identity development that can help inform the therapist and guide the treatment, and (b) a clear, well-conceptualized sociopolitical and historical understanding of racism in our culture. Both are necessary and dependent on each other. Without a clear model of racial identity development, the therapist and client may find themselves fumbling, unable to move beyond the cognitive recognition of racial inequities with no clear direction in the process. Without the ability to examine racism from a systemic viewpoint, they may become mired down with unanswerable questions, and the frustrated search for answers can lead the client to blaming the victim and settling on an identity that assumes racial superiority. A sociopolitical and historical understanding of racism helps explain perplexing dynamics, cultural norms, and personal attitudes. It also allows the patient to consider the issue cognitively before being thrust into the heat of feeling. Individuals who realize that they have been indoctrinated into a system beyond their control may be better prepared for the guilt that often accompanies growing awareness of their role in racism.

An Analysis of Racism

The following analysis is provided as a guide to a sociopolitical and historical understanding of racism in the United States. Since the specter of racism is beyond the scope of individual experience or personal behavior, and encompasses both the oppression of people of color and the advantages afforded to Whites (Fine, 1997), it can be hard to locate or define. Racism is simultaneously embedded in our society and culture, and deeply entrenched in our psyches (Jones & Carter, 1996). In order to effectively use an analysis of racism as a tool in psychotherapy, it is important to have an understanding of its dynamics.

Franklin, Boyd-Franklin, and Kelly (this volume) give a solid overview of many aspects of how racism is enacted. Stated simply, however, racism can be understood as race prejudice plus power (Chisom & Washington, 1997), a definition that is best appreciated in the context of lessons in American history and the social and political development of American culture. The following summarizes some of my own study and is not meant to be an historical tome. In an effort to briefly outline the development of racism, many important aspects of our country's development are omitted. Citations are provided not only to support my conclusions, but also to encourage readers to pursue more in-depth learning.

Whites, the European settlers/conquerors of the "New World," created the concept of race in order to classify all other races as being inferior, thus establishing and maintaining privilege and power (Banton, 1999; Hacker, 2003; Horsman, 1999). From the beginning, the economic development of the Americas was important to Europe, as many European countries were laying claim to the land. The race-based social order was, in part, a response to the need to encourage economically poor people from Europe to risk everything to come to the "New World" and settle the vast wilderness. The Colonies needed cheap labor for production and growing families to populate the land, but the poor of Europe would not necessarily come just to be poor in the Colonies. It was important to entice them with the promise of equality and the opportunity for riches, neither of which were possible in their home countries.

The economic development of the Colonies, however, would not have been feasible if it had only relied upon the inexpensive labor of the early European immigrants. As many societies did at that time, the early Colonists turned to slavery as the most economical source of manual labor. The first attempts to enslave the native peoples of the land failed, and the African slave trade took hold. The extent and inhumanity of the African slave trade, however, far exceeded the accepted norms of the time (Zinn, 2003). To protect against social backlash and justify the cruel policies, Europeans developed the social construct of race, and later created pseudoscience to support the notion of superiority of the White people (Mosse, 1999; Poliakov, 1999).

Racism is not about individual acts of malice or prejudice, but refers to a systemic power arrangement that provides Whites with unearned privilege and oppresses people of color (Hitchcock, 2002; McIntosh, 1988; Tatum, 1997). Some elements of racism are visible and actively hurt people of color, and thus give the illusion of being easy to identify and eradicate. Racism continues to be less visibly perpetuated, however, by systems and institutions that confer unearned privilege and opportunity on White people. White people are taught not to see that we have any unearned advantages, but to believe that we have the best because we have worked hard and earned it. Our children are taught in a primary and secondary educational system that slants the story of our nation's history in a manner that supports White superiority and seemingly legitimizes our dominance (Loewen, 1995; Zinn, 2003). Thus, the dynamics of oppression are obscured and woven into the fabric of the institutional culture.

Our nation was founded on principles and a worldview that justified– even *required*–racism (Fredrickson, 1999; Hacker, 2003; Loewen, 1995). All of our fundamental societal institutions were created in this context. Thus, racism permeates every institution in American society and continues as a force of oppression to this day. Unless an organization is intentionally antiracist, everything it does will disproportionately benefit White people and perpetuate racism, as discussed by several authors in this volume (see Geller, Miller, & Churchill, this volume;

McGlade & Ackerman, this volume; Peacock & Daniels, this volume). People run these institutions, of course, and not all of those people are White. Just as White people are taught to accept the status quo as normal and internalize a sense of racial dominance, people of color can internalize racial oppression. By not examining internalized oppression, people of color may unconsciously and unwittingly participate in perpetuating racist policies and practices (Helms, 1995), making reality even harder to see clearly.

Racism in Psychological Theories

Psychotherapy is a product of White and Jewish cultures (Langman, 1997), and this cultural bias has been embedded into our understanding of the etiology and definitions of mental disorders and pathology (Rollock & Gordon, 2000). Since mental health and social services have been designed based on these culturally biased ideas (Carter, 1995; Sue, 2003), using these theories or models to inform our work without critical analysis perpetuates racism. To counteract this, a sophisticated understanding of the cultural assumptions embedded in our theories, aided by a thorough knowledge of the sociopolitical climate at the time and place of the theory's development, can expose unintentional racism and cultural bias.

AN ANTIRACIST FRAMEWORK FOR MENTAL HEALTH

An antiracist framework proposes that to achieve optimal mental and emotional health, all people need to develop a healthy, well-integrated racial identity (Carter, 1997). Racial identity is as fundamental as identity related to gender, spirituality, sexuality/sexual orientation, body image, and other important aspects of personhood. Fundamental to the development of a healthy racial identity is the need to understand race issues and racism, including how they impact self, family, and community. Clients are encouraged to examine how they are impacted by racism, including looking at how they function in ways that at times perpetuates racism, and at other times work to undo it.

How Is the White Client Helped by Understanding Racism?

When both therapist and client are White, there is often an unconscious and unspoken collusion that racial identity does not matter, and that racism is not taking its toll. Just as we are taught not to see the privileges afforded us because of our skin color, White people are generally taught not to see how we are hurt by racism. When a society is structured on the basis of race, however, conformity to the norms of racial roles maintains both inequitable treatment of its people and pathological relations between them (Bowser & Hunt, 1996). All members of society are hurt by the dynamic of oppressor versus oppressed (McIntosh, 1988). Race and racism may have been invented *for* us, but it is also something that is done *to* us. Participating in a racist society without conscious awareness of its institutional systems of oppression, and one's position and role in the process, prohibits healthy development for all members of that society. As very eloquently stated by Nelson Mandela (1994) about his revelations upon his release from prison,

> I knew as well as I knew anything that the oppressor must be liberated just as surely as the oppressed. A man who takes away another man's freedom is a prisoner of hatred, he is locked behind the bars of prejudice and narrow-mindedness. I am not truly free if I am taking away someone else's freedom, just as surely as I am not free when my freedom is taken from me. The oppressed and the oppressor alike are robbed of their humanity. (p. 544)

Developing comfort in asking White clients about racial identity takes time and a few awkward tries before the therapist develops his or her own language and style. Experienced therapists already have the skills to do this because we are well-versed in asking very personal questions about issues not likely to come up in the course of everyday conversation. We listen attentively for clues as to when it will be therapeutically appropriate to move closer to sensitive topics for further exploration. When working from an antiracist framework, we add the component of racial identity and listen attentively for the cue to begin exploration about race.

I typically start by looking for an opening to talk about racial identity from the moment my new client and I meet, and I often find some way to work it into the conversation naturally. When that opening does not appear in the first or second session, I may say something like, "In order to really be of help to you, I need to get to know the full scope of who you are, not just the problem that brought you here. So we've already talked a bit about your family, your parents, your spouse, your job. I'm getting a good sense of who you are in the world in a lot of ways, the quality of these relationships and what they mean to you. But we haven't yet talked about race, how you identify yourself racially and ethnically, what it means for you to be a White person in our world, in our city." It is not unusual for the White client to respond superficially, or be somewhat flummoxed by the query. Once the question has been raised, however, it usually piques their interest and curiosity and places race in the room, available for further exploration. What follows are some examples of discussions with White patients that show their phase of racial identity development in the context of the therapeutic work.

Reintegration Status and Trauma Recovery and Grief

Gary is a 46-year-old gay man who entered therapy when his lover of 25 years committed suicide. Initially, helping him through this trauma superceded focus in other areas, and issues of race did not come up. As the shock began to wear off and he started to work through the grief, he naturally began to reminisce about their life together. He began recalling how they met and fell in love, recounted the process of coming out to his family, and shared the highs and lows of their 25-year-long partnership, living in the same Bronx neighborhood in which Gary had grown up. It was during this time that identity issues came into play, but at first focused only on sexual identity, homophobia, and his feelings about the gay community in New York City.

My attempts to initiate consideration of racial identity were repeatedly ignored or dismissed–until he started reevaluating his current situation and questioning whether he wanted to remain in New York. Gary was speaking in vague, general terms about feeling like he did not belong. He was feeling unanchored without his partner, certainly, but it seemed that he was reaching to articulate something else that was not being said clearly. I prodded him with some warm, gentle teasing, "I know you're trying to tell me something important here, Gary, but to be honest, I'm looking at a good-looking White gay man, single in New York City–and you're telling me you feel like you don't belong?!" At first he smiled; then, looking down and shaking his head, started in, with anger,

> You know what's it's like to be a White gay man in this city? Forget I'm too old to be a buffed out Chelsea-boy. I didn't want that when I was young enough to enjoy it. It's being the only White guy on the train by the time I get to my stop, feeling like a foreigner in my own neighborhood. When I was a kid–up until 10 years ago– my neighborhood was all German and Italian. And the *Italians*

were the coloreds! Then the Puerto Ricans, the Jamaicans. I walk
down the street and I don't even know what language they're
speaking, the foods they sell at the stores. We don't even have
delis anymore–they're "bodegas." And it's dirtier now, not safe
when you walk around–they've ruined it. I know you'll think I'm a
racist, but you're White, you know what I mean. Or maybe you
live in Manhattan so you're not as bothered by it. But me, working-
class White guy living in some black. . . I don't know. . .

Long pause, I take a deep breath. Recognizing that Gary has landed
squarely in the reintegration phase, my task in the racial identity piece
of the work is to help him move toward pseudo-independence. In the
broader context of the grief work, however, I am aware of the multiple
losses he is identifying: loss of his familiar neighborhood, loss of his
sense of belonging, loss of the security of sameness and continuity. All
of the things that he has counted on to give him definition are gone now,
along with his life-partner. Racial identity development is important in
this instance because Gary is not only in the process of putting his life
back together, he is putting *himself* back together. How he comes to understand his racial identity is critical to his sense of self-worth since he
will not be able to feel truly good about himself if he carries hatred and
fear about those around him.
   I also recognize the risk he is taking with me and hear his words
clearly, "you'll think I'm racist, but you're White, you know what I
mean." I sense he feels shame and anxiety at what he is expressing and
fears being rejected by me. He needs to know that I understand him, but I
cannot support his prejudice. I begin by offering him a simple reframing,
attempting to align with his pain and sense of disorientation while not
aligning with this racial bigotry. "So being a gay man in the City isn't the
thing, it's being White in an area where you've become the minority,
where you feel out of place. You look over the last 10 years and see how
your relationship was crumbling, even though you didn't know it, and
now you look around you and it feels like everything around you has
crumbled, too. Even in both of us being White, though, we have different
views, different experiences of similar things. I look around neighborhoods like yours and see color and it looks beautiful to me, exciting, interesting, thriving. You look around and see negatives, like the anger–the
rage–and sadness you have in your soul right now gets projected out to all
those Black and brown faces of your neighbors." At this he begins crying,
admitting that he does not want to hate, but he does not know how to contain his rage or how to live with his sense of alienation. Having brought

racial identity fully into the work, we can now begin the process of weaving it into the big picture as we progress through the grief recovery process, helping Gary to formulate a well-integrated sense of self. As Gary returns to these issues, a socio-historical analysis of racism will help us explore the questions about inequities in our society that often come up in this process in a context that incorporates the dynamics of power and privilege along with looking at individual abilities and life circumstance.

Pseudo-Independent Status and Dealing with Mental Illness

Tzapora is a 37-year-old Orthodox Jewish woman who lives with severe bipolar disorder. She lives in a New York City neighborhood that is traditionally Jewish, where she has family and many friends who share her faith and traditions. As a married woman, she covers her head with a scarf and wears modest clothing that does not show her arms or legs, and thus becomes a visible member of her Jewish community. She works, however, in an adjoining neighborhood that is primarily African American.

Tzapora has a long history of mental illness, including a handful of hospitalizations, and maintains a fragile psychiatric stability with the help of medication and ongoing psychotherapy. Our work centers on her efforts to manage the functional and emotional demands of her life and her struggle to find her place in her community, where she feels highly stigmatized by her mental illness. She was very sheltered as a child and adolescent, and now has a keen curiosity about people who are different from those with whom she grew up. Relationships, however, are very difficult for her because she is easily confused by interpersonal conflict, and this threatens her psychiatric stability. Having been encouraged to do so early in our work together, she often brings up issues of race, along with religious and cultural identity. She worries a great deal about being identified with a group that has tense and sometimes hostile relations with Black people in our city.

In describing her experience in the neighborhood in which she works, she said,

> Sometimes I feel like everybody is staring at me, and other times I feel like I'm invisible. And LaShonda, this woman I work with, she can be so rude. I just complimented her on her hair–she has dreadlocks I think they're called, and they're really beautiful. She just *looked* at me. I don't know–is it me? I try to be so nice to them. I don't mean to be rude when I say "them." Is that rude? I want to

be respectful. I don't feel . . . I'm really not prejudice, but I feel like they're prejudice toward me. I wish I could make them understand that we have more in common than we have differences: our people have been enslaved, we've been victims of genocide, and even today we're kept outside of the mainstream.

An important shift is evident here: in reintegration, Gary's struggle was in dealing with "the other" and feeling out of place, focusing on others as the source of his discomfort in his racial identity. Tzapora's issues, in the pseudo-independent phase, begin to locate the concern within herself. Her wish seems to be that we could live in a color-blind world, where differences do not matter, or can be glossed over in the effort to find unity.

The therapeutic work has been to help Tzapora move into the depth and complexity of racial identity exploration and progress toward the immersion/emergence phase. Since she is so fragile emotionally and psychiatrically, however, this has been a delicate process. Offering a perspective on race and race relations based on socio-political and historical information has been important in helping her to understand and come to terms with the differences between her community's experience and that of African Americans. Today, approximately two years after she made the statement quoted here, she has continued her exploration of race and culture on a significantly more emotional level. She has greater self-awareness and understanding of how others may view her, and more appreciation of what it means to be White, in addition to being Jewish. The examination of racial identity and the dynamics of racism have also provided us with a way to explore conflict, confusion, ambiguity, and subjectivity–all issues that cause her trouble in interpersonal relationships–from a standpoint that has combined intellectual processing and emotional experience. As a result, she expresses feeling stronger about her own Jewish identity, less stigmatized by her mental illness, and enjoys improved social relationships.

Immersion/Emergence Status and Issues of Emerging Adulthood

Clark is a 24-year-old musician who grew up in the mostly White, middle-class suburbs of a large metropolitan area. His music and genuine curiosity about people and other ways of being in the world often led him to encounter people and situations outside of his home environment, and eventually led him to move to New York City. He came to therapy when an accidental overdose of recreational drugs led to a hospitalization and a re-evaluation of his life and relationships. Core identity issues are often a theme in his sessions–Who am I? What is my purpose? Are my artistic contributions valuable or just self-indulgent?

Our first in-depth discussion of racial identity was initiated when I asked him about his several tattoos. At first he mumbled something about the beauty of body art and then paused and added, looking down, "I just needed to make my statement, to be different from them. I don't even know who 'them' is . . ." he glanced up, chuckled a bit and said with a dramatic flair, "suburban drones, the masses I guess–everything I don't want to be but fear that I am." I responded by adding the racial component, "You don't want to be just another middle-class White guy." He perked up and made eye contact,

> Yeah. That's it. I don't even know what it is to be White–I don't want to be associated with "them": racists, "the man," people who just parade around flaunting all their fucking privilege and don't even know what the rest of the world is like. I even question my music. Is rock even relevant anymore? Maybe hip-hop, telling the real experience of poverty, what racism is, what life is like for people who don't have privilege, what our society creates when it holds people down, maybe that's all that's relevant right now. I'm not sure where I can fit in, *if* I fit in, if I want to. I feel so fucked up about it.

The theme of "them" resurfaces here, but "they" are now other Whites and the search for identity has now turned solidly inward. Clark's struggle is to know who he is and figure out how to place himself in the White world while maintaining his integrity and antiracist, anti-oppression ideals. My role is to help guide him through this process and move toward autonomy, incorporating racial identity with all the other important aspects of identity that he is naturally struggling with as he moves toward mature adulthood. Intrigued by our conversations about race, he has done a good deal of reading on his own and has become more aware of the interplay of power, authority, and racism. As a result, he has chosen to become involved in local political activities. He recently completed his first solo album and handed me a copy, saying, "What's on here is the most honest I know how to be. I still don't know if it's relevant, or if anybody is going to buy it, but that doesn't matter. So I'm just another White guy with punk rage, poetic longing, whatever. That's what I've got right now."

Autonomy Status and Life Adjustment Issues

Carole is a 62-year-old social worker who came to therapy because she was experiencing acute anxiety attacks that began when she and her longtime live-in partner decided to live separately due to problems in their relationship. For most of our initial session, she focused on her immediate concerns: the discomfort of the anxiety and the difficulty in her relationship. In the course of this, however, she mentioned that she had two grown children, stating almost dismissively, "I raised two successful, healthy Black men–long story." This, of course, gave me my opening. I worded my response to pick up on the racial identity piece, "So what was it like for you, a White woman, to raise these Black sons who became so healthy and successful?"

Her response made it clear that she had done a good deal of personal work in this area in her life. She also told me later that she was grateful I picked up on the issue of racial identity. She had become so accustomed to other people's limited understanding of Whiteness and racism that she was afraid to bring it up with me because she did not want to be disappointed with me as a therapist. In this sense, she began therapy with the same defensiveness that many people of color carry when they start treatment with a White therapist.

Over 35 years before, Carole had been married to a Black man and had two children with him. When he died, she suddenly found herself the single mother of two very young Black children. She intuitively understood that in order to help them grow up strong and healthy, she needed to go through a transformative process of her own to be the parent they needed.

> I knew I couldn't just model my parenting style after my mother or my friends. These boys needed something different, needed me to *be* something different. When my husband was alive, I just assumed–I guess we assumed–that he would teach them. Then he died and *I* needed to find a way to teach them about how to be Black, how to deal with racism, how to be gentle men. Fortunately, I had his family to help, but I had to learn, I had to figure out how to be with them in a way that they would forget that I was there, or that they would trust me enough so that they could talk about race the way Black people talk when there aren't White people in the room listening. I knew I had to do this for my sons, but it was hard, really hard. I had these two babies, I was completely unprepared for being a single mom, and . . . I don't know how to describe it . . .

She trailed off, and I replied, "You're talking about what you had to 'do' and what you had to 'learn,' but bigger than that I hear you trying to articulate a process of evolution, or transformation. You had to *become* somebody different, somebody you didn't expect to be, with no road map, no direction from other White people." Her eyes welled up with tears, "And I've felt so alone ever since."

Over the coming sessions, she talked more about her racial identity development, her activist work in the 1960s and 1970s, her ongoing commitment to social justice as reflected in her social work career, and the multiracial social network she built for herself over the years. While reviewing this time in her life, she once said, "I often thought it ironic that I started this whole journey to help my sons in being Black, and in the meantime I learned a whole lot about being White. More about being White, I guess, because that is what I am, and in this odd way it's become the only part of who I am that I'm truly at peace with." She often returned, however, to the profound sense of aloneness she would experience in the company of White "sincere antiracists who couldn't recognize their own racism" or people of color who "had just been too hurt, or taught to hate, and would never trust me."

As we revisited this area of her identity and the issues connected with it, Carole began to understand how her sense of aloneness and isolation was contributing to her anxiety. Her partner had been one of the few White people whom she could really trust in racial identity issues. Without him, she feared she would be overwhelmingly alone. Prior to entering therapy, she had already made the first layer of connection: the distance in the relationship with her longtime life-partner was triggering feelings about the loss of her husband. But it was not until we spent time focusing on the identity transformation she had gone through, and how she felt that process made it difficult to find others with whom she felt a trusted kinship, that she connected with the source of the profound sense of loss and isolation she had been carrying for years. Our discussions about race helped bring a more holistic view to her current situation and became integral to her ability to feel at peace in other areas of her life and identity.

CURRENT LITERATURE AND NEED FOR FURTHER STUDY

Most of the sources for this paper come from social science, sociology, education, history, and, ironically, Black or multicultural studies, all of which provide rich resources for the study of Whiteness. Michelle Fine, Lois Weis, and a few other research psychologists have contributed excellent work on the social construction of Whiteness. I found very little written about White identity, however, in the clinical or counseling psychology and social work fields, and even less that was written by Whites about Whites. Janet Helms, whose White Racial Identity Model was chosen for this paper because it has the most empirical support of the models available, is a Black woman. Robert Carter, Chalmer Thompson, both Black men, and Helen Neville, a Black woman, have all published extensively on racism and mental health with examinations of White racial identity, and are among the few resources in the mental field I could find directly related to my topic.

There is always the danger that studies on Whiteness can degenerate into a self-absorption that detracts from the persistent issues of racism in our society. The study of White identity must be done only for the purposes of undoing the ideology of color-blindness that provides legitimacy to the persistence of racism (Doane & Bonilla-Silva, 2003). In this context, there are some White people in the mental health field who are contributing important work: Michael D'Andrea, Julie Ancis, Lisa Spanierman, and a few others. Taken as a whole, however, the field lacks empirical inquiry and theoretical advancement that opens up the dialogue about the role of White racial identity development in overall mental and emotional health, and in relation to specific issues. While this paper suggests that the answers to the following questions are "yes," it would be useful to the field if these questions could be adopted for consideration as research questions or hypotheses. Is there a significant correlation between a therapist's effectiveness and his or her racial identity development status? Does the integration of racial identity issues in psychotherapy contribute to the development of positive self-esteem in the White patient? Do White patients in psychotherapy who are encouraged to explore racial identity issues exhibit or express different rates of resolution of intra-psychic conflict, guilt, shame, generalized anxiety, or depression than White patients who are not encouraged to explore racial identity issues? Does exploration of White racial identity have an impact on the patient's inter-personal functioning and the quality of their social contacts?

CAN RACISM BE CURED?

In some ways, this question belongs to my four-year-old self, the little girl sitting dumfounded with her mother, wanting this ugly question to just go away. Racism is a pathology of a nation, a culture, a socio-political-economic system. Individuals are hurt by it, but do not have the individual power to "cure" it. Ultimately, racism can only be undone through the collective power of community organizing, which includes the education and empowerment of individuals and whole communities or organizations (Chisom & Washington, 1997). Most therapists do not engage directly in community organizing activities. We do, however, have a profound impact on the lives of the people who pass through our offices. Many of them have jobs where they hold the function of gate-keepers, people who control access to resources. Our clients may run companies, manage departments, or teach school. Even those who do not hold positions of power are likely to be part of work or social groups, or worship with a faith community where they have influence. I am not suggesting that we force an advocate role on our clients, but people with a well-integrated, healthy racial identity will make decisions in their everyday life that reflect their worldview. Thus, we have an opportunity to plant seeds of antiracism education and empowerment, even in the context of individual, family, or group psychotherapy that is based on psychodynamic, behavioral, or other theoretical constructs.

For those of us who hold dual roles, as therapists and as administrators in social service agencies or educators in the profession, we also hold a dual obligation. We have the opportunity to promote the paradigm of antiracist community organization in program development, service delivery, and curriculum development, as well as in psychosocial intervention. Part of our responsibility is to understand and address the racism in our programs and the agencies or the systems with which we collaborate. We have the opportunity to engage in "community organizing" through reaching out, educating, and challenging those in power who maintain the status quo. Antiracist organizing and education can be done with all members of the staff of our programs, as well as the hierarchy of the agency. For those connected with educational institutions, there is a powerful opportunity to educate and influence future generations of mental health and social service professionals.

So, for anyone looking for a ridiculously expensive, totally impractical, longitudinal study that would be impossible to control, the big question is: Is there a "tipping point" where enough White people in our country move beyond the pseudo-independent phase so that racism becomes a thing of the past?

REFERENCES

Anderson, M. L. (2003). Whitewashing race: A critical perspective on Whiteness. In A. W. Doane & E. Bonilla-Silva (Eds.), *White out: The continuing significance of racism* (pp. 21-34). New York: Routledge.

Banton, M. (1999). The racializing of the world. In M. Bulmer & J. Solomos (Eds.), *Racism* (pp. 34-40). New York: Oxford University Press.

Bowser, B. P., & Hunt, R. G. (Eds.) (1996). *Impacts of racism on White Americans* (2nd ed.). Thousand Oaks: Sage Publications.

Carter, R. T. (1995). *The influence of race and racial identity in psychotherapy: Toward a racially inclusive model.* New York: John Wiley & Sons, Inc.

Carter, R. T. (1997). Is White a race? Expressions of White racial identity. In M. Fine, L. Weis, L. C. Powell, & L. M. Wong (Eds.), *Off White: Readings on race, power, and society* (pp. 198-209). New York: Routledge.

Chisom, R., & Washington, M. (1997). *Undoing racism: A philosophy of international social change.* New Orleans: The People's Institute Press.

Doane, A. W., & Bonilla-Silva, E. (2003). *White out: The continuing significance of racism.* New York: Routledge.

Fine, M. (1997). Witnessing Whiteness. In M. Fine, L. Weis, L. C. Powell, & L. M. Wong (Eds.), *Off White: Readings on race, power, and society* (pp. 57-65). New York: Routledge.

Franklin, A. J., Boyd-Franklin, N., & Kelly, S. (2006). Racism and invisibility: Race-related stress, emotional abuse and psychological trauma for people of color. *Journal of Emotional Abuse, 6*(2/3), 9-30.

Fredrickson, G. (1999). Social origins of American racism. In M. Bulmer & J. Solomos (Eds.), *Racism* (pp. 70-82). New York: Oxford University Press.

Geller, J., Miller, J., & Churchill, P. (2006). Triple trouble: Battered women of color – "Being black, being battered and being female . . . I ask myself, where do I begin?" *Journal of Emotional Abuse, 6*(2/3), 77-96.

Hacker, A. (2003). *Two nations: Black and White, separate, hostile, unequal.* New York: Scribner.

Hartman, H. (1964). *Ego psychology.* New York: International University Press.

Helms, J. E. (1995). An update of Helm's White and people of color racial identity models. In J. G. Ponteroto, J. M. Casas, L. A. Suzuki, & C. M. Alexander (Eds.), *Handbook of multicultural counseling* (pp. 181-198). Thousand Oaks: Sage Publications.

Hitchcock, J. (2002). *Lifting the White veil: An exploration of White American culture in a multiracial context.* New Jersey: Crandall, Dostie & Douglas Books, Inc.

Horsman, R. (1999). Superior and inferior races. In M. Bulmer & J. Solomos (Eds.), *Racism* (pp. 45-49). New York: Oxford University Press.

Jones, J. M., & Carter, R. T. (1996). Racism and White racial identity: Merging realities. In B. P. Bowser & R. G. Hunt (Eds.), *Impacts of racism on White Americans* (2nd ed.; pp. 1-23). Thousand Oaks: Sage Publications.

Kernberg, O. F. (1976). *Object-relations theory and clinical psychoanalysis.* New York: Aronson.

Kohl, B. G., Jr. (2006). Can you feel me now? Worldview, empathy and racial identity in a therapy dyad. *Journal of Emotional Abuse, 6*(2/3), 173-196.

Langman, P. F. (1997). White culture, Jewish culture, and the origins of psychotherapy. *Psychotherapy: Theory, Research, Practice, Training, 34,* 207-218.

Loewen, J. W. (1995). *Lies my teacher told me: Everything your American history textbook got wrong.* New York: Simon & Schuster.

Mandela, N. (1994). *Long walk to freedom: The autobiography of Nelson Mandela.* Boston: Little Brown.

McGlade, K., & Ackerman, J. (2006). A hope for foster care: Agency executives in partnerships with parent leaders. *Journal of Emotional Abuse, 6*(2/3), 97-112.

McIntosh, P. (1988). *White privilege and male privilege: A personal account of coming to see the correspondences through work in women's studies*. Wellesley, MA: Center for Research on Women.

Mosse, G. (1999). Eighteenth-century foundations. In M. Bulmer & J. Solomos (Eds.), *Racism* (pp. 40-44). New York: Oxford University Press.

Ottavi, T. M., Pope-Davis, D. B., & Dings, J. G. (1994). Relationship between White racial identity attitudes and self-reported multicultural counseling competencies. *Journal of Counseling Psychology, 41*, 149-154.

Peacock, C., & Daniels, G. (2006). Applying an antiracist framework to a residential treatment center: Sanctuary®, a model for change. *Journal of Emotional Abuse, 6*(2/3), 135-154.

Poliakov, L. (1999). Gobineau and his contemporaries. In M. Bulmer & J. Solomos (Eds.), *Racism* (pp. 51-56). New York: Oxford University Press.

Pope-Davis, D. B., Menefee, L. A., & Ottavi, T. M. (1993). The comparison of White racial identity attitudes among faculty and students: Implications for professional psychologists. *Professional Psychology: Research and Practice, 24*, 443-449.

Rollock, D., & Gordon, E. W. (2000). Racism and mental health into the 21st century: Perspectives and parameters. *American Journal of Orthopsychiatry, 70*, 5-13.

Sue, S. (2003). In defense of cultural competency in psychotherapy and treatment. *American Psychologist, 58*, 964-970.

Tatum, B. D. (1997). *Why are all the Black kids sitting together in the cafeteria? And other conversations about race*. New York: Basic Books.

Thompson, C. E., & Neville, H. A. (1999). Racism, mental health, and mental health practice. *The Counseling Psychologist, 27*, 155-223.

Zinn, H. (2003). *A people's history of the United States*. New York: HarperCollins Publishers.

doi:10.1300/J135v06n02_15

Index

BOOK ORDER FORM!

Order a copy of this book with this form or online at:
http://www.HaworthPress.com/store/product.asp?sku= 5933

Racism and Racial Identity
Reflections on Urban Practice in Mental Health and Social Services

—— in softbound at $36.00 ISBN-13: 978-0-7890-3109-9 / ISBN-10: 0-7890-3109-4.
—— in hardbound at $55.00 ISBN-13: 978-0-7890-3108-2 / ISBN-10: 0-7890-3108-6.

COST OF BOOKS _____

POSTAGE & HANDLING _____
US: $4.00 for first book & $1.50
for each additional book
Outside US: $5.00 for first book
& $2.00 for each additional book.

SUBTOTAL _____

In Canada: add 6% GST. _____

STATE TAX _____
CA, IL, IN, MN, NJ, NY, OH, PA & SD residents
please add appropriate local sales tax.

FINAL TOTAL _____
If paying in Canadian funds, convert
using the current exchange rate,
UNESCO coupons welcome.

❑ **BILL ME LATER:**
Bill-me option is good on US/Canada/
Mexico orders only; not good to jobbers,
wholesalers, or subscription agencies.

❑ **Signature** _____

❑ **Payment Enclosed: $**_____

❑ **PLEASE CHARGE TO MY CREDIT CARD:**
❑ Visa ❑ MasterCard ❑ AmEx ❑ Discover
❑ Diner's Club ❑ Eurocard ❑ JCB

Account #_____

Exp Date_____

Signature_____
(Prices in US dollars and subject to change without notice.)

PLEASE PRINT ALL INFORMATION OR ATTACH YOUR BUSINESS CARD
Name
Address
City   State/Province   Zip/Postal Code
Country
Tel   Fax
E-Mail

May we use your e-mail address for confirmations and other types of information? ❑Yes ❑No We appreciate receiving
your e-mail address. Haworth would like to e-mail special discount offers to you, as a preferred customer.
We will never share, rent, or exchange your e-mail address. We regard such actions as an invasion of your privacy.

Order from your **local bookstore** or directly from
The Haworth Press, Inc. 10 Alice Street, Binghamton, New York 13904-1580 • USA
Call our toll-free number (1-800-429-6784) / Outside US/Canada: (607) 722-5857
Fax: 1-800-895-0582 / Outside US/Canada: (607) 771-0012
E-mail your order to us: orders@HaworthPress.com

For orders outside US and Canada, you may wish to order through your local
sales representative, distributor, or bookseller.
For information, see http://HaworthPress.com/distributors

(Discounts are available for individual orders in US and Canada only, not booksellers/distributors.)

The Haworth Press Inc.

Please photocopy this form for your personal use.
www.HaworthPress.com   BOF06